SIGFSM Workshop on Statistical NLP and Weighted Automata

Held at ACL 2016

Berlin, Germany
12 August 2016

ISBN: 978-1-5108-2771-4

ACL 2016

The 54th Annual Meeting of the Association for Computational Linguistics

Proceedings of the SIGFSM Workshop on Statistical NLP and Weighted Automata

August 12, 2016
Berlin, Germany

Preface

The past 20 years have seen a fundamental paradigm shift in the field of automated natural language processing: though long dominated by rule-based techniques, the vast majority of contemporary approaches are now based on statistical models. This trend can be observed not only in traditional tasks such as machine translation or morphological analysis, but also in new research areas such as topic modelling. The reasons for such a paradigm shift can be attributed above all to the steadily growing pool of large, high-quality manually annotated training material as well as the availability of suitable statistical methods and easily accessible implementations thereof.

The purpose of the Workshop on Statistical Natural Language Processing and Weighted Automata (StatFSM) was to bring together researchers interested in statistical natural language processing, automata theory and application. We are pleased to say that the program of the workshop reflected in this proceedings volume met these expectations.

These proceedings contain the contributions presented at the StatFSM workshop held on August 12, 2016 in conjunction with ACL 2016 in Berlin, Germany. The workshop was a meeting of the ACL Special Interest Group on Finite-State Methods (SIGFSM). In total, 12 papers (seven long and five short papers) were submitted to a doubly blind refereeing process. Each paper was reviewed by three members of the program committee, which consisted of highly esteemed researchers from the field of automata theory and applications. In the end, 9 papers were selected for presentation at the workshop, and those contributions are included in this volume. They discuss topics ranging from weighted finite-state transducers to weighted tree automata and to devices on even more complicated structures. In addition, the contributions strike the right balance between purely theoretic foundational investigations as well as considerations and solutions to problems entirely motivated from practice.

The workshop would not have been possible without the help of a lot of support. First, we would like to thank the program committee members for providing their expertise and valuable feedback during the review process. We also want to express our gratitude to JASON EISNER for his inspiring keynote lecture. The constant efforts of the ACL administration and the local organizers made this workshop possible. Last but not least we want to thank the authors and the participants who above all others have made this workshop a success.

Bryan Jurish
Andreas Maletti
Uwe Springmann
Kay-Michael Würzner

Organizers:

Bryan Jurish, Berlin-Brandenburg Academy of Sciences and Humanities, Germany
Andreas Maletti, University of Stuttgart, Germany
Uwe Springmann, Ludwig-Maximilians-Universität München, Germany
Kay-Michael Würzner, Berlin-Brandenburg Academy of Sciences and Humanities, Germany

Program Committee:

Borja Balle, Lancaster University, UK
Francisco Casacuberta, Instituto Tecnológico de Informática, Spain
Simon Clematide, University of Zurich, Switzerland
Gregory Crane, University of Leipzig, Germany
Frank Drewes, Umeå University, Sweden
Jason Eisner, Johns Hopkins University, Baltimore, MD, USA
Colin de la Higuera, Nantes University, France
Mans Hulden, University of Colorado, Boulder, CO, USA
Krister Lindén, University of Helsinki, Finnland
Kevin Knight, University of Southern California, CA, USA
Marcus Eichenberger-Liwicki, University of Kaiserslautern, Germany
Stoyan Mihov, Bulgarian Academy of Sciences, Sofia, Bulgaria
Mark-Jan Nederhof, University of St Andrews, UK
Michael Riley, Google Inc., USA
Martin Reynaert, Tilburg University, The Netherlands
Brian Roark, Google Inc., USA
Richard Sproat, Google Inc., USA
Heiko Vogler, Dresden University of Technology, Germany
Bruce Watson, Stellenbosch University, South Africa

Invited Speaker:

Jason Eisner, Johns Hopkins University, Baltimore, MD, USA

Table of Contents

Conference Program

Friday, August 12, 2016 (continued)

14:00–15:30   Weighted finite-state transducers

14:00–14:30   *Distributed representation and estimation of WFST-based n-gram models*
Cyril Allauzen, Michael Riley and Brian Roark

14:30–15:00   *Learning transducer models for morphological analysis from example inflections*
Markus Forsberg and Mans Hulden

15:00–15:30   *Data-driven spelling correction using weighted finite-state methods*
Miikka Silfverberg, Pekka Kauppinen and Krister Lindén

15:30–16:00   Afternoon break

16:00–17:30   Various weighted automata

16:00–16:30   *EM-training for weighted aligned hypergraph bimorphisms*
Frank Drewes, Kilian Gebhardt and Heiko Vogler

16:30–17:00   *On the correspondence between compositional matrix-space models of language and weighted automata*
Shima Asaadi and Sebastian Rudolph

17:00–17:30   *Pynini: A Python library for weighted finite-state grammar compilation*
Kyle Gorman

Equivalences between Ranked and Unranked Weighted Tree Automata via Binarization

Toni Dietze
Faculty of Computer Science
Technische Universität Dresden
01062 Dresden, Germany
`toni.dietze@tu-dresden.de`

Abstract

Encoding unranked trees to binary trees, henceforth called binarization, is an important method to deal with unranked trees. For each of three binarizations we show that weighted (ranked) tree automata together with the binarization are equivalent to weighted unranked tree automata; even in the probabilistic case. This allows to easily adapt training methods for weighted (ranked) tree automata to weighted unranked tree automata.

1 Introduction

When dealing with trees, tree grammars, and formal languages of trees, a restriction to binary trees is often beneficial, e.g. for improved generalization when generating grammars from treebanks, or for reduced parsing complexity. A *binarization* maps any (unranked) tree to a binary tree such that the original tree can be reconstructed from the result.

In this paper we investigate three different binarizations inspired by Matsuzaki et al. (2005, Fig. 6). For each of these binarizations we show that a weighted unranked tree language is recognizable by a weighted unranked tree automaton (wuta) iff the binarization of the language is recognizable by a weighted tree automaton (wta). This even holds with restriction to probabilistic automata. To support this result we show that for any $\mathbb{R}_{\geq 0}$-weighted finite state automaton with the sum of weights of all words being 1, there is an equivalent probabilistic finite state automaton. This implies that the class of weighted string languages recognizable by probabilistic finite state automata is closed under reversal.

These results suggest that by adding binarization to training methods for wta we effectively get training methods for wuta. Alterations to the weights and the state behaviour while training then carry over to wuta. This also gives an explanation for why the performance of the training by Matsuzaki et al. (2005) is rather independent from the used binarization.

Related Work. Fülöp and Vogler (2009) give an overview over wta, and Droste and Vogler (2011) introduced wuta. For the unweighted case binarizations (also called encodings) were investigated by, e.g., Comon et al. (2007, Section 8.3). Their first-child-next-sibling encoding is similar to our left-branching binarization. Their extension encoding is also used to define stepwise tree automata (Carme et al., 2004). A stepwise tree automaton is defined like a (ranked) tree automaton. It accepts an unranked tree, if it accepts the extension encoding of the tree while the automaton is interpreted as a (ranked) tree automaton. Högberg et al. (2009, Lemmas 4.2 and 6.2) extend this connection to the weighted case and show that weighted stepwise tree automata and wuta are equally powerful.

Our results for weighted and for probabilistic finite state automata are a special case of *renormalization* of weighted or of probabilistic context-free grammars (Abney et al., 1999; Chi, 1999; Nederhof and Satta, 2003). We provide alternative proofs for this special case.

2 Preliminaries

Let A and B be sets, and $R \subseteq A \times B$ a relation. By $R(a)$ we denote the set $\{b \in B \mid (a, b) \in R\}$ for every $a \in A$. The *inverse relation of R* is defined by $R^{-1} = \{(b, a) \mid (a, b) \in R\}$. Occasionally we identify a function $f \colon A \to B$ with the relation $\{(a, f(a)) \mid a \in A\}$.

An *alphabet* is a finite, non-empty set. Let Σ be an alphabet. The *set of words over Σ* is denoted

Proceedings of the ACL Workshop on Statistical NLP and Weighted Automata, pages 1–10,
Berlin, Germany, August 12, 2016. ©2016 Association for Computational Linguistics

by Σ^*. The length of a word $w \in \Sigma^*$ is denoted by $|w|$. The *empty word*, denoted by ε, is the word of length 0. The set of *unranked trees over* Σ, denoted by U_Σ, is the smallest set U such that for every $\sigma \in \Sigma$, $k \in \mathbb{N}$, and $t_1, \ldots, t_k \in U$ we have $\sigma(t_1, \ldots, t_k) \in U$. We abbreviate $\sigma() \in \mathrm{U}_\Sigma$ by σ. Let $t = \sigma(t_1, \ldots, t_k) \in \mathrm{U}_\Sigma$. We call σ the *root symbol of* t. The *root rank of* t is defined by $\mathrm{rk}(t) = k$. The *set of positions of* t is recursively defined by $\mathrm{pos}(t) = \varepsilon \cup \bigcup_{i \in \{1, \ldots, k\}} \{i\rho \mid \rho \in \mathrm{pos}(t_i)\}$. Let $\rho \in \mathrm{pos}(t)$. The *subtree of* t *at* ρ is recursively defined by $t|_\rho = t$ if $\rho = \varepsilon$ and $t|_\rho = t_i|_{\rho'}$ if $\rho = i\rho'$. The *symbol of* t *at* ρ, denoted by $t(\rho)$, is defined as the root symbol of $t|_\rho$. The *rank of* t *at* ρ is defined as $\mathrm{rk}(t|_\rho)$.

Let S be a non-empty set (of *sorts*). An *S-sorted alphabet* is a family $\Sigma = (\Sigma^{(s)} \mid s \in S)$ of pairwise disjoint sets such that their union is non-empty and finite. For families of sets we often use the same identifier for denoting the family and the union of its members. Let Σ be an $(S \times S^*)$-sorted alphabet. The *family of (S-sorted) trees over* Σ, denoted by $\mathrm{T}_\Sigma = (\mathrm{T}_\Sigma^{(s)} \mid s \in S)$, is defined as the smallest family $(T^{(s)} \mid s \in S)$ such that for every $(s_0, s_1 \ldots s_k) \in (S \times S^*)$, for every $\sigma \in \Sigma^{(s_0, s_1 \ldots s_k)}$, for every $t_1 \in T^{(s_1)}, \ldots, t_k \in T^{(s_k)}$, we have $\sigma(t_1, \ldots, t_k) \in T^{(s_0)}$. If S is a singleton, this is equivalent to the usual definition of ranked trees. Note that $\mathrm{T}_\Sigma \subseteq \mathrm{U}_\Sigma$, so all notions for unranked trees are also valid for sorted trees. Also note that, for sorted trees, the symbol at a position determines the rank at this position; therefore we will use rk also for symbols from Σ.

A commutative semiring is an algebraic structure $\Re = (R, +, \cdot, 0, 1)$ such that $(R, +, 0)$ and $(R, \cdot, 1)$ are commutative monoids, $\cdot$ is distributive over $+$, and 0 is annihilating w.r.t. $\cdot$. We often write $\Re$ instead of R. Let A be a set and $f \colon A \to \Re$ be a mapping. The *support of* f is defined by $\mathrm{supp}(f) = \{a \in A \mid f(a) \neq 0\}$.

In the following we will define devices to associate weights with sorted trees, words, or unranked trees. We will use weights from an arbitrary commutative semiring. Therefore, if we use addition, multiplication, 0, and 1, then these are operations from that semiring. We will call two such devices equivalent, if their (yet to define) semantics $\llbracket \cdot \rrbracket$ is the same.

Definition 1 (wsta)**.** Let S be a set of sorts and $\Re$ be a commutative semiring. An $\Re$-*weighted S-sorted tree automaton* ($\Re$-*S-wsta*) is a tuple

(Q, Σ, I, Δ) where
- Q is an S-sorted alphabet (of *states*),
- Σ is an $(S \times S^*)$-sorted alphabet (of *terminals*),
- $I \colon Q \to \Re$ is a mapping (*root weights*), and
- $\Delta = (\Delta^{(\sigma)} \colon Q^{(s_0)} \times \ldots \times Q^{(s_k)} \to \Re \mid (s_0, s_1 \ldots s_k) \in S \times S^*, \sigma \in \Sigma^{(s_0, s_1 \ldots s_k)})$ is a family of mappings (*transition weights*). $\square$

Let $\mathcal{M} = (Q, \Sigma, I, \Delta)$ be an $\Re$-S-wsta. The *size of* $\mathcal{M}$ is defined by $\mathrm{size}(\mathcal{M}) = \mathrm{supp}(I) + \sum_{\sigma \in \Sigma} \mathrm{supp}(\Delta^{(\sigma)})$. For some $s \in S$, we call $\mathcal{M}$ *s-rooted*, if for every $s' \in S \setminus \{s\}$ and $q \in Q^{(s')}$ we have that $I(q) = 0$. We define the relation $\mathrm{run}_\mathcal{M}$ that contains (t, r), if $t \in \mathrm{T}_\Sigma$, $r \colon \mathrm{pos}(t) \to Q$, and for every $\rho \in \mathrm{pos}(t)$ we have $r(\rho) \in Q^{(s_0)}$, if $t(\rho) \in \Sigma^{(s_0, s_1 \ldots s_k)}$, i.e., the sorts of states and terminals at the same position match. We say that r *is a run of* $\mathcal{M}$ *on* t.

Definition 2 (semantics of wsta)**.** Let $\mathcal{M} = (Q, \Sigma, I, \Delta)$ be an $\Re$-S-wsta and $t \in \mathrm{T}_\Sigma$. The *weight of* t *under* $\mathcal{M}$ is defined by $\llbracket \mathcal{M} \rrbracket(t) = \sum_{r \in \mathrm{run}_\mathcal{M}(t)} \llbracket \mathcal{M} \rrbracket(t, r)$ where

$$\llbracket \mathcal{M} \rrbracket(t, r) = I(r(\varepsilon))$$
$$\cdot \prod_{\rho \in \mathrm{pos}(t)} \Delta^{(\sigma)}(r(\rho), r(\rho 1), \ldots, r(\rho k))$$
$$\text{and } \sigma = t(\rho) \text{ and } k = \mathrm{rk}(\sigma). \quad \square$$

Note: If S is a singleton set, then S-wsta are equivalent to weighted tree automata over ranked alphabets (Fülöp and Vogler, 2009). The sorts just add syntactic restrictions that will help us in the following.

Definition 3 (wfsa)**.** Let $\Re$ be a commutative semiring. An $\Re$-*weighted finite state automaton* ($\Re$-*wfsa*) is a tuple (P, Σ, J, Π, F) where
- P is an alphabet (of *states*),
- Σ is an alphabet (of *terminals*),
- $J \colon P \to \Re$ is a mapping (*initial weights*),
- $\Pi \colon P \times \Sigma \times P \to \Re$ is a mapping (*transition weights*), and
- $F \colon P \to \Re$ is a mapping (*final weights*). $\square$

By $\mathrm{wfsa}(\Re, \Sigma)$ we denote the set of all $\Re$-wfsa with terminal alphabet Σ. Let $\mathcal{N} = (P, \Sigma, J, \Pi, F)$ be an $\Re$-wfsa. The *size of* $\mathcal{N}$ is defined by $\mathrm{size}(\mathcal{N}) = \mathrm{supp}(J) + \mathrm{supp}(\Pi) + \mathrm{supp}(F)$. We define the relation $\mathrm{run}_\mathcal{N}$ that contains (w, r), if $w \in \Sigma^*$ and $r \colon \{0, \ldots, |w|\} \to P$. We say that r *is a run of* $\mathcal{N}$ *on* t.

Definition 4 (semantics of wfsa)**.** Let $\mathcal{N} = (P, \Sigma, J, \Pi, F)$ be an $\Re$-wfsa and $w =$

$w_1 \ldots w_k \in \Sigma^*$ for some $k \in \mathbb{N}$. The *weight of w under $\mathcal{N}$* is defined by $[\![\mathcal{N}]\!](w) = \sum_{r \in \mathrm{run}_{\mathcal{N}}(w)} [\![\mathcal{N}]\!](w, r)$ where

$$[\![\mathcal{N}]\!](w, r) = J(r(0))$$
$$\cdot \Big(\prod_{i \in \{1, \ldots, |w|\}} \Pi(r(i-1), w_i, r(i)) \Big)$$
$$\cdot F(r(|w|)). \qquad \Box$$

Definition 5 (wuta). Let $\Re$ be a commutative semiring. An *$\Re$-weighted unranked tree automaton ($\Re$-wuta)* is a tuple (Q, Σ, I, Δ) where

- Q is an alphabet (of *states*),
- Σ is an alphabet (of *terminals*),
- $I \colon Q \to \Re$ is a mapping (*root weights*), and
- $\Delta \colon Q \times \Sigma \to \mathrm{wfsa}(\Re, Q)$ is a mapping. $\quad \Box$

Let $\mathcal{M} = (Q, \Sigma, I, \Delta)$ be an $\Re$-wuta. The *size of $\mathcal{M}$* is defined by $\mathrm{size}(\mathcal{M}) = \mathrm{supp}(I) + \sum_{q \in Q, \sigma \in \Sigma} \mathrm{size}(\Delta(q, \sigma))$. The *number of states of $\mathcal{M}$* is defined as $|Q|$ plus the numbers of states of all wfsa in the image of Δ. We define the relation $\mathrm{run}_{\mathcal{M}}$ that contains (t, r), if $t \in \mathrm{U}_{\Sigma}$ and $r \colon \mathrm{pos}(t) \to Q$. We say that *$r$ is a run of $\mathcal{M}$ on t*.

Definition 6 (semantics of wuta). Let $\mathcal{M} = (Q, \Sigma, I, \Delta)$ be an $\Re$-wuta. Let $t \in \mathrm{U}_{\Sigma}$. The *weight of t under $\mathcal{M}$* is defined by $[\![\mathcal{M}]\!](t) = \sum_{r \in \mathrm{run}_{\mathcal{M}}(t)} [\![\mathcal{M}]\!](t, r)$ where

$$[\![\mathcal{M}]\!](t, r) = I(r(\varepsilon))$$
$$\cdot \prod_{\rho \in \mathrm{pos}(t)} [\![\Delta(r(\rho), \sigma)]\!](r(\rho 1) \ldots r(\rho k))$$
$$\text{and } \sigma = t(\rho) \text{ and } k = \mathrm{rk}(t|_{\rho}). \quad \Box$$

By exploiting distributivity it is easy to find the following equivalent formulation. Let $P_{\mathcal{M}}$ be the set of all states of all wfsa in the image of Δ. We define the relation $\mathrm{ex\text{-}run}_{\mathcal{M}}$ that contains (t, e), if $t \in \mathrm{U}_{\Sigma}$ and $e = (r, s)$ where $r \in \mathrm{run}_{\mathcal{M}}(t)$ and $s \colon \mathrm{pos}(t) \to \bigcup_{n \in \mathbb{N}} P_{\mathcal{M}}{}^{\{0, \ldots, n\}}$ such that $s(\rho) \in \mathrm{run}_{\Delta(r(\rho), t(\rho))}(r(\rho 1) \ldots r(\rho \, \mathrm{rk}(t|_{\rho})))$ for every $\rho \in \mathrm{pos}(t)$. We say that *e is an extended run of $\mathcal{M}$ on t*. We have $[\![\mathcal{M}]\!](t) = \sum_{e \in \mathrm{ex\text{-}run}_{\mathcal{M}}(t)} [\![\mathcal{M}]\!](t, e)$ where

$$[\![\mathcal{M}]\!](t, (r, s)) = I(r(\varepsilon)) \cdot \prod_{\rho \in \mathrm{pos}(t)} J_{\rho}(s(\rho)(0))$$
$$\cdot \Big(\prod_{i=1}^{\mathrm{rk}(t|_{\rho})} \Pi_{\rho}\big(s(\rho)(i-1), r(\rho i), s(\rho)(i)\big) \Big)$$
$$\cdot F_{\rho}\big(s(\rho)(\mathrm{rk}(t|_{\rho}))\big)$$

and $(P_{\rho}, Q, J_{\rho}, \Pi_{\rho}, F_{\rho}) = \Delta(r(\rho), t(\rho))$. A similar result was stated by Droste and Vogler (2011, Def. 6.7 and Obs. 6.8).

3 Equivalences via Binarizations

In this section we will present three different surjective mappings $h \colon \mathrm{T}_{\Gamma} \to \mathrm{U}_{\Sigma}$ where Σ is an alphabet and Γ is a sorted alphabet with the maximum rank of a symbol being 2. We call h a *binarization* and we *binarize* a tree by using h backwards. Note that this allows several representations for a single unranked tree. Occasionally we also say that *t' is a binarization of t* if $t' \in \mathrm{T}_{\Gamma}$ and $t = h(t')$.

We show that wsta together with any of the presented binarizations and wuta are equally powerful; more formally for every wuta $\mathcal{M}$ there is a wsta $\mathcal{M}'$ and vice versa such that $[\![\mathcal{M}]\!](t) = \sum_{t' \in h^{-1}(t)} [\![\mathcal{M}']\!](t')$ for every $t \in \mathrm{T}_{\Sigma}$.

3.1 Left-branching Binarization

Our first binarization is inspired by the LEFT binarization of Matsuzaki et al. (2005, Fig. 6). It is similar to first-child-next-sibling encoding (Comon et al., 2007, Sec. 8.3.1). It transforms an unranked branch into a sequence of branches growing rightwards (cf. Figure 1).

Let Σ be an alphabet and let $S = \{\mathrm{T}, \mathrm{H}\}$ be a set of sorts. Intuitively, T will be the sort for trees and H will be the sort for hedges (sequences of trees). Based on Σ and assuming $\mathrm{CONS}, \mathrm{NULL} \notin \Sigma$, we define the $(S \times S^*)$-sorted alphabet Γ by $\Gamma^{(\mathrm{T}, \mathrm{H})} = \Sigma$, $\Gamma^{(\mathrm{H}, \mathrm{TH})} = \{\mathrm{CONS}\}$, $\Gamma^{(\mathrm{H}, \varepsilon)} = \{\mathrm{NULL}\}$.

There is a unique homomorphism h from the S-sorted term algebra over Γ into the S-sorted algebra $((A^{(s)} \mid s \in S), (\theta_{\sigma} \mid \sigma \in \Gamma))$ where $A^{(\mathrm{T})} = \mathrm{U}_{\Sigma}$, $A^{(\mathrm{H})} = (\mathrm{U}_{\Sigma})^*$,

$$\forall \sigma \in \Sigma \colon \theta_{\sigma}(t_1 \ldots t_k) = \sigma(t_1, \ldots, t_k),$$
$$\theta_{\mathrm{CONS}}(t_0, t_1 \ldots t_k) = t_0 t_1 \ldots t_k,$$
$$\theta_{\mathrm{NULL}}() = \varepsilon.$$

Figure 1 (ignoring the states for now) illustrates h. Note that h is a bijection, where $h(\xi')(\rho) = \xi'(12^{\rho_1 - 1} 1 \cdots 12^{\rho_n - 1} 1)$ for every $\xi' \in \mathrm{T}_{\Gamma}^{(\mathrm{T})}$ and $\rho = \rho_1 \cdots \rho_n \in \mathrm{pos}(h(\xi'))$.

Now let $\mathcal{M}' = (Q', \Gamma, I', \Delta')$ be a T-rooted $\Re$-S-wsta and $\mathcal{M} = (Q, \Sigma, I, \Delta)$ be an $\Re$-wuta such that Q and the state sets of the wfsa defined by Δ are pairwise disjoint. We say that *$\mathcal{M}$ and $\mathcal{M}'$ are*

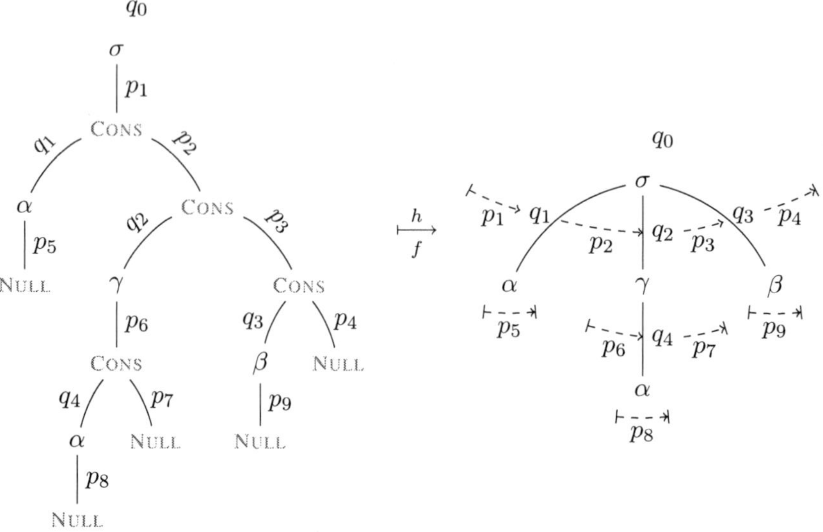

Figure 1: Trees with runs of related wsta and wuta.

$$\llbracket \mathcal{M} \rrbracket(t, e)$$

$$= I(r(\varepsilon)) \cdot \prod_{\rho \in \mathrm{pos}(t)} J_\rho(s(\rho)(0))$$

$$\cdot \left(\prod_{i=1}^{\mathrm{rk}(t|_\rho)} \Pi_\rho\big(s(\rho)(i-1), r(\rho i), s(\rho)(i)\big) \right) \cdot F_\rho\big(s(\rho)(\mathrm{rk}(t|_\rho))\big)$$

$$= I'(r(\varepsilon)) \cdot \prod_{\rho \in \mathrm{pos}(t)} \Delta'^{(t(\rho))}(r(\rho), s(\rho)(0))$$

$$\cdot \left(\prod_{i=1}^{\mathrm{rk}(t|_\rho)} \Delta'^{(\mathrm{CONS})}(s(\rho)(i-1), r(\rho i), s(\rho)(i)) \right)$$

$$\cdot \Delta'^{(\mathrm{NULL})}(s(\rho)(\mathrm{rk}(t|_\rho)))$$

(by definition of related)

$$= I'(r'(\varepsilon)) \cdot \prod_{\substack{\rho \in \mathrm{pos}(t), \\ \rho' = 12^{\rho_1 - 1}1 \cdots 12^{\rho_{|\rho|} - 1}1, \\ k = \mathrm{rk}(t|_\rho)}} \Delta'^{(t'(\rho'))}(r'(\rho'), r'(\rho'1))$$

(by definition of h and f)

$$\cdot \left(\prod_{i=1}^{k} \Delta'^{(t'(\rho'12^{i-1}))}(r'(\rho'12^{i-1}), r'(\rho'12^{i-1}1), r'(\rho'12^i)) \right)$$

$$\cdot \Delta'^{(t'(\rho'12^k))}(r'(\rho'12^k))$$

$$= I'(r'(\varepsilon)) \cdot \prod_{\rho \in \mathrm{pos}(t')} \Delta'^{(t'(\rho))}(r'(\rho), r'(\rho 1), \ldots, r'(\rho\,\mathrm{rk}(t'|_\rho)))$$

(by commutativity of $\cdot$ and definition of h)

$$= \llbracket \mathcal{M}' \rrbracket(t', r')$$

Figure 2: Showing that $\llbracket \mathcal{M} \rrbracket(t, e) = \llbracket \mathcal{M}' \rrbracket(t', r')$ for proof of Theorem 7, where $(t, e) = f(t', r')$, $(r, s) = e$, and $(P_\rho, Q, J_\rho, \Pi_\rho, F_\rho) = \Delta(r(\rho), t(\rho))$ for every $\rho \in \mathrm{pos}(t)$.

related, if $Q'^{(\mathrm{T})} = Q$, $Q'^{(\mathrm{H})}$ is the union of the state sets of all wfsa defined by Δ, and for every $\sigma \in \Sigma$, $q_0, q \in Q$, and $p, p' \in P$ we have

$$I'(q) = \begin{cases} I(q) & \text{if } q \in Q, \\ 0 & \text{otherwise,} \end{cases}$$

$$\Delta'^{(\sigma)}(q_0, p) = J(p),$$

$$\Delta'^{(\mathrm{CONS})}(p, q, p') = \Pi(p, q, p'),$$

$$\Delta'^{(\mathrm{NULL})}(p) = F(p),$$

where $(P, Q, J, \Pi, F) = \Delta(q_0, \sigma)$. Note that $\mathcal{M}'$ is T-rooted.

Theorem 7. *If $\mathcal{M}$ and $\mathcal{M}'$ are related, then $[\![\mathcal{M}']\!](t) = [\![\mathcal{M}]\!](h(t))$ for every $t \in \mathrm{T}_\Gamma$.*

Proof. Assume that $\mathcal{M}$ and $\mathcal{M}'$ are related. Figure 1 shows an example tree and its image under h. Moreover it shows a run and its image under the function $f \colon \mathrm{run}_{\mathcal{M}'} \to \mathrm{ex\text{-}run}_{\mathcal{M}}$ that is defined as follows: For every $(t', r') \in \mathrm{run}_{\mathcal{M}'}$ and $\rho \in \mathrm{pos}(h(t))$ we let $\rho' = 12^{\rho_1 - 1} 1 \cdots 12^{\rho_{|\rho|} - 1} 1$ and define $f(t', r') = (h(t'), (r, s))$ where $r(\rho) = r'(\rho')$ and $s(\rho)(i) = r'(\rho' 12^i)$ for every $i \in \{0, \ldots, \mathrm{rk}(t|_\rho)\}$. Note that f is a bijection.

Let $(t', r') \in \mathrm{run}_{\mathcal{M}'}$ and $(t, e) = f(t', r')$. In Figure 2 we show that $[\![\mathcal{M}]\!](t, e) = [\![\mathcal{M}']\!](t', r')$. This immediately implies that $[\![\mathcal{M}]\!](t) = [\![\mathcal{M}']\!](t')$. q.e.d.

It is easy to see that a wuta and a wsta have the same size and number of states, if they are related.

3.2 Right-branching Binarization

Our second binarization is based on the RIGHT binarization of Matsuzaki et al. (2005, Fig. 6).

In comparison to left-branching binarization we make the following changes. We define Γ by $\Gamma^{(\mathrm{T},\mathrm{H})} = \Sigma$, $\Gamma^{(\mathrm{H},\overline{\mathrm{H}}\mathrm{T})} = \{\mathrm{SNOC}\}$, and $\Gamma^{(\mathrm{H},\varepsilon)} = \{\mathrm{NULL}\}$. To define h we replace the definition of θ_{CONS} by $\theta_{\mathrm{SNOC}}(t_1 \ldots t_k, t_{k+1}) = t_1 \ldots t_k t_{k+1}$. In the definition for *related*, we just replace CONS by SNOC and reverse the wfsa, i.e. we interchange J and F and swap the states in transitions. Theorem 7 still holds with these changes; the proof works analogously.

3.3 Mixed Binarization

We now have a look at a binarization where the direction of growth may be flipped at arbitrary positions from rightwards to leftwards; cf. CENTER-PARENT and CENTER-HEAD binarization of Matsuzaki et al. (2005, Fig. 6). For this purpose,

let $S = \{\mathrm{T}, \mathrm{H}, \overline{\mathrm{H}}\}$. Based on Σ and assuming FLIP, CONS, NULL, SNOC, $\overline{\mathrm{NULL}} \notin \Sigma$, we define the $(S \times S^*)$-sorted alphabet Γ by

$$\Gamma^{(\mathrm{T},\mathrm{H})} = \Sigma, \qquad \Gamma^{(\mathrm{H},\overline{\mathrm{H}}\mathrm{T})} = \{\mathrm{FLIP}\},$$

$$\Gamma^{(\mathrm{H},\varepsilon)} = \{\mathrm{NULL}\}, \qquad \Gamma^{(\mathrm{H},\mathrm{T}\mathrm{H})} = \{\mathrm{CONS}\},$$

$$\Gamma^{(\overline{\mathrm{H}},\varepsilon)} = \{\overline{\mathrm{NULL}}\}, \qquad \Gamma^{(\overline{\mathrm{H}},\overline{\mathrm{H}}\mathrm{T})} = \{\mathrm{SNOC}\}.$$

There is a unique homomorphism h from the S-sorted term algebra over Γ into the S-sorted algebra $((A^{(s)} \mid s \in S), (\theta_\sigma \mid \sigma \in \Gamma))$ where $A^{(\mathrm{T})} = \mathrm{U}_\Sigma$, $A^{(\mathrm{H})} = A^{(\overline{\mathrm{H}})} = (\mathrm{U}_\Sigma)^*$, and

$$\forall \sigma \in \Sigma \colon \theta_\sigma(t_1 \ldots t_k) = \sigma(t_1, \ldots, t_k),$$

$$\theta_{\mathrm{CONS}}(t_0, t_1 \ldots t_k) = t_0 t_1 \ldots t_k,$$

$$\theta_{\mathrm{FLIP}}(t_1 \ldots t_k, t_{k+1}) = t_1 \ldots t_k t_{k+1},$$

$$\theta_{\mathrm{SNOC}}(t_1 \ldots t_k, t_{k+1}) = t_1 \ldots t_k t_{k+1},$$

$$\theta_{\mathrm{NULL}}() = \theta_{\overline{\mathrm{NULL}}}() = \varepsilon.$$

Unfortunately, this homomorphism is just surjective, but not bijective. That means, there may be several possible binarizations of an unranked tree. Given a wsta $\mathcal{M}'$ we will construct a wuta $\mathcal{M}$, such that the weight of an unranked tree t under $\mathcal{M}$ is the sum of weights of all binarizations $h^{-1}(t)$ under $\mathcal{M}'$.

Figure 4 shows an unranked node with the three subtrees t_1, t_2, t_3 and Figure 3 shows one possible binarization with the binarized subtrees t_1', t_2', t_3'. Note that in Figure 3 the rightmost subtree t_3' is attached to the node labeled FLIP, yet this node is located in the middle of the tree. Therefore, if we follow the path from the root to the leaf labeled $\overline{\mathrm{NULL}}$, we find t_1', t_3', and t_2' in this order. For the indicated run, we find the states in the order p_0, p_1, p_3, p_2.

Conversely, in the unranked case we find the subtrees in the order t_1, t_2, t_3. This is indicated by the arrow in Figure 3. Therefore, in a run of a wfsa from the constructed wuta, we have to pass along the information that we visited the state p_1, because we need it at the rightmost subtree t_3. Additionally, since each transition of the wfsa deals with one subtree, but the $\overline{\mathrm{NULL}}$ node has no subtrees, we have to guess a child and pass on this guess in the state. The constructed run is depicted in Figure 4.

Construction 8. For this construction, we use Σ, Γ, and S as defined above.

Let $\mathcal{M}' = (Q', \Gamma, I', \Delta')$ be a T-rooted $\Re$-S-wsta. We construct the $\Re$-wuta $\mathcal{M} =$

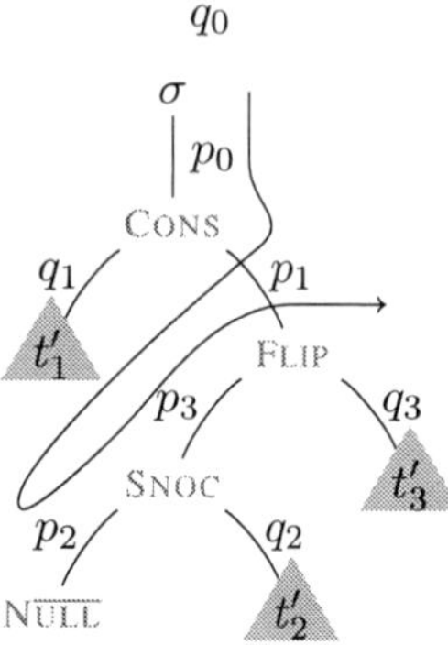

Figure 3: A binarization of Figure 4. The arrow indicates the processing order of the constructed wuta (cf. Construction 8). Note that the arrow touches p_1 twice.

$(Q'^{(\mathrm{T})}, \Sigma, I, \Delta)$ where, for every $q_0 \in Q'^{(\mathrm{T})}$ and $\sigma \in \Sigma$, we set $I(q_0) = I'(q_0)$ and $\Delta(q_0, \sigma) = (P, Q'^{(\mathrm{T})}, J, \Pi, F)$ where $P = Q'^{(\mathrm{H})} \cup \{\bar{p}_{q,s} \mid \bar{p} \in Q'^{(\overline{\mathrm{H}})}, q \in Q'^{(\mathrm{T})}, s \in Q'^{(\mathrm{H})}\}$, and for every $p, r, s \in Q'^{(\mathrm{H})}, \bar{p}, \bar{r} \in Q'^{(\overline{\mathrm{H}})}$, and $q, q' \in Q'^{(\mathrm{T})}$ we set

$$J(p) = \Delta'^{(\sigma)}(q_0, p),$$
$$\Pi(p, q, r) = \Delta'^{(\mathrm{CONS})}(p, q, r),$$
$$\Pi(s, q, \bar{r}_{q,s}) = \Delta'^{(\overline{\mathrm{NULL}})}(\bar{r}),$$
$$\Pi(\bar{p}_{q',s}, q, \bar{r}_{q,s}) = \Delta'^{(\mathrm{SNOC})}(\bar{r}, \bar{p}, q'),$$
$$F(\bar{p}_{q,s}) = \Delta'^{(\mathrm{FLIP})}(s, \bar{p}, q),$$
$$F(p) = \Delta'^{(\mathrm{NULL})}(p).$$

Every other weight is set to 0. □

Theorem 8. *For $\mathcal{M}$ and $\mathcal{M}'$ from Construction 8, we have $[\![\mathcal{M}]\!](t) = \sum_{t' \in h^{-1}(t)} [\![\mathcal{M}']\!](t')$ for every $t \in T_\Sigma$.*

Proof. Analogously to the proof of Theorem 7, we define a function $f \colon \mathrm{run}_{\mathcal{M}'} \to \mathrm{ex\text{-}run}_{\mathcal{M}}$. Figures 3 and 4 visualize this mapping. Note in contrast to h that f is injective.

By construction of $\mathcal{M}$, we have that $[\![\mathcal{M}']\!](t', r') = [\![\mathcal{M}]\!](f(t', r'))$ for every $t' \in T_\Gamma$ and $r' \in \mathrm{run}_{\mathcal{M}'}(t')$. For every (t, e) not in the image of f we have $[\![\mathcal{M}]\!](t, e) = 0$.

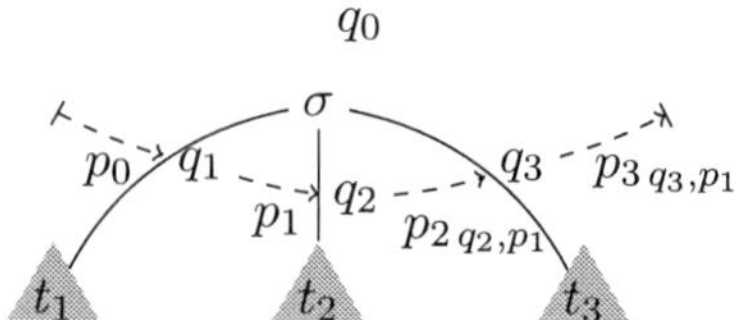

Figure 4: Unranked node with three subtrees.

All in all we have

$$[\![\mathcal{M}]\!](t) = \sum_{e \in \mathrm{ex\text{-}run}_{\mathcal{M}}(t)} [\![\mathcal{M}]\!](t, e)$$
$$= \sum_{e \in \mathrm{ex\text{-}run}_{\mathcal{M}}(t) \cap \mathrm{im}(f)} [\![\mathcal{M}]\!](t, e)$$
$$= \sum_{e \in \mathrm{ex\text{-}run}_{\mathcal{M}}(t) \cap \mathrm{im}(f)} [\![\mathcal{M}']\!](f^{-1}(t, e))$$
$$= \sum_{t' \in h^{-1}(t)} \sum_{r' \in \mathrm{run}_{\mathcal{M}'}(t')} [\![\mathcal{M}']\!](t', r')$$
$$= \sum_{t' \in h^{-1}(t)} [\![\mathcal{M}']\!](t'). \qquad \text{q.e.d.}$$

In Construction 8, the number of states of a single wfsa of $\mathcal{M}$ is in $\mathcal{O}(|Q'|^3)$ and its size is in $\mathcal{O}(|Q'|^2 \cdot \mathrm{size}(\mathcal{M}'))$. Since there is a wfsa for every state and terminal of $\mathcal{M}$, the number of states of $\mathcal{M}$ is in $\mathcal{O}(|Q'|^4 \cdot |\Sigma|)$ and its size is in $\mathcal{O}(|Q'|^3 \cdot |\Sigma| \cdot \mathrm{size}(\mathcal{M}'))$. Note that Π and F are the same for every constructed wfsa, so it might be beneficial to share them in an implementation.

For the other direction, i.e. when constructing a wsta given a wuta such that Theorem 8 holds, note that trees resulting from left-branching and right-branching binarization may also result from mixed binarization (modulo different node labels). Therefore the results from the previous sections can be applied.

4   The Probabilistic Case

For this section, we consider the semiring of non-negative reals with addition and multiplication. Note that every element different from 0 has an inverse with respect to multiplication. We will use this fact later on. Since our semiring is fixed, we will not mention it anymore in this section.

If we only consider weights between 0 and 1, and some additional conditions are met, these weights can be intuitively interpreted as probabilities. With this idea in mind we start with investigating wfsa since they form the core of wuta.

4.1 Probabilistic Automata

A wfsa $\mathcal{N} = (P, \Sigma, J, \Pi, F)$ is called

- *out-probabilistic*, if for every $p \in P$ we have
  $F(p) + \sum_{\sigma \in \Sigma, p' \in P} \Pi(p, \sigma, p') = 1$,
- *semi-probabilistic*, if it is out-probabilistic and
  $\sum_{p \in P} J(p) = 1$,
- *convergent*, if $\sum_{w \in \Sigma^*} [\![\mathcal{N}]\!](w)$ is finite,
- *consistent*, if this sum is 1,
- *probabilistic*, if it is semi-probabilistic and consistent, and
- *reduced*, if for every state $p \in P$ there is a word
  $w \in \Sigma^*$, a run $r \in \mathrm{run}_{\mathcal{N}}(w)$, and an index
  $i \in \{0, \dots, |w|\}$ such that $[\![\mathcal{N}]\!](w, r) > 0$ and
  $r(i) = p$.

These notions are strongly influenced by Dupont et al. (2005). If a semi-probabilistic wfsa is reduced, then it is consistent and, hence, probabilistic (Dupont et al., 2005, cf. Def. 9 and Prop. 2). Note that you can construct an equivalent reduced wfsa from any wfsa by removing those states p that violate the above condition. These states can be effectively determined.

Related Work   For the remainder of this section we investigate a special case of *renormalization* of weighted or of probabilistic context-free grammars (Abney et al., 1999; Chi, 1999; Nederhof and Satta, 2003). We restrict our investigations to wfsa and give alternative proofs.

In the following, we give an alternative view on wfsa by using matrices. Let A be a matrix. The matrix entry in the i-th row and the j-th column is denoted by $(A)_{i,j}$. If A has just a single row or column, we write $(A)_i$ for the entry in the i-th column or row, respectively. A matrix with just a single entry is identified with this entry. A *diagonal matrix* is a matrix that has non-zero entries only on its diagonal. For some vector X, by $\mathrm{diag}(X)$ we denote the diagonal matrix that has the entries of X on its diagonal. The *identity matrix*, denoted by Id, is $\mathrm{diag}(1 \dots 1)$; the dimensions of Id will always be clear from the context.

Let (P, Σ, J, Π, F) be a wfsa. We may assume w.l.o.g. that $P = \{1, \dots, |P|\}$. We will interpret J as a $1 \times |P|$ matrix, F as a $|P| \times 1$ matrix, and we will write $\Pi^{(\sigma)}$ for the $|P| \times |P|$ matrix defined as $(\Pi^{(\sigma)})_{p,p'} = \Pi(p, \sigma, p')$ for every $\sigma \in \Sigma, p, p' \in P$.

Observation 9. *Let $\mathcal{N} = (P, \Sigma, J, \Pi, F)$ be a wfsa and $w = w_1 \dots w_k \in \Sigma^*$. The weight of*

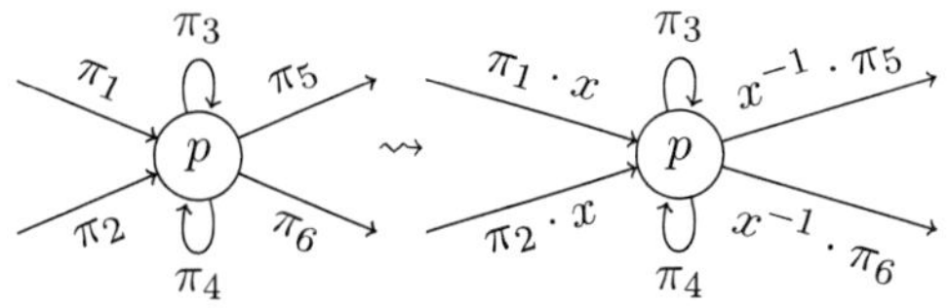

Figure 5: Changing weights $\pi_1, \dots, \pi_6$ at state p of a wfsa with a positive real x.

w under $\mathcal{N}$ can be alternatively calculated by

$$[\![\mathcal{N}]\!](w) = J \cdot \left(\prod_{i=1}^{|w|} \Pi^{(w_i)} \right) \cdot F.$$

The idea of the next lemma is to locally change weights of a wfsa without changing its semantics. For this purpose, the weights of "incoming" transitions (including initial weights) of some state p are scaled by some factor x while the weights of "outgoing" transitions (including final weights) of p are scaled by x^{-1}. Weights of transitions from p to p itself do not change. Figure 5 visualizes this idea. Lemma 10 applies this idea to all states simultaneously.

Lemma 10. *Let $\mathcal{N} = (P, \Sigma, J, \Pi, F)$ be a wfsa and let $X \in (\mathbb{R}_{>0})^{|P|}$. Construct the wfsa*

$$\mathcal{N}' = (P, \Sigma, J \cdot \mathrm{diag}(X), \Pi', \mathrm{diag}(X)^{-1} \cdot F)$$

with $\Pi'^{(\sigma)} = \mathrm{diag}(X)^{-1} \cdot \Pi^{(\sigma)} \cdot \mathrm{diag}(X)$ for every $\sigma \in \Sigma$. The wfsa $\mathcal{N}$ and $\mathcal{N}'$ are equivalent.

Proof. Let $w \in \Sigma^*$. If we calculate $[\![\mathcal{N}']\!](w)$ as presented in Observation 9, it is easy to see that for every factor $\mathrm{diag}(X)$ there is the adjacent factor $\mathrm{diag}(X)^{-1}$ and vice versa.   q.e.d.

Construction 11. Let $\mathcal{N} = (P, \Sigma, J, \Pi, F)$ be a convergent and w.l.o.g. reduced wfsa, and let $A = \sum_{\sigma \in \Sigma} \Pi^{(\sigma)}$. Then $\mathrm{Id} - A$ is invertible and an out-probabilistic wfsa $\mathcal{N}'$ equivalent to $\mathcal{N}$ can be constructed by applying Lemma 10 to $\mathcal{N}$ with $X = (\mathrm{Id} - A)^{-1} \cdot F$.   □

Theorem 11. *For every convergent wfsa there is an equivalent out-probabilistic wfsa.*

Proof. Note that $\sum_{w \in \Sigma^*} [\![\mathcal{N}]\!](w) = \sum_{j \in \mathbb{N}} J \cdot A^j \cdot F$. Hence, for every $p, p' \in P$ and $i, k \in \mathbb{N}$ we have

$$\infty > \sum_{j \in \mathbb{N}} J \cdot A^j \cdot F \qquad \text{(by convergence)}$$

$$\geq \sum_{j \geq i+k} J \cdot A^j \cdot F = \sum_{j \in \mathbb{N}} J \cdot A^i \cdot A^j \cdot A^k \cdot F$$

$$\geq \sum_{j \in \mathbb{N}} (J \cdot A^i)_p \cdot (A^j)_{p,p'} \cdot (A^k \cdot F)_{p'}$$

$$= (J \cdot A^i)_p \cdot \left(\sum_{j \in \mathbb{N}} (A^j)_{p,p'} \right) \cdot (A^k \cdot F)_{p'}.$$

Since $\mathcal{N}$ is reduced, there are $i, k \in \mathbb{N}$ such that $(J \cdot A^i)_p > 0$ and $(A^k \cdot F)_{p'} > 0$; therefore $\sum_{j \in \mathbb{N}} (A^j)_{p,p'} < \infty$ for every $p, p' \in P$. Hence, $\sum_{j \in \mathbb{N}} A^j$ is a converging Neumann series. This implies that the inverse of $\mathrm{Id} - A$ exists and is equal to this sum; this seems to be a well known result in the field of functional analysis; e.g. cf. Heuser (2006, Thm. 12.4).

Now we need a vector X to apply Lemma 10 such that the resulting wfsa is out-probabilistic, i.e., $\mathrm{diag}(X)^{-1} \cdot A \cdot \mathrm{diag}(X) \cdot (1 \ \ldots \ 1)^{\mathrm{T}} + \mathrm{diag}(X)^{-1} \cdot F = (1 \ \ldots \ 1)^{\mathrm{T}}$. This equation can easily be transformed into $(\mathrm{Id} - A) \cdot X = F$. Since $\mathrm{Id} - A$ is invertible, the equation is solved by $X = (\mathrm{Id} - A)^{-1} \cdot F$.

It remains to be shown that every entry of X is strictly positive. Recall that every entry of A is non-negative and that for every $p \in P$ there is a $j \in \mathbb{N}$ such that $(A^j \cdot F)_p > 0$. This implies that every entry of $(\mathrm{Id} - A)^{-1} = \sum_{j \in \mathbb{N}} A^j$ is non-negative and that every entry of $X = (\sum_{j \in \mathbb{N}} A^j) \cdot F$ is strictly positive. $\hfill$ q.e.d.

Theorem 12. *For every consistent wfsa there is an equivalent probabilistic wfsa.*

Proof. Since consistency implies convergence we can apply Construction 11 and obtain $\mathcal{N}' = (P, \Sigma, J', \Pi', F')$. By Lemma 10 $\mathcal{N}'$ is consistent. It remains to be shown that $\mathcal{N}'$ is also semi-probabilistic. By Construction 11 $\mathcal{N}'$ is already out-probabilistic, so we just have to show that $\sum_{p \in P} J'(p) = 1$.

For $p \in P$, let $\mathcal{N}_p = (P, \Sigma, J_p, \Pi', F')$ where J_p is the $1 \times |P|$ matrix where $(J_p)_p = 1$ and every other entry is 0. Obviously $\mathcal{N}_p$ is semi-probabilistic. Let $\mathcal{N}'_p$ be the equivalent reduced wfsa that is created from $\mathcal{N}_p$ just by removing states. It is easy to see that $\mathcal{N}'_p$ is also semi-probabilistic. Since $\mathcal{N}'_p$ is semi-probabilistic and

reduced, it is also consistent, hence, by equivalency, also $\mathcal{N}_p$ is consistent. That means

$$1 = \sum_{w \in \Sigma^*} [\![\mathcal{N}_p]\!](w) = \sum_{w \in \Sigma^*} J_p \cdot \left(\prod_{i=1}^{|w|} \Pi'^{(w_i)} \right) \cdot F'$$

$$= \sum_{w \in \Sigma^*} \left(\left(\prod_{i=1}^{|w|} \Pi'^{(w_i)} \right) \cdot F' \right)_p.$$

Since p was chosen arbitrarily, we have $1 = \sum_{w \in \Sigma^*} [\![\mathcal{N}']\!](w) = J' \cdot (1 \ \ldots \ 1)^{\mathrm{T}}$. $\hfill$ q.e.d.

Corollary 13. *The class of weighted languages recognizable by probabilistic wfsa is closed under reversal.*

Proof. A wfsa can easily be reversed by transposing the transition matrices and interchanging initial and final weights. The corollary follows by Theorem 12. $\hfill$ q.e.d.

Related Work. Paz (1971, Chapter III, Section A, Theorem 1.8) presents the same result for his probabilistic automata, which are slightly different from our probabilistic wfsa. His construction requires an exponential number of states in comparison to the given automaton. Our definition of probabilistic wfsa allows the presented construction, which does not change the state set at all. Paz' construction can be easily adapted to our case, yet it is unclear if our construction can also be adapted to his case.

4.2 Probabilities and Tree Automata

The notions probabilistic, semi-probabilistic, convergent, consistent, and reduced can be easily generalized to wsta and wuta. Note that in the tree case semi-probabilistic and reduced do not generally imply consistent. We now investigate what happens to these properties when constructing a wuta given a wsta or vice versa as presented in Section 3.

If the input is reduced, so is the output, except in case of mixed binarization when going from wsta to wuta; yet the output can easily be reduced. In case of left-branching binarization, if the input is semi-probabilistic, the output is also semi-probabilistic. Note that in any case, if the input is semi-probabilistic and reduced, then the wfsa in the wuta are consistent. Hence, in case of right-branching binarization, if the input is semi-probabilistic and reduced, the output is reduced and by Theorem 12 we can find an equivalent automaton that is also semi-probabilistic. In case of mixed binarization the direction from wuta to wsta is subsumed by the previous cases. Starting with a semi-probabilistic and reduced wsta, we can apply Construction 8, reduce the wfsa in the wuta without breaking consistency, and apply Theorem 12, ending up with a semi-probabilistic and reduced wuta.

Theorems 7 and 8 imply that if the input is convergent or even consistent, so is the output. Hence in the previous paragraph we may replace semi-probabilistic by probabilistic and the statements still hold.

5 Outlook: Implications on Training Methods

For each of three binarizations we have shown that wsta together with a binarization are equally powerful to wuta.

Our results suggest training methods for wuta: By binarizing a wuta, training the resulting wsta, and undoing the binarization, it is possible to use training algorithms designed for wsta also on wuta. The training may even alter the state behaviour, e.g. by splitting or merging states; cf. e.g. Matsuzaki et al. (2005) and Petrov et al. (2006). *Merging* (for example two) states q_1 and q_2 to a new state q means to replace every occurrence of q_1 and q_2 by q; the state set, the initial weights and the transition weights have to be adapted appropriately. The opposite direction is the *splitting* of a state q into (for example two) new states q_1 and q_2, which means to replace every occurrence of q by q_1 or q_2 in every possible combination, e.g., if there is a transition with two occurrences of q before splitting, then there are four transitions with different occurrences of q_1 and q_2 after splitting. Note that q, q_1, and q_2 need to have the same sort, otherwise there would be incompatibilities with the sorts of the (unchanged) terminals after splitting or merging.

These results formally explain why the performance of the training by Matsuzaki et al. (2005) is rather independent from the used binarization. Note that they used probabilistic context-free grammars with latent annotations (pcfg-la) while we used wsta, but it is easy to see that both formalisms are equally powerful. Additionally our binarizations use different node labels and introduced additional unary nodes as well as NULL and

NULL; but again this does not change the power of the formalism. Note that while changing latent annotations for pcfg-la it is not necessary to deal with sorts, because a latent annotation is always considered together with the terminal[1] it is attached to.

References

Steven Abney, David McAllester, and Fernando Pereira. 1999. Relating probabilistic grammars and automata. In *Proceedings of the 37th Annual Meeting of the Association for Computational Linguistics on Computational Linguistics*, ACL '99, page 542–549, Stroudsburg, PA, USA. Association for Computational Linguistics. DOI: 10.3115/1034678.1034759.

Julien Carme, Joachim Niehren, and Marc Tommasi. 2004. Querying unranked trees with stepwise tree automata. In Vincent van Oostrom, editor, *Rewriting Techniques and Applications*, volume 3091 of *Lecture Notes in Computer Science*, page 105–118. Springer Berlin Heidelberg. DOI: 10.1007/978-3-540-25979-4_8.

Zhiyi Chi. 1999. Statistical properties of probabilistic context-free grammars. *Computational Linguistics*, 25(1):131–160, March. URL: http://dl.acm.org/citation.cfm?id=973215.973219.

Hubert Comon, Max Dauchet, Remi Gilleron, Christof Löding, Florent Jacquemard, Denis Lugiez, Sophie Tison, and Marc Tommasi. 2007. Tree automata techniques and applications, October. URL: http://tata.gforge.inria.fr/.

Manfred Droste and Heiko Vogler. 2011. Weighted logics for unranked tree automata. *Theory of Computing Systems*, 48(1):23–47. DOI: 10.1007/s00224-009-9224-4.

Pierre Dupont, François Denis, and Yann Esposito. 2005. Links between probabilistic automata and hidden Markov models: probability distributions, learning models and induction algorithms. *Pattern Recognition*, 38(9):1349–1371. Grammatical Inference. DOI: 10.1016/j.patcog.2004.03.020.

Zoltán Fülöp and Heiko Vogler, 2009. *Handbook of Weighted Automata*, chapter Weighted Tree Automata and Tree Transducers, pages 313–403. Springer Berlin Heidelberg, Berlin, Heidelberg. DOI: 10.1007/978-3-642-01492-5_9.

Harro Heuser. 2006. *Funktionalanalysis / Theorie und Anwendung*. Teubner, fourth edition. URL: https://www.springer.com/9783835100268.

---

[1]We stick to the notion of terminal as it is used in this paper. In the context of pcfg-la, nullary terminals are called terminal symbols while the other terminals are called nonterminal symbols.

Johanna Högberg, Andreas Maletti, and Heiko Vogler. 2009. Bisimulation minimisation of weighted automata on unranked trees. *Fundamenta Informaticae*, 92(1-2):103–130, January. DOI: 10.3233/FI-2009-0068.

Takuya Matsuzaki, Yusuke Miyao, and Jun'ichi Tsujii. 2005. Probabilistic CFG with latent annotations. In *Proceedings of the 43rd Annual Meeting on Association for Computational Linguistics*, ACL '05, pages 75–82, Stroudsburg, PA, USA. Association for Computational Linguistics. DOI: 10.3115/1219840.1219850.

Mark-Jan Nederhof and Giorgio Satta. 2003. Probabilistic parsing as intersection. In *8th International Workshop on Parsing Technologies*, page 137–148.

Azaria Paz. 1971. *Introduction to Probabilistic Automata*. Academic Press. URL: http://www.sciencedirect.com/science/book/9780125476508.

Slav Petrov, Leon Barrett, Romain Thibaux, and Dan Klein. 2006. Learning accurate, compact, and interpretable tree annotation. In *Proceedings of the 21st International Conference on Computational Linguistics and the 44th annual meeting of the Association for Computational Linguistics*, ACL-44, pages 433–440, Stroudsburg, PA, USA. Association for Computational Linguistics. DOI: 10.3115/1220175.1220230.

Adaptive Importance Sampling from Probabilistic Tree Automata

Christoph Teichmann
University of Potsdam

Kasimir Wansing
Leipzig University

Alexander Koller
University of Potsdam

{chriteich|akoller}@uni-potsdam.de
kasimir.wansing@uni-leipzig.de

Abstract

We present a general importance sampling technique for approximating expected values based on samples from probabilistic finite tree automata. The algorithm uses the samples it produces to adapt rule probabilities for the automaton in order to improve sample quality.

1 Introduction

Natural language processing (NLP) often requires the computation of expected values $\mathbb{E}_{G(T)}[f(T)] = \sum_{t \in L_A} G(T = t) f(t)$ where the random variable T takes values from the language L_A of a probabilistic regular tree automaton (pRTA) A, f measures a quantity of interest and G is a probability distribution on L_A. A tree automaton provides a natural generalization of acyclic hypergraphs and latent variable grammars that are often used in natural language processing to express e.g. a parse chart or all the ways a word could be decomposed into morphemes. For different choices of G and f we obtain e.g. (Li and Eisner, 2009):

Feature Expectations for conditional random fields.

Kullback-Leibler Divergence to compare the predictions of different probability models.

Expected Loss for minimum risk decoding.

Log-Likelihood for predicting the next word in language models.

Gradients of those quantities for optimization.

Exact computation of these values is feasible if L_A is small or additional assumptions can be made, e.g. if the expected value is defined via semiring operations on the automaton defining L_A (Li and Eisner, 2009).

Li and Eisner (2009) give an exact semiring solution if two key assumptions can be made. First the definition of the probability $G(T)$ must decompose into smaller derivation steps along the rules of A. Second the number of rules of A cannot be too large, as they must all be visited. The first assumption is violated when e.g. non-local features (Huang, 2008) are used to define probabilities or when probabilities are defined by recurrent neural nets that use hidden states derived from whole subtrees (Socher et al., 2013; Dyer et al., 2016). The second assumption is violated when e.g. tree automata are used to represent parse charts for combinatorially complex objects like in graph parsing (Groschwitz et al., 2015).

When semiring techniques are not applicable, it is necessary to use approximation techniques. One popular technique is the use of Monte Carlo methods, i.e. sampling. It is often based on Markov Chain Monte Carlo (Gamerman and Lopes, 2006) or Particle Monte Carlo (Cappé et al., 2007) approaches and requires minimal knowledge about the expected value being approximated. In this work we develop an importance sampler based on pRTAs which can be used to approximate expected values in settings where exact solutions are infeasible. One can efficiently sample from a pRTA making it a suitable tool for generating proposals for importance sampling, as we show in Section 3.2.

Good performance of importance sampling requires choosing rule probabilities for the pRTA to closely approximate the target distribution. One can attempt to derive rule probabilities that achieve this by analyzing the target distribution a priori or by using a proposal that is known to be a good fit (Dyer et al., 2016). We present a technique for self-adaption in Section 4 that allows the

Proceedings of the ACL Workshop on Statistical NLP and Weighted Automata, pages 11–20,
Berlin, Germany, August 12, 2016. ©2016 Association for Computational Linguistics

sampler to learn a good proposal distribution on its own. Following recent advances in adaptive importance sampling (Ryu and Boyd, 2014; Douc et al., 2007) our technique picks the best possible rule probabilities for the pRTA according to an appropriate quality measure.

Both the generation of proposals from a pRTA and the adaption procedure we propose allow for a lazy implementation that only needs to visit states seen when drawing a sample. Therefore our algorithm can deal with very large automata.

2 Tree Automata

A signature Σ is a set of *functors*, for which any $l \in \Sigma$ is assigned a positive integer as an *arity* denoted by $rank(l)$. A *well formed tree* over Σ has the form $l(t_1, \ldots, t_{rank(l)})$ where $l \in \Sigma$ and each t_i is also a well formed tree.

2.1 Regular Tree Automata

A *probabilistic regular tree automaton* (pRTA) (Comon et al., 2007) is a tuple $A = \langle \Sigma, Q, R, q_S, \theta \rangle$ with Σ a signature, Q a finite set of *states* and $q_S \in Q$ the *start state*. R is a finite set of *rules* that have the form $q_0 \to l(q_1, \ldots, q_{rank(l)})$ with each q_i taken from Q and l from Σ.

The rules in R are mapped one to one to integers in $[1, |R|]$ so that we can say, e.g. r_i is the i-th rule. $\theta \in \mathbb{R}^{|R|}$ is a vector of *parameters* for the rules and θ_i is the parameter for r_i. We call the values of θ parameters because we use them indirectly to derive probabilities. By using a vector θ and defining probabilities indirectly, we deviate from standard notation for pRTA. We do this in order to more easily express the optimization problem we will later have to solve during adaption. For a rule $r = q \to l(\ldots)$ we call $lhs(r) = q$ the *left hand side* of r and use $sis(r)$ to denote the set of rules with the same left hand side as r. For pRTA A with parameters θ we define the probability $P_A^q(R = r_i)$ of using a rule r_i given a state q as 0 if $lhs(r_i) \neq q$ and otherwise as:

$$\frac{e^{\theta_i}}{\sum_{r_j \in sis(r)} e^{\theta_j}} \tag{1}$$

The probabilities sum to 1 for q if there is at least one rule r with $lhs(r) = q$ and therefore θ can take any value in $\mathbb{R}^{|R|}$. We shorten $P(X = x_1, \ldots | Y_1 = y_1, \ldots)$ to $P(x_1, \ldots | y_1, \ldots)$ if random variables are clear from the context.

As an example for a pRTA we will use $A_{ex} = \langle \{l, l'\}, \{q_0\}, \{r_1 = q_0 \to l(q_0, q_0), r_2 = q_0 \to l'()\}, q_0, \langle 1, 2 \rangle \rangle$. By our definition $P_{A_{ex}}^{q_0}(r_1) = \frac{e^1}{e^1 + e^2}$.

2.2 Derivations

At the core of our paper are *derivations* for a pRTA A, which are easily sampled. They are well formed trees for a signature Σ_R that is derived by using the rules of A as functors with $rank(q_0 \to l(q_1, \ldots)) = rank(l)$. A derivation d for A must have a rule r with $lhs(r) = q_S$ as its root functor and any node in d with a functor of the form $q_0 \to l(q_1, \ldots, q_n)$, must have an i-th child with a root functor of the form $q_i \to l'(\ldots)$. For A_{ex} one derivation is $d_{ex} = r_1(r_2, r_2)$.

We say a derivation *maps* to a tree t, denoted by $m(d) = t$, if replacing all the rules in d by their functor produces t. For A_{ex} we have $m(d_{ex}) = l(l', l')$. The set of derivations from a pRTA A that map to a tree t is denoted as Δ_A^t.

The language of A is $L_A = \{t | \Delta_A^t \neq \emptyset\}$. If $|\Delta_A^t| \leq 1$ for every t then A is said to be *unambiguous*. Assuming unambiguous automata simplifies most of our discussion and we do so throughout. Therefore we can denote the single derivation for a tree t as d_t. Many tree automata used in NLP, e.g. parse charts, are unambiguous. An extension to the ambiguous case is straightforward but laborious and is left for future work.

We denote by $R(d)$ the multi-set of all the rules that occur in the derivation d, e.g. $R(d_{ex}) = \{r_1, r_2, r_2\}$. For $A = \langle \Sigma, Q, R, q_S, \theta \rangle$ we define the joint probability $P_A(T = t, D = d)$ of a derivation d and a tree t as 0 if $m(d) \neq t$ and otherwise as:

$$\prod_{r \in R(d)} P_A^{lhs(r)}(r) \tag{2}$$

Lack of ambiguity implies $P_A(t) = P_A(t, d_t)$.

2.3 Sampling Derivations

For almost all Monte Carlo techniques it is of great importance that one can efficiently generate proposals and compute their probability. This is very easy for pRTAs which is why we use them here. One can draw a sample $\langle t, d \rangle$ from $P_A(T, D)$ if it is possible to sample rules given their left hand state. Begin with a tree consisting of only the start state q_S. Until we have a derivation we replace the leftmost state q_l in our tree with a rule

$q_l \rightarrow l(q_1, \ldots, q_n)$ drawn according to $P_A^{q_l}(R)$ and make $q_1, \ldots, q_n$ its children. This produces a derivation d and tree t given by $m(d)$. Note that the probability of generating any derivation-tree pair $\langle t, d \rangle$ this way is given by the multiplication of rule probabilities matching the definition of $P_A(T, D)$. For our case this means that we can also sample $P_A(t)$.

The sampling of derivations can fail in three ways. First, there may be states for which there are no rules to expand them. The sampling procedure we have outlined is undefined when such a state is reached. Secondly, it is possible that a pRTA is deficient[1] (Nederhof and Satta, 2006). This means that there is a non-zero probability that the sampling procedure we have outlined keeps expanding without ever stopping. Finally the number of rules for a single state might be so large that it is impossible to iterate over them efficiently to select one for a sample. The techniques for solving these problems are outside the scope of this paper and we therefore make three additional assumptions in addition to our condition that a pRTA A is unambiguous:

1. For every state q in A there is at least one rule r with $lhs(r) = q$.

2. A is cycle free, i.e. no state can be expanded to reach the same state. This restricts us to finite tree languages and removes the possibility of deficiency.

3. For each state q in A we can efficiently list all the rules r with $lhs(r)$.

3 Importance Sampling

3.1 Problem Setting

The formulation for the problem we want to solve is as follows. We have access to some pRTA A, the language L_A of which is the domain over which we are trying to compute an expected value. We are also given a probability function $G(T)$ defined over L_A and some function f, which measures some quantity of interest, e.g. the number of times a certain functor occurs as a leaf in a tree, whether a constituent appears in a parse tree or the count of a feature used for training a model. We want to compute the value of $\mathbb{E}_{G(T)}[f(T)]$. Note that many problem domains in NLP can be expressed as the language of a pRTA as they can express

charts that occur e.g. in context free parsing and also graph parsing (Groschwitz et al., 2015).

Li and Eisner (2009) give an algorithm for this problem that computes the expected frequency of seeing every rule in L_A under G and then exactly computes $\mathbb{E}_{G(T)}[f(T)]$ rule by rule. The algorithm they present is not applicable if G does not decompose according to the rules of the A or if A is too large to compute expectations efficiently. It can also be the case that we cannot compute $G(T)$ and instead have to use a proportional function $g(t)$ with $G(t) = \frac{g(t)}{Z}$ where Z is some normalization constant. This is the case if we are using e.g. a discriminate model that defines probabilities based on global normalization such as Conditional Random Fields (Lafferty et al., 2001). It also happens whenever we are only interested in the probability of a tree given an observation, e.g. when we want to know the probability of a parse tree given an observed sentence for EM training. If g is defined using non-local features (Huang, 2008) or using e.g. recurrent neural network structures (Dyer et al., 2016; Vinyals et al., 2014), then it is often infeasible to compute either Z or G.

The algorithm by Li and Eisner (2009) also requires f to decompose with the rules of A, which may not be the case if we are computing e.g. complex losses in loss aware training (Gimpel and Smith, 2010).

There are therefore situations in which we need a sampling algorithm that uses A to generate an approximation for $\mathbb{E}_{\frac{g(T)}{Z}}[f(T)]$ using only evaluations of g and f on single trees. This algorithm should work without computing Z or visiting all rules of A.

3.2 Solution with Importance Sampling

Importance sampling (Robert and Casella, 2004) is a well known technique based on the following fundamental equalities that hold for any set L and *auxiliary* probability distribution $P(T)$:[2]

$$\mathbb{E}_{G(T)}[f(T)] = \sum_{t \in L} \frac{G(t)f(t)}{P(t)} P(t) \quad (3)$$

$$= \mathbb{E}_{P(T)}\left[\frac{G(T)f(T)}{P(T)}\right] \quad (4)$$

On this basis we can approximate any expected value we are interested in by generating independent samples $s = t_1, \ldots, t_n$ from P, defining:

---

[1] Also called inconsistent.

[2] We assume $P(t) \neq 0$ for all $t \in L$

$$\mathbb{S}_{\langle t_1,\ldots,t_n \rangle}[h(t_i)] = \frac{1}{n}\sum_{i=1}^{n} h(t_i) \qquad (5)$$

and using $\mathbb{S}_s\left[\frac{G(t_i)f(t_i)}{P(t_i)}\right]$ as our approximation. Under mild conditions the law of large numbers tells us that this approximation will almost surely become arbitrarily close to the correct value as the number of samples increases.

As stated before, we might be unable to compute the normalizer Z to derive G from g. We can also estimate Z from samples. Note that:

$$Z = \sum_{t \in L} \frac{g(t)}{P(t)}P(t) \qquad (6)$$

$$= \mathbb{E}_{P(T)}\left[\frac{g(T)}{P(t)}\right] \qquad (7)$$

and we can estimate Z in a similar way to how we estimate $\mathbb{E}_{G(T)}[f(T)]$. In practice Z is estimated from the same sample s used to compute $\mathbb{S}_s\left[\frac{G(t_i)f(t_i)}{P(t_i)}\right]$. For a sample $s = t_1,\ldots,t_n$ from P we therefore approximate $\mathbb{E}_{G(T)}[f(T)]$ through the self normalized importance sampling estimate (Cappé et al., 2004) defined by :

$$\mathbb{S}_s^{\mathrm{norm}}\left[\frac{g(t_i)f(t_i)}{P(t_i)}\right] = \sum_{i=1}^{n} \frac{f(t_i)g(t_i)\sum_{j=0}^{n}\frac{P(t_j)}{g(t_j)}}{P(t)} \qquad (8)$$

If P^n is the probability of generating a sample $s = t_1,\ldots,t_n$ through independent draws from P then $\mathbb{E}_{P^n(S)}\left[\mathbb{S}_S^{\mathrm{norm}}\left[\frac{g(t_i)f(t_i)}{P_A(t_i)}\right]\right]$ may not equal $\mathbb{E}_{G(T)}[f(T)]$ as nested estimates can create systematic bias. But the law of large numbers ensures that Z converges to its true value with increasing n and the self normalized importance sampling estimate converges on $\mathbb{E}_{G(T)}[f(T)]$.

If we want to use importance sampling over a set of trees then we need a way to specify P that allows us easy sampling and evaluation of $P(t)$ for any tree t. As we saw in Section 2 pRTAs meet these requirements. Therefore we will use P_A with respect to some unambiguous pRTA A as our proposal distribution. It must be true that $L \subseteq L_A$ and such an automaton is usually given by the problem setting, e.g. one would directly use a parse chart when computing expected values over parses. We draw samples from P_A and compute an approximation according to equation 8. Note that this algorithm does not require us to know much about

f or g, we only have be be able to evaluate them both on the trees that occur in our sample, which will usually cover a small fraction of L_A. Most importantly g and f do not need to decompose for any sub-parts of t, as is often required in dynamic programming based techniques.

While the technique we have outline works no matter how we set rule probabilities for A, the term:

$$\frac{G(t_i)f(t_i)}{P_A(t_i)} \qquad (9)$$

may be become comparatively small when $P_A(t_i) >> G(t_i)$ so t_i contributes almost nothing to the estimate. It may also become relatively large if $P_A(t_i) << G(t_i)$ which can lead to a single t_i "dominating" the sample, again allowing other t_j almost no contribution. In both cases we will have to draw much more samples to obtain a good estimate (Robert and Casella, 2004). Therefore we would prefer P_A to not be too different from G. Choosing rule weights to set P_A to be close to G through analysis of G may be difficult and would have to be solved for every new problem instance. Therefore we develop an algorithm that automatically adapts P_A to improve sample quality.

4   Proposal Optimization

In this section we will discuss how to learn the auxiliary distribution P_A. We will use one out of a family A_θ of pFTAs with the form $\langle \Sigma, Q, R, q_S, \theta \rangle$ for which Σ, Q, R and q_S are fixed and we only adjust θ. We write $\theta^{(i)}$ with $i \in \mathbb{N}$ to denote a fixed choice for the parameters. $A_{\theta^{(i)}}$ denotes the member of the family with $\theta = \theta^{(i)}$. As in other recent research on adaptive importance sampling (Lian, 2011; Douc et al., 2007; Gu et al., 2015) we try to find a $\theta^{(i)}$ that minimizes a measure for how bad the fit between $P_{A_{\theta^{(i)}}}$ and G is. A natural measure from information theory is the Kullback-Leibler Divergence between P_{A_θ} and G:

$$D_{KL}(G||P_{A_\theta}) = \mathbb{E}_{G(T)}\left[\log\left(\frac{G(T)}{P_{A_\theta}(T)}\right)\right] \qquad (10)$$

If we subtract $G(t)\log(G(t))$ – which does not vary with θ – and replace $G(t) = \frac{g(t)}{Z}$ with just $g(t)$ we do not change the values of θ for which minima are obtained. A simpler function with the same minima would therefore be:

$$\mathbf{o}\left(\theta\right) = \sum_{t \in L_A} \left(-g(t) \left(\sum_{r_i \in R(d_t)} \theta_i - \log \left(\sum_{r_j \in sis(r_i)} e^{\theta_j} \right) \right) \right) + \frac{\|\theta\|^2}{2\lambda} \tag{11}$$

$$\frac{\partial \mathbf{o}\left(\theta^{(n)}\right)}{\partial \theta_k} = \sum_{t \in L_A} \left(-g(t) \left(\sum_{r_i \in R(d_t)} 1(i = k) - P_{A_{\theta^{(n)}}}^{lhs(r_i)}(r_k) \right) \right) + \frac{\theta_k^{(n)}}{\lambda} \tag{12}$$

$$o_{\langle \theta^{(n)}, k \rangle}(t) = -g(t) \left(\sum_{r_i \in R(d_t)} 1(i = k) - P_{A_{\theta^{(n)}}}^{lhs(r_i)}(r_k) \right) \tag{13}$$

$$\sum_{t \in L_A} -g(t) \left(\log \left(P_{A_\theta}(t) \right) \right) \tag{14}$$

Note that this function is no longer dependent on the complicated normalization constant Z and we can therefore ignore Z for our optimization algorithm. We will attempt to find the optimal θ iteratively. To ensure that any estimate $P_{A_{\theta^{(i)}}}$ assigns nonzero weight to any tree in L_A we add a regularization term to our objective. As a result we are going to attempt to find parameters θ that minimize the objective function given by (11). λ is a configuration parameter used to trade off between fitting G and spreading out rule probabilities evenly. Note that unambiguous automata are important to derive this convex objective function.

4.1 Optimization

Like Ryu and Boyd (2014) we use *stochastic gradient descent* (SGD) (Bottou, 1998). In SGD we attempt to find a minimum for $\mathbf{o}\left(\theta\right)$ by generating a series $\theta^{(1)}, \ldots, \theta^{(m)}$ of approximations to a stationary point according to:

$$\theta^{(n+1)} = \theta^{(n)} - \left(\alpha^{(n)} \odot \overline{\nabla \mathbf{o}\left(\theta^{(n)}\right)} \right) \tag{15}$$

Here $\overline{\nabla \mathbf{o}\left(\theta^{(n)}\right)}$ is an approximation of the gradient of $\mathbf{o}\left(\theta\right)$ at the point $\theta^{(n)}$, $\alpha^{(n)}$ is a vector of pre-set learning rates and $\odot$ denotes element-wise multiplication of the two arguments to the operator. If we can efficiently obtain an estimate for $\nabla \mathbf{o}\left(\theta^{(n)}\right)$ then we can run SGD for a number of iterations and optimize θ. Standard derivative rules show that the kth dimension of $\nabla \mathbf{o}\left(\theta^{(n)}\right)$ takes the form given by (12), where $1(x)$ is 1 if x is true and 0 otherwise. Note that, if we ignore the contribution of the regularization term, the gradient becomes smaller the more the probability of a rule given its left hand side matches the same

---

Given G, f, A_θ and population size ps

1. set $\theta^{(1)} = \mathbf{0}$

2. for $n \in [1, m]$ do:

    (a) generate a sample of trees
    $s^{(n)} = t_1^n, \ldots, t_{ps}^n$ from $P_{A_{\theta^{(n)}}}$

    (b) estimate gradient $\overline{\nabla \mathbf{o}\left(\theta^{(n)}\right)}_k$ as

    $$\mathbb{S}_{s^{(n)}} \left[\frac{o_{\langle \theta^{(n)}, k \rangle}(t_i)}{P_{A_{\theta^{(n)}}}(t_i)} \right] + \frac{\theta_k^{(n)}}{\lambda}$$

    (c) generate learning rates $\alpha^{(n)}$
    (d) set $\theta^{(n+1)}$ according to (15)

3. compute an importance estimate for $\mathbb{E}_{G(T)}\left[f(T)\right]$.

Algorithm 1: The adaptive importance sampling algorithm for pRTAs.

value according to $G(T)$. Intuitively this means that the rule weights adapt to match the expected frequency of a rule given its parent which is reminiscent of the use of expected rule counts in the technique of (Li and Eisner, 2009).

The gradient is a sum over a fairly simple function of trees and we can denote the "contribution" from a single tree t to a gradient dimension k by $o_{\langle \theta^{(n)}, k \rangle}(t)$ given by (13). We therefore use the iterative procedure given in Figure 1 for to chose a good $A_{\theta^{(n)}}$ and produce an estimate.

For the last step in our algorithm we can generate an additional final sample from $A_{\theta^{(m)}}$. A more efficient use of computation resources is to use all the samples $s^{(n)}$ to create m importance sampling estimates for $\mathbb{E}_{G(T)}\left[f(T)\right]$ and then take a weighted average. The use of a weighed average is due to the fact that early values for $\theta^{(n)}$ are likely to be of poorer quality than the final ones and there might be less merit to their contribution. The number of iteration steps m, the number ps of samples drawn in each iteration and the learning rates $\alpha^{(n)}$ must be specified externally. The parameters that need to be configured are usually much easier to set than values for θ, e.g. ps and m should simply be set as large as computationally feasible for optimal performance.

At first it may seem as if Step 2d requires us to adjust all parameters of the automaton at the same time. This would make it expensive to apply our algorithm to large automata. However we can add the gradient contribution of the regularization in a lazy fashion as in Carpenter (2008). This means that we only update rules seen in the sample. The regularization also forces parameters that have not been updated for a while towards 0, allowing us to remove these from explicit storage. As a result we can sample with very large pRTAs as proposal distributions.

4.2 Convergence

Before we give evaluation results we should make some statements on the convergence behavior of our algorithm. By the law of large numbers we can state:

Theorem 1. *In Algorithm 1 we almost surely have for each n:* $\displaystyle\lim_{ps\to\infty} \mathbb{S}^{norm}_{s^{(n)}}\left[\frac{g(t_i)f(t_i)}{P_{A_{\theta^{(n)}}}}\right] = \mathbb{E}_{G(T)}[f(T)].$

Estimates will converge to $\mathbb{E}_{G(T)}[f(T)]$ as stated by Theorem 1 even if SGD did not improve the fit between P_{A_θ} and G. But it would be reassuring if we could show that the $\theta^{(n)}$ tend towards a minimum for $\mathbf{o}(\theta)$ as n increases towards infinity. This can be shown by standard convergence conditions for SGD. The objective function given by equation 11 is actually strictly convex. This is the case because the square norm is strictly convex and a logarithm over a sum of exponentials is convex. All other terms in the formula are either constant or linear in θ and therefore also convex. The following conditions ensure convergence to an optimal setting of θ (for details see Bottou (1998)):

1. For every dimension k and sample size ps:

$$\mathbb{E}_{P^{ps}_{A_{\theta^{(n)}}}(S)}\left[\mathbb{S}_{s^{(n)}}\left[\frac{o_{\langle\theta^{(n)},k\rangle}(t_i)}{P_{A_{\theta^{(n)}}}(t_i)}\right]\right]$$

equals $\overline{\nabla\mathbf{o}\left(\theta^{(n)}\right)}_k$

2. $\mathbf{o}(\theta)$ is bounded from below.

3. For every dimension k it is true that $\alpha^{(n)}_k > 0$ for all n and $\sum_{n=0}^\infty (\alpha^{(n)}_k)^2 < \infty$, $\sum_{n=0}^\infty \alpha^{(n)}_k = \infty$.

4. The second moment of our estimate for $\nabla\mathbf{o}\left(\theta^{(n)}\right)$ is bounded by a linear function of $\|\theta^{(n)}\|^2$.

Condition 3 depends only on the α which may be chosen by the user to be i.e. $\frac{1}{n}$ to meet the requirement. Condition 2 is true as the Kullback-Leibler Divergence is never smaller than 0 and the same is true for the Euclidean norm. Condition 4 can be verified by inspecting the gradient and noting that L_A is finite by the assumptions we made in Section 2 and that all the terms in the sum are bounded by either 1,-1 or $\theta^{(n)}$. Condition 1 can be verified by simple algebra from our exposition of importance sampling. As a result we can state:

Theorem 2. *For Algorithm 1 we almost surely have:*

$$\lim_{n\to\infty} \theta^{(n)} = \operatorname*{argmin}_\theta \mathbf{o}(\theta)$$

This means that the rule probabilities converge towards values that are optimal as measured by the Kullback-Leibler Divergence.

5 Evaluation

We created an implementation of our approach in order to investigate its behavior. It, along with all evaluation data and documentation, is available via `https://bitbucket.org/tclup/alto/wiki/AdaptiveImportanceSampling` as part of Alto, an Interpreted Regular Tree Grammar (Koller and Kuhlmann, 2011) toolkit. We encourage readers to use the sampler in their own experiments. In this section we will evaluate the ability of our algorithm to learn good proposal weights in an artificial data experiment that specifically focuses on this aspect. This will show whether the theoretical guarantees correspond to practical benefits. In future work we will evaluate the algorithm in End-to-End NLP experiments to see how it interacts with a larger tool chain.

5.1 Evaluation Problem

We tested our approach by computing a constant expected value $\mathbb{E}_{G(T)}[1]$. The ratio $\frac{1*G(T)}{P_{A_\theta}(T)}$ be-

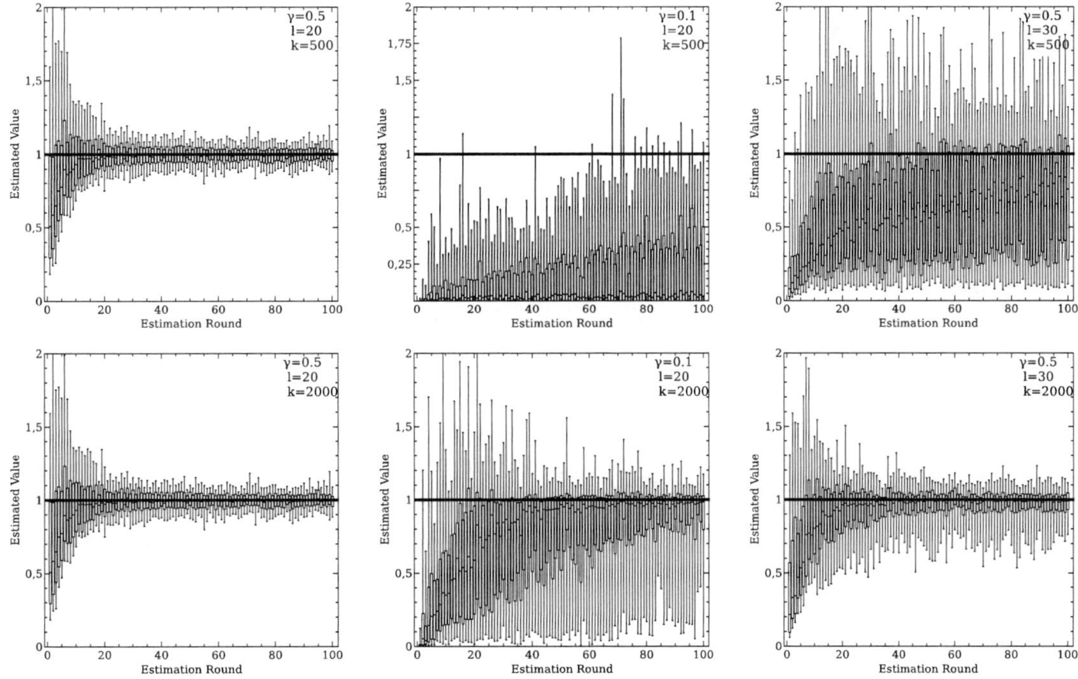

Figure 1: Convergence plots for different problem settings.

comes 1 if P_{A_θ} perfectly matches G and a single sample would suffice for an exact estimate. Therefore any error in the estimate is directly due to a mismatch between G and P_{A_θ}. We defined G through a pRTA with the same structure as the automaton we are sampling from. Therefore it is possible for P_{A_θ} to exactly match G. If we were told the correct parameters for θ then we would obtain a perfect sample in the first step and a good sample should be generated if the SGD steps successfully move θ from $\mathbf{0}$ to the values defining G.

The parameters for G were randomly chosen so that the resulting probabilities for rules given their left hand sides where distributed according to a symmetric Dirichlet Distribution. This is a good model for probability distributions that describe natural language processes (Goldwater et al., 2011). The symmetric Dirichlet Distribution is parametrized by a concentration parameter γ. The rule weights become more likely to be concentrated on a few of the rules for each left hand side as γ goes toward 0. Therefore many trees will be improbable according to G.

We obtain a complete evaluation problem by giving the structure of the automata used. As stated, we use the same automaton to specify G and A_θ save for θ which we initialize to be 0

for all entries. We chose a structure similar to a CKY parse chart for the underlying rules and states (Younger, 1967). Given a *length parameter* $l \in \mathbb{N}$ we added to the automaton all states of the form $\langle i, j \rangle$ with $0 \le i < j \le l$. The automaton has all rules of the form $\langle i, i+1 \rangle \to i()$ and all rules $\langle i, j \rangle \to *(\langle i, h \rangle, \langle h, j \rangle)$ with $0 \le i < h < j \le l$ and $*$ an arbitrary functor. Therefore the parameters for our evaluation problems are l and γ.

A central concern in making SGD based algorithms efficient is the choice of $\alpha^{(n)}$. We use an adaptive strategy for configuring the learning rates (Duchi et al., 2010; Schaul et al., 2012). These schemes usually have convergence proofs that require much stricter conditions than "vanilla" SGD and we therefore cannot claim that $\theta^{(n)}$ will converge with these approaches, but in practice they often perform well. Concretely, we use the technique for setting learning rates that was introduced by Duchi et al. (2010) which uses α' and divides it by the sum of all the gradient estimates seen so far to obtain the learning rate for each dimension. α' is fixed ahead of time – we chose 0.5 and we found that values between 1.0 and 0.1 could be used interchangeably to obtain the best performance. We set the regularization parameter λ in our objective $\mathbf{o}(\theta)$ to 100 for comparatively weak regularization.

5.2 Evaluation Results

Figure 1 plots the convergence behavior of the algorithm for different problem settings with fixed parameters l and γ. The upper row shows experiments with 500 samples and the lower uses 2000 samples. Each plot gives results for a single example automaton. Experiments with different automata showed the same trends. Each graph shows 100 repetitions of the experiment as box plots. Different random number seed were used for the repetitions. The box plots show how well the expected value was approximated in each of the $m = 100$ rounds of adaption. The value in each round/repetition n is computed only for the sample $s^{(n)}$ drawn in that round/repetition. Whiskers indicate the 9th and 91th percentile value.

Note the tendency towards underestimation in all experiments. This indicates that the algorithm proposes many trees with low probability under G and has to adapt in order to find more likely trees.

For $l = 20$ and $\gamma = 0.5$ and $k = 500$ the sampler converges in 40 iterations. Note that performance after four steps with $k = 500$ is better than with one step of $k = 2000$. This shows that adapting parameters provides a benefit over simply increasing the sample size. With $\gamma = 0.1$, $l = 20$ and $k = 500$ the samples improve much more slowly. This is to be expected as there are more than 1 billion trees in L_A and only very few of them will be assigned large probabilities by the more peaky rule probabilities. Therefore the algorithm has to randomly find these few trees to produce a good estimate both for the evaluated value and for the gradient used in adaptation. When $k = 2000$ there are faster improvements as the algorithm has a better gradient estimate.

Convergence is also slower when l is increased to 30 as the number of trees to consider rises and the amount of parameters in θ grows in the order of $O(l^3)$. Convergence speed again increases if we set the sample size $k = 2000$.

Overall we can see that the adaption steps improve the quality of our importance sampler and lead to a simple, yet versatile algorithm for approximating expected values.

6 Related Work

Sampling in NLP is most often implemented via Markov Chain Monte Carlo methods that either have to move through the relevant domain with small steps (Chung et al., 2013) or use a good proposal distribution in order to generate new trees (Johnson et al., 2007). Because it is difficult to adapt Markov Chain Monte Carlo algorithms (Liang et al., 2010) the proposal distribution for generating new trees needs to be specified by the user in advance. Particle Monte Carlo Methods (Cappé et al., 2007; Börschinger et al., 2012) are related to importance sampling and would allow for more adaptive proposals, but have not been used this way for the structured outputs used in natural language processing. The idea of using adaptive versions of importance sampling has become much more prevalent in the last years (Douc et al., 2007; Lian, 2011; Ryu and Boyd, 2014). Ryu and Boyd (2014) discussed the use of SGD to optimize a convex function in order to improve an importance sampler. They discussed applications where the proposal distribution is from the exponential family of distributions and used the variance of their sampler as the optimization objective. Douc et al. (2007) and Lian (2011) used an objective based on Kullback-Leibler divergence, but they used techniques other than SGD to optimize the objective. It is also possible to use more complex models to generate proposals (Gu et al., 2015) at the price of less efficient training.

7 Conclusion

We have presented an adaptive importance sampler that can be used to approximate expected values taken over the languages of probabilistic regular tree automata. These values play a central role in many natural language processing applications and cannot always be computed analytically. Our sampler adapts itself for improved performance and only requires the ability to evaluate all involved functions on single trees. To achieve adaptiveness, we have introduced a convex objective function which does not depend on a complex normalization term. We hope that this simple technique will allow researchers to use more complex models in their research.

Acknowledgments. We thank the anonymous reviewers for their comments. We thank the workshop organizers for their patients in waiting for our final version. We received valuable feedback from Jonas Groschwitz and Martn Villalba. This work was supported by the DFG grant KO 2916/2-1.

References

Benjamin Börschinger, Katherine Demuth, and Mark Johnson. 2012. Studying the effect of input size for Bayesian Word Segmentation on the Providence Corpus. In *Proceedings of COLING 2012*, pages 325–340.

Léon Bottou. 1998. Online Algorithms and stochastic approximations. In David Saad, editor, *Online Learning in Neural Networks*, pages 9–13. Cambridge University Press. revised, oct 2012.

Olivier Cappé, Arnaud Guillin, Jean-Michel Marin, and Christian Robert. 2004. Population Monte Carlo. *Journal of Computational and Graphical Statistics*, 13(4):907–929.

Olivier Cappé, Simon J. Godsill, and Eric Moulines. 2007. An overview of existing methods and recent advances in Sequential Monte Carlo. In *Proceedings of the IEEE*, volume 95, pages 899–924.

Bob Carpenter. 2008. Lazy sparse Stochastic Gradient Descent for Regularized Multinomial Logistic Regression. Technical report, Alias-i, Inc.

Tagyoung Chung, Licheng Fang, Daniel Gildea, and Daniel Štefankovič. 2013. Sampling tree fragments from forests. *Computational Linguistics*, 40(1):203–229.

Hubert Comon, Max Dauchet, Rémi Gilleron, Florent Jacquemard, Denis Lugiez, Sophie Tison, Marc Tommasi, and Christof Löding. 2007. *Tree Automata techniques and applications*. published online - http://tata.gforge.inria.fr/.

Randal Douc, Arnaud Guillin, Jean-Michel Marin, and Christian Robert. 2007. Convergence of adaptive mixtures of Importance Sampling schemes. *The Annals of Statistics*, 35(1):420–448.

John Duchi, Elad Hazan, and Yoram Singer. 2010. Adaptive Subgradient methods for Online Learning and stochastic optimization. In *COLT 2010 - The 23rd Conference on Learning Theory*, pages 257–269.

Chris Dyer, Adhiguna Kuncoro, Miguel Ballesteros, and Noah A. Smith. 2016. Recurrent Neural Network grammars. In *Proceedings of the 2016 Conference of the North American Chapter of the Association for Computational Linguistics: Human Language Technologies*, pages 199–209.

Dani Gamerman and Hedibert F. Lopes. 2006. *Markov Chain Monte Carlo - Stochastic Simulation for Bayesian Inference*. Chapman & Hall/CRC.

Kevin Gimpel and Noah A. Smith. 2010. Softmax-Margin Training for structured Log-Linear Models. Technical report, Carnegie Mellon University.

Sharon Goldwater, Thomas L. Griffiths, and Mark Johnson. 2011. Producing Power-Law Distributions and damping Word Frequencies with two-stage language models. *Journal of Machine Learning Research*, 12:2335–2382.

Jonas Groschwitz, Alexander Koller, and Christoph Teichmann. 2015. Graph parsing with S-graph Grammars. In *Proceedings of the 53rd Annual Meeting of the Association for Computational Linguistics and the 7th International Joint Conference on Natural Language Processing*, pages 1481–1490.

Shixiang Gu, Zoubin Ghahramani, and Richard E. Turner. 2015. Neural adaptive Sequential Monte Carlo. In *Advances in Neural Information Processing Systems 28*, pages 2629–2637.

Liang Huang. 2008. Forest reranking: Discriminative parsing with non-local features. In *Proceedings of ACL-08: HLT*, pages 586–594.

Mark Johnson, Thomas L. Griffiths, and Sharon Goldwater. 2007. Bayesian Inference for PCFGs via Markov Chain Monte Carlo. In *Human Language Technology Conference of the North American Chapter of the Association of Computational Linguistics*, pages 139–146. The Association for Computational Linguistics.

Alexander Koller and Marco Kuhlmann. 2011. A generalized view on parsing and translation. In *Proceedings of the 12th International Conference on Parsing Technologies*, pages 2–13.

John D. Lafferty, Andrew McCallum, and Fernando C. N. Pereira. 2001. Conditional Random Fields: Probabilistic models for segmenting and labeling sequence data. In *Proceedings of the Eighteenth International Conference on Machine Learning*, pages 282–289.

Zhifei Li and Jason Eisner. 2009. First- and second-order Expectation Semirings with applications to Minimum-Risk training on Translation Forests. In *Proceedings of the 2009 Conference on Empirical Methods in Natural Language Processing*, pages 40–51.

Heng Lian. 2011. Stochastic adaptation of Importance Sampler. *Statistics*, 46(6):777–785.

Faming Liang, Chuanhai Liu, and Raymond Carroll. 2010. *Advanced Markov Chain Monte Carlo Methods*. John Wiley and Sons Ltd.

Mark-Jan Nederhof and Giorgio Satta. 2006. Estimation of consistent Probabilistic Context-free Grammars. In *Proceedings of the Human Language Technology Conference of the North American Chapter of the ACL*, pages 343–350.

Christian P. Robert and George Casella. 2004. *Monte Carlo statistical methods*. Springer, 2 edition.

Ernest K. Ryu and Stephen P. Boyd. 2014. Adaptive Importance Sampling via stochastic Convex Programming. *CoRR, abs/1412.4845*.

Tom Schaul, Sixin Zhang, and Yann LeCun. 2012. No more pesky learning rates. *CoRR*, abs/1206.1106.

Richard Socher, John Bauer, Christopher D. Manning, and Andrew Y. Ng. 2013. Parsing with Compositional Vector Grammars. In *Proceedings of the 51st Annual Meeting of the Association for Computational Linguistics*, pages 455–465.

Oriol Vinyals, Lukasz Kaiser, Terry Koo, Slav Petrov, Ilya Sutskever, and Geoffrey E. Hinton. 2014. Grammar as a foreign language. *CoRR*, abs/1412.7449.

Daniel H. Younger. 1967. Recognition and parsing of Context-Free Languages in time n^3. *Information and Control*, 10:189–208.

Transition-based dependency parsing as latent-variable constituent parsing

Mark-Jan Nederhof
School of Computer Science
University of St Andrews, UK

Abstract

We provide a theoretical argument that a common form of projective transition-based dependency parsing is less powerful than constituent parsing using latent variables. The argument is a proof that, under reasonable assumptions, a transition-based dependency parser can be converted to a latent-variable context-free grammar producing equivalent structures.

1 Introduction

Over the last decade, transition-based dependency parsers have received much attention, to a large extent due to Nivre (2003), Nivre and Scholz (2004), Nivre et al. (2004) and following publications. The theory represented in these publications seems to differ significantly from traditional automata theory, on which the theory of constituent parsing is based. Differences lie in notation, in terminology and in the overall conceptual framework.

An explanation for this cannot immediately be found by contrasting the foundations of dependency parsing and constituent parsing. Some of the earliest literature on dependency parsing (Hays, 1964; Gaifman, 1965) discusses the two kinds of parsing on an equal footing. Also more recent literature (Carroll and Charniak, 1992; Klein and Manning, 2004) discusses dependency parsing as closely related to constituent parsing. The concept of bilexical context-free grammars (Eisner and Satta, 1999) establishes further explicit connections between phrase-structure grammar and dependency grammar. See also Rambow (2010) for a discussion about the relation between constituent and dependency structures.

One advantage of dependency grammar is the ease with which the definition of parse struc-

tures can be generalized from the projective case to the non-projective case, but also this cannot explain the divergence from the theory of constituent parsing, as much the same style is used for describing projective dependency parsing and for non-projective dependency parsing; cf. Nivre (2009) for the latter. Furthermore, discontinuity has also been explored for constituent parsing (Kallmeyer and Maier, 2010; van Cranenburgh et al., 2011). Close links between discontinuous constituent parsing and non-projective dependency parsing follow from the work of, among others, Kallmeyer and Kuhlmann (2012) and Kuhlmann (2013).

Recent literature on dependency parsing has a strong emphasis on parsing speed. Often, parsing algorithms are close to linear-time, or close to quadratic-time in the worst case (Covington, 2001). However, there is also a considerable body of literature on speeding up constituent parsing (Lavie and Tomita, 1993; Goodman, 1997; Caraballo and Charniak, 1998). Deterministic parsing algorithms for constituent parsing were proposed by e.g. Wong and Wu (1999), Kalt (2004), Sagae and Lavie (2005) and Nederhof and McCaffery (2014), while the parser of Ratnaparkhi (1997) is close to linear time; for deterministic chunk parsing, see Tsuruoka and Tsujii (2005). Seneff (1989) suggests that deterministic constituent parsing was more or less the norm at the end of the 1980s. Conversely, transition-based dependency parsing has been generalized to non-deterministic parsing (Kuhlmann et al., 2011; Huang and Sagae, 2010).

An empirical connection between constituent parsing and dependency parsing has been established by several investigations of conversion between constituent structures and dependency structures. Transformation from constituent structures to dependency structures is addressed by Lin (1998), Collins (2003), Yamada and Matsumoto

Proceedings of the ACL Workshop on Statistical NLP and Weighted Automata, pages 21–31,
Berlin, Germany, August 12, 2016. ©2016 Association for Computational Linguistics

(2003) and Hall and Novák (2005). Dependency parsers have been used to perform constituent parsing (Ma et al., 2010). Transformations from unlabeled dependency structures to constituent structures were discussed by Johnson (2007), and transformations from labeled dependency structures were discussed by Miyao et al. (2008). It has been observed that constituent parsers used to perform dependency parsing can be at least as accurate as dedicated dependency parsers, although they are generally slower (Cer et al., 2010; Candito et al., 2010).

The present article aims to elucidate part of the relation between the theory of transition-based dependency parsing and the theory of constituent parsing. We will focus on a particular form of constituent parsing that is based on latent-variable probabilistic context-free grammars, which currently offers state-of-the-art accuracy. One apparent complication is that there are competing ways of obtaining such grammars, roughly divided into forms of EM training (Matsuzaki et al., 2005; Petrov et al., 2006) or of spectral learning (Narayan and Cohen, 2015). We circumvent this complication by looking at the general class of *non-probabilistic* latent-variable context-free grammars, and show that these have sufficient formal power to subsume deterministic transition-based dependency parsing. The implication is that latent-variable *probabilistic* context-free grammars, obtained through EM training, spectral learning, or any other method still to be developed, have the potential to be at least as accurate as deterministic transition-based dependency parsing.

This paper intentionally limits the scope to projective parsing. The reason is that the literature on non-projectivity (discontinuity) has not yet converged, and new approaches are discovered with some regularity. This makes it hard to offer formal evidence that non-projective dependency parsing can generally be realized via discontinuous constituent parsing. At best, one can highlight one or two typical implementations of dependency parsing and constituent parsing and argue that the mechanisms for dealing with non-projectivity are comparable in nature, awaiting precise arguments relating their formal power.

One well-established approach to dealing with non-projective dependency structure is commonly referred to as *pseudo-projectivity* (Kahane et al.,

1998; Nivre and Nilsson, 2005). The idea is that a first phase of projective parsing is followed by a *lifting* operation that rearranges edges to make them cross one another. A related idea for discontinuous constituent parsing is the reversible splitting conversion of Boyd (2007).

A related but different approach is due to Nivre (2009). Here, the usual one-way input tape is replaced by a buffer. A non-topmost element from the parsing stack, which holds a word previously read from the input sentence, can be transferred back to the buffer, and thereby input positions can be effectively swapped, and non-projective structures result. We see no reason why the same idea would not equally well apply to constituent parsing.

This paper has the following structure. After fixing notation in Section 2, we present a formal model of deterministic parsing in Section 3, in terms of oracle automata. These automata appear at first sight to be biased towards constituent parsing, but Section 4 shows that they allow a clean formalization of arc-standard and arc-eager transition-based dependency parsing. It is shown in Section 5 that oracle automata can, under reasonable assumptions, be transformed into latent-variable context-free grammars. Section 6 further explores these assumptions as relating to common implementations of transition-based dependency parsing. As shown in Section 7, the results carry over to probabilistic automata and grammars.

2 Preliminaries

In this paper, a *tree* refers to a term built of leaf symbols, from the alphabet Σ_{leaf}, and internal symbols, from the alphabet Σ_{intern}. A symbol $a \in \Sigma_{leaf}$ by itself is a tree, and if $A \in \Sigma_{intern}$ and $t_1, \ldots, t_k$ are trees, then $A(t_1 \cdots t_k)$ is a tree. (In this paper, we assume the number k of children of an internal node is non-zero.) The set of all trees with given alphabets Σ_{leaf} and Σ_{intern} is denoted by $\mathcal{T}(\Sigma_{leaf}, \Sigma_{intern})$. We will use the symbol t for trees and symbol τ for sequences of trees. The empty sequence is denoted by ε. We define the *root* of a tree by $root(a) = a$ and $root(A(t_1 \cdots t_k)) = A$. We define the *yield* of a tree by $yield(a) = a$ and $yield(A(t_1 \cdots t_k)) = yield(t_1) \cdots yield(t_k)$. We define $first(aw) = a$ and $last(wa) = a$, for $a \in \Sigma_{leaf}$ and $w \in \Sigma_{leaf}^*$, $first(\varepsilon)$ and $last(\varepsilon)$ are undefined, and $first(t) = first(yield(t))$ and $last(t) = last(yield(t))$ for

$t \in \mathcal{T}(\Sigma_{leaf}, \Sigma_{intern})$.

As usual, a *context-free grammar* (CFG) is represented by a 4-tuple (Σ, N, S, R), where Σ and N are two disjoint finite sets of *terminals* and *nonterminals*, respectively, $S \in N$ is the *start symbol*, and R is a finite set of *rules*, each of the form $A \to \alpha$, where $A \in N$ and $\alpha \in (\Sigma \cup N)^*$. By *grammar symbol* we mean a terminal or nonterminal. We use symbols $A, B, C, \ldots$ for nonterminals, $a, b, c, \ldots$ for terminals, $v, w, x, \ldots$ for strings of terminals, and $\alpha, \beta, \gamma, \ldots$ for strings of grammar symbols. To simplify the discussion we will assume that all rules are of the form $A \to B_1 \cdots B_k$, where $k \geq 1$, or of the form $A \to a$. We also assume that S does not occur in the right-hand side of any rule.

A *latent-variable* CFG (L-CFG) differs from a CFG in that each nonterminal, except the start symbol $S^\dagger$, is of the composite form $A^{(\ell)}$, where A is a *surface* symbol and ℓ is a *latent* symbol. We denote the set of latent symbols by L, the set of surface symbols by N and the set of composite nonterminals by N^L. A L-CFG has one or more rules of the form $S^\dagger \to S^{(\ell)}$, some $\ell \in L$.

The intuition behind L-CFG is that the surface symbols are those that occur in parse trees used to represent syntactic structure, these being trees in $\mathcal{T}(\Sigma, N)$, while the purpose of the latent symbols is to restrict derivations and help define probability distributions over parse trees, once we extend rules with probabilities.

L-CFGs are intimately related to regular tree grammars (Brainerd, 1969; Gécseg and Steinby, 1997), which is apparent from the definition of their 'derives' relation. Fix a L-CFG G. For $t, t' \in \mathcal{T}(\Sigma \cup N^L, N)$, we let $t \Rightarrow_G t'$ if t' results from t by replacing some occurrence of $A^{(\ell)}$ by $A(\alpha)$, for some rule $A^{(\ell)} \to \alpha$. A *parse tree* of G is a tree $t \in \mathcal{T}(\Sigma, N)$ such that $S^{(\ell)} \Rightarrow_G^* t$, for some ℓ.

A *canonical* L-CFG is formed from a CFG by having a singleton set $L = \{\ell\}$, enhancing each nonterminal occurrence with an additional superscript (ℓ), and adding rule $S^\dagger \to S^{(\ell)}$. The parse trees of this canonical L-CFG concur with the standard definition of parse tree of a CFG. The set of all parse trees is called the *tree language* of a CFG or L-CFG.

It is often convenient to distinguish a subset of the composite nonterminals as not producing any surface symbols in parse trees. For example, if we binarize a long rule $A \to B\ C\ D$ from a CFG into two rules $A^{(\ell_A)} \to E^{(\ell_E)}\ D^{(\ell_D)}$ and $E^{(\ell_E)} \to B^{(\ell_B)} C^{(\ell_C)}$ of a L-CFG, then we may wish to mark $E^{(\ell_E)}$ as not producing any trace in the parse tree. In terms of the derives relation, this means $A^{(\ell_A)} \Rightarrow_G A(E^{(\ell_E)} D^{(\ell_D)}) \Rightarrow_G A(B^{(\ell_B)} C^{(\ell_C)} D^{(\ell_D)})$, etc. The same principle may be used to avoid spurious ambiguity in the representation of dependency structures using bilexical context-free grammars (Section 4).

3 Oracle automata

We define an *oracle automaton* as a variant of a traditional shift-reduce parser, in which an oracle uniquely determines the next parser action. The oracle is a partial function Ω that maps a sequence of trees (the current content of the *stack*, see below) and a terminal (the *lookahead*) to a rule that is to be applied next. It is constrained by:

1. if $\Omega(\tau, a) = (A \to b)$, then $a = b$; and

2. if $\Omega(\tau, a) = (A \to B_1 \cdots B_k)$, then τ can be written as $\tau' t_1 \cdots t_k$, where $root(t_i) = B_i$ for each i $(1 \leq i \leq k)$.

The first constraint says that reduction of terminal b to nonterminal A should only be suggested if that terminal is the lookahead. The second constraint says that reduction by a rule with right-hand side of length k should only be suggested if the roots of the top-most k subtrees on the stack match the right-hand side of that rule.

For CFG G and oracle Ω, the oracle automaton $\mathcal{M}$ manipulates configurations of the form $(\tau, v\$)$, where τ is the stack, and v is the remaining input. The symbol $\$$ is the end-of-sentence marker, which we will need for technical reasons. For given input w, the initial configuration is $(\varepsilon, w\$)$. The allowable steps are:

shift $(\tau, av\$) \vdash_\mathcal{M} (\tau A(a), v\$)$, if $\Omega(\tau, a) = (A \to a)$; and

reduce $(\tau t_1 \cdots t_k, v\$) \vdash_\mathcal{M} (\tau A(t_1 \cdots t_k), v\$)$ if $\Omega(\tau t_1 \cdots t_k, first(v\$)) = (A \to B_1 \cdots B_k)$.

If a configuration is $(\tau, av\$)$ and $\Omega(\tau, a)$ is undefined, then parsing fails. Acceptance happens upon reaching a configuration $(t, \$)$ with $root(t) = S$. By a *computation* we mean a sequence $(\tau, vw\$) \vdash_\mathcal{M}^* (\tau', w\$)$ of zero or more steps.

It is easy to see that if $(\varepsilon, w\$) \vdash^*_{\mathcal{M}} (t, \$)$ then $yield(t) = w$. The set of all t such that $(\varepsilon, w\$) \vdash^*_{\mathcal{M}} (t, \$)$ and $root(t) = S$ is the *tree language* of $\mathcal{M}$, and is a subset of the tree language of G. This may be a *strict* subset. In particular, if t is a parse tree of G and $w = yield(t)$, then there is at most one computation of the form $(\varepsilon, w\$) \vdash^*_{\mathcal{M}} (t', \$)$, for some t' with $root(t') = S$, but t' may or may not be equal to t, depending on the definition of Ω.

In practice, the value $\Omega(\tau, a)$ is not an arbitrary function of τ and a. It will typically depend on only a bounded number of features that can be extracted from τ. As τ becomes longer and as trees in τ become deeper, through application of reductions, more and more details of these trees will be outside the reach of these features. This observation is formalized through the notion of a *stack congruence* $\equiv_{st}$, which is an equivalence relation on stacks, with additional constraints. These additional constraints are to capture the intuition that once details of a stack have become irrelevant to the features, they remain so. It was inspired by Pereira and Wright (1997).

In order to define $\equiv_{st}$, we also need a *tree congruence* $\equiv_{tr}$, which is an equivalence relation on trees, again with an additional constraint. This constraint on $\equiv_{tr}$ says that if $t_1 \equiv_{tr} t'_1, \ldots, t_k \equiv_{tr} t'_k$, then $A(t_1 \cdots t_k) \equiv_{tr} A(t'_1 \cdots t'_k)$ for each A. The intuition is that once we have decided that some aspects of trees $t_1, \ldots t_k$ are no longer useful for the oracle, this remains so when these trees become part of a deeper tree, by adding A as root.

The constraint on $\equiv_{st}$ now says that if $\tau \equiv_{st} \tau'$ and $t \equiv_{tr} t'$ then also $\tau t \equiv_{st} \tau' t'$. We further say that $\equiv_{st}$ is *consistent* with oracle Ω if $\tau \equiv_{st} \tau'$ implies $\Omega(\tau, a) = \Omega(\tau', a)$ for every a. The equivalence class of tree t is denoted by $[t]_{\equiv_{tr}} = \{t' \mid t' \equiv_{tr} t\}$, or simply $[t]$. Similarly, the equivalence class of stack τ is denoted by $[\tau]_{\equiv_{st}}$ or $[\tau]$.

Trivial tree and stack congruences result by equivalence classes that each contain a single tree or stack, respectively. This would entail an infinite number of equivalence classes. As argued above however, we may reasonably assume that the number of equivalence classes is finite, considering typical oracles would use a bounded number of features. These features are likely to investigate only a bounded number of top-most trees on the

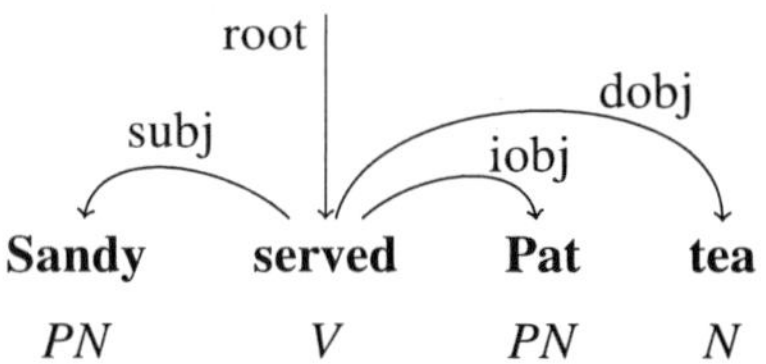

Figure 1: Example dependency structure.

stack, and for any such tree, the focus of interest is likely to be the root, or leaves at the extreme ends of the yields. Features are further discussed in Section 6.

For technical reasons, we will assume $t \equiv_{tr} t'$ implies $first(t) = first(t')$. This is without loss of generality: in the worst case, one needs to split up each existing equivalence class into several, one for each terminal.

4 Oracle automata and transition-based dependency parsing

As our oracle automata were defined in terms of context-free grammars, it deserves an explanation how we can use them to perform dependency parsing. The most straightforward solution is to assume a bilexical context-free grammar, with a single delexicalized nonterminal A. Concretely, for every pair of words a and b, we assume two rules $A_a \to A_a A_b$ and $A_a \to A_b A_a$. In the first rule, the first member in the right-hand side is the *head*, and in the second rule, the second member is the *head*. (The critical reader may object this definition is inconsistent if $a = b$; this could be fixed by having two versions of each nonterminal A_a.) For each terminal, we also have the rule $A_a \to a$ and the rule $S \to A_a$.

With grammars of this form, we obtain what is commonly known as *spurious ambiguity*. That is, there may be several parse trees that correspond to the same dependency structure. For example, the dependency structure in Figure 1 can be obtained by a left-most derivation: $A_{\text{served}} \Rightarrow A_{\text{Sandy}} A_{\text{served}} \Rightarrow$ **Sandy** $A_{\text{served}} \Rightarrow$ **Sandy** $A_{\text{served}} A_{\text{tea}} \Rightarrow$ **Sandy** $A_{\text{served}} A_{\text{Pat}} A_{\text{tea}} \Rightarrow^*$ **Sandy served Pat tea.** Two more left-most derivations exist however that correspond to the same dependency structure, both starting with $A_{\text{served}} \Rightarrow A_{\text{served}} A_{\text{tea}}$.

In practice, this spurious ambiguity is not a

problem. It is the oracle that ensures that only one structure is produced. Spurious ambiguity of transition-based dependency parsing is discussed at length by Goldberg and Nivre (2012).

If we apply oracle automata on the above bilexical context-free grammars, we obtain what Nivre et al. (2007) call the *arc-standard* strategy of transition-based dependency parsing. This contrasts with the *arc-eager* strategy. The latter has a *shift* operation, which corresponds exactly to our shift. The *left-arc* operation corresponds to reduction with a rule $A_a \rightarrow A_b A_a$, or in other words, a step $(\tau A_b(\tau_b) A_a(\tau_a), v\$) \vdash (\tau A_a(A_b(\tau_b) A_a(\tau_a)), v\$)$. The formulation of e.g. Nivre et al. (2007) has the top of the stack as part of the remaining input, which is largely an inconsequential notational difference, although it does affect the way features address elements in the stack or in remaining input; we will return to this issue in Section 6.

Contrary to what one may expect, the *right-arc* operation is not the mirror image of the left-arc operation but then for the rule $A_a \rightarrow A_a A_b$. The easiest way of looking at the right-arc operation is as making an early commitment to do the actual *reduce* operation with the rule $A_a \rightarrow A_a A_b$, before all the dependents of b have been processed.

In terms of bilexical grammars, this 'early commitment' made by the right-arc operation can be expressed by marking a nonterminal occurrence, to enforce that it (or its ancestors) will end up as the second member (as opposed to the first) in the right-hand side of a rule. We will use a bar-symbol for this mark. Concretely, we may construct the following rules:

- $S \rightarrow A_a$, $A_a \rightarrow a$ and $\overline{A}_a \rightarrow A_a$, for each a, and

- $A_a \rightarrow A_b A_a$, $A_a \rightarrow A_a \overline{A}_b$ and $\overline{A}_a \rightarrow \overline{A}_a \overline{A}_b$, for each pair a and b.

A reduction with rule $\overline{A}_a \rightarrow A_a$ now corresponds to a right-arc operation, and a reduction with $A_a \rightarrow A_a \overline{A}_b$ or $\overline{A}_a \rightarrow \overline{A}_a \overline{A}_b$ corresponds to what is called a reduce in the arc-eager model.

Having a representation of 'early commitment' by bar-symbols does not change the information available to an oracle, relative to the formulation of the right-arc operation in the cited literature. In the worst case, it will require a different way of addressing elements in the stack. Thereby the conclusions we will draw in Section 6 are unaffected.

5 Construction of a L-CFG from an oracle automaton

Let us assume an oracle automaton $\mathcal{M}$ for a CFG G and an oracle Ω. We also assume a tree congruence $\equiv_{tr}$ and a stack congruence $\equiv_{st}$ consistent with Ω, both with a finite number of equivalence classes. We will construct a L-CFG $G_{\mathcal{M}}$ as follows. The terminals of $G_{\mathcal{M}}$ are those of G. The nonterminals of $G_{\mathcal{M}}$ are S and composite nonterminals of the form $A^{(\ell)}$, where A is a nonterminal from G and the latent symbol ℓ is a triple $([\tau], [t], a)$ consisting of an equivalence class of stacks, an equivalence class of trees, and a lookahead symbol. Intuitively, $[\tau]$ represents context to the left of the occurrence of A, $[t]$ captures internal properties of a derivation of A, and a represents the first terminal of context immediately to the right of the occurrence of A.

There are three types of rules in $G_{\mathcal{M}}$. The first is:

$$S^\dagger \rightarrow S^{([\varepsilon],[t],\$)}$$

for every class $[t]$. This is easily justified, as initially the stack is empty, and the first symbol after an occurrence of S must be $\$$. The second is:

$$A^{([\tau],[A(a)],b)} \rightarrow a$$

for every class $[\tau]$, terminals a and b, and rule $(A \rightarrow a) = \Omega(\tau, a)$. The third is:

$$A^{([\tau_0],[t_0],a_0)} \rightarrow B_1^{([\tau_1],[t_1],a_1)} \cdots B_k^{([\tau_k],[t_k],a_k)}$$

for all classes $[\tau_0], [\tau_1], \ldots, [\tau_k]$, classes $[t_0], [t_1], \ldots, [t_k]$, terminals $a_0, a_1, \ldots, a_k$, and rule $(A \rightarrow B_1 \cdots B_k) = \Omega(\tau_k, a_0)$ such that:

- $[\tau_1] = [\tau_0]$ and $[\tau_i] = [\tau_{i-1} t_{i-1}]$ for each i $(1 < i \leq k)$,

- $[t_0] = [A(t_1 \cdots t_k)]$,

- $a_i = \text{first}(t_{i+1})$ for each i $(1 \leq i < k)$ and $a_k = a_0$.

Note that the definitions are all well-defined. For example, $[\tau_i] = [\tau_{i-1} t_{i-1}]$ uniquely denotes an equivalence class, regardless of the choice of τ_{i-1} from $[\tau_{i-1}]$ and the choice of t_{i-1} from $[t_{i-1}]$, because of $\equiv_{st}$ being a stack congruence. Similarly, $a_i = \text{first}(t_{i+1})$ is well-defined by the additional assumption on tree congruences. The above construction is reminiscent of covering of LR(k) grammars by LR(1) grammars (Sippu and Soisalon-Soininen, 1990).

Theorem 1 *The tree language of $G_\mathcal{M}$ equals the tree language of $\mathcal{M}$.*

Proof. It is easy to see that if $A^{([\tau],[t'],b)} \Rightarrow^*_{G_\mathcal{M}} t$, for some A, t', b and t, then $[t'] = [t]$. We now need to show that $(\varepsilon, w\$) \vdash^*_\mathcal{M} (t, \$)$ if and only if $S^{([\varepsilon],[t],\$)} \Rightarrow^*_{G_\mathcal{M}} t$, for every $t \in \mathcal{T}(\Sigma, N)$, where $w = yield(t)$.

In the 'only if' direction, it suffices to prove by induction on the length of computations that $(\tau, vw\$) \vdash^*_\mathcal{M} (\tau t, w\$)$ implies $A^{([\tau],[t],b)} \Rightarrow^*_{G_\mathcal{M}} t$, where $A = root(t)$ and $b = first(w\$)$.

The base case applies if $v = a$ and the computation consists of a shift $(\tau, aw\$) \vdash_\mathcal{M} (\tau A(a), w\$)$, where $\Omega(\tau, a) = (A \to a)$. Then $G_\mathcal{M}$ must include a rule $A^{([\tau],[A(a)],b)} \to a$, where $b = first(w\$)$. Hence $A^{([\tau],[A(a)],b)} \Rightarrow_{G_\mathcal{M}} A(a)$.

Otherwise, we have a computation:

$$(\tau_0, v_1 \cdots v_k w\$) \vdash^*_\mathcal{M}$$
$$(\tau_0 t_1, v_2 \cdots v_k w\$) \vdash^*_\mathcal{M} \cdots \vdash^*_\mathcal{M}$$
$$(\tau_0 t_1 \cdots t_{k-1}, v_k w\$) \vdash^*_\mathcal{M}$$
$$(\tau_0 t_1 \cdots t_k, w\$) \vdash_\mathcal{M} (\tau_0 A(t_1 \cdots t_k), w\$)$$

where $\Omega(\tau_0 t_1 \cdots t_k, a_0) = (A \to B_1 \cdots B_k)$, with $a_0 = first(w\$)$ and $B_i = root(t_i)$ for each i ($1 \le i \le k$).

Let further $\tau_1 = \tau_0$ and $\tau_i = \tau_{i-1} t_{i-1}$ for each i ($1 < i \le k$), let $t_0 = A(t_1 \cdots t_k)$, let $a_i = first(t_{i+1})$ for each i ($1 \le i < k$) and let $a_k = a_0$. Then $G_\mathcal{M}$ must include a rule:

$$A^{([\tau_0],[t_0],a_0)} \to B_1^{([\tau_1],[t_1],a_1)} \cdots B_k^{([\tau_k],[t_k],a_k)}$$

We can now use the inductive hypothesis, which tells us that $B_i^{([\tau_i],[t_i],a_i)} \Rightarrow^*_{G_\mathcal{M}} t_i$ for each i ($1 \le i \le k$). Hence $A^{([\tau_0],[t_0],a_0)} \Rightarrow^*_{G_\mathcal{M}} t_0$.

In the 'if' direction, it suffices to prove by induction on the tree depth that $A^{([\tau],[t],b)} \Rightarrow^*_{G_\mathcal{M}} t$ implies $(\tau, vw\$) \vdash^*_\mathcal{M} (\tau t, w\$)$ for every w with $b = first(w\$)$, where $v = yield(t)$.

The base case applies if the derivation is $A^{([\tau],[A(a)],b)} \Rightarrow_{G_\mathcal{M}} A(a)$. Due to existence of $A^{([\tau],[A(a)],b)} \to a$, and because $\equiv_{st}$ is consistent with Ω, we must have $\Omega(\tau, a) = (A \to a)$. Hence $(\tau, aw\$) \vdash_\mathcal{M} (\tau A(a), w\$)$ for every w, regardless of whether $b = first(w\$)$.

Otherwise, we have a derivation:

$$A^{([\tau_0],[t_0],a_0)} \Rightarrow_{G_\mathcal{M}}$$
$$A(B_1^{([\tau_1],[t_1],a_1)} \cdots B_k^{([\tau_k],[t_k],a_k)}) \Rightarrow^*_{G_\mathcal{M}}$$
$$A(t_1 \cdots t_k)$$

for some stack τ_0, trees t_1, ..., t_k, and terminal a_0 such that $\Omega(\tau_k, a_0) = (A \to B_1 \cdots B_k)$, where $\tau_1 = \tau_0$, $\tau_i = \tau_{i-1} t_{i-1}$ for each i ($1 < i \le k$), $t_0 = A(t_1 \cdots t_k)$, $a_i = first(t_{i+1})$ for each i ($1 \le i < k$) and $a_k = a_0$.

Let $v_i = yield(t_i)$ for each i ($1 \le i \le k$). Choose w such that $first(w\$) = a_0$. This means $a_i = first(v_{i+1} \cdots v_k w\$)$ for each i ($1 \le i \le k$). We can now apply the inductive hypothesis on $B_i^{([\tau_i],[t_i],a_i)} \Rightarrow^*_{G_\mathcal{M}} t_i$ for each i ($1 \le i \le k$), and assemble the desired computation:

$$(\tau_0, v_1 \cdots v_k w\$) \vdash^*_\mathcal{M}$$
$$(\tau_0 t_1, v_2 \cdots v_k w\$) \vdash^*_\mathcal{M} \cdots \vdash^*_\mathcal{M}$$
$$(\tau_0 t_1 \cdots t_{k-1}, v_k w\$) \vdash^*_\mathcal{M}$$
$$(\tau_0 t_1 \cdots t_k, w\$) \vdash_\mathcal{M} (\tau_0 A(t_1 \cdots t_k), w\$)$$

Note that we made implicit use of $\equiv_{st}$ being consistent with Ω, so that, for example, the choice of τ_0 from a class $[\tau_0]$ is irrelevant. $\blacksquare$

Our construction may result in a L-CFG that is not reduced, that is, it may contain unreachable or unproductive rules. This can be solved by reduction algorithms for CFGs (Harrison, 1978).

If probabilistic L-CFGs are desired, one may assign probabilities in an arbitrary way, for example by assigning probability $1/n$ to each rule that shares its left-hand side with $n - 1$ other rules. This does not change the tree language however, and the grammar remains unambiguous, that is, for each string, there is at most one tree.

We make no claim that the construction of L-CFGs as given here has practical benefits over methods for obtaining L-PCFGs via EM training or spectral learning. The main purpose of our construction was to show that L-(P)CFGs are at least as powerful as oracle automata.

6 Features

We now present a formalization of common features. Recall *root* as defined in Section 2. We introduce $\bot$ to denote the undefined value. We assume a function applied on the undefined value evaluates to the undefined value; for example $root(\bot) = \bot$.

We define *child* and *nth* by
$$child(i, A(t_1 \cdots t_k)) = child(-i, A(t_k \cdots t_1))$$
$$= nth(i, t_1 \cdots t_k) = nth(-i, t_k \cdots t_1) = t_i, \text{ for}$$
$1 \le i \le k$. In words, the first argument is an index, which counts from the left if it is positive and from the right if it is negative. For arguments

not covered by the above, the function values are $\perp$.

We now define a *feature* to be a function F from sequences of trees (stacks) to $\Sigma_{leaf} \cup \Sigma_{intern} \cup \{\perp\}$. We will first consider a simple kind of feature of the form $F = root(child(i_\ell, child(i_{\ell-1}, \ldots, child(i_1, nth(i_0, \cdot) \ldots)))$, some $\ell \geq 0$. Here $\cdot$ is a placeholder for the stack as argument. In words, the feature value for a stack $t_1 \cdots t_k$ is found by considering t_{i_0} if $i_0 > 0$ or t_{k+1+i_0} if $i_0 < 0$. The subtree at index i_1 is then taken (distinguishing between $i_1 > 0$ and $i_1 < 0$ as before), etc. Of the subtree obtained by the final application of $child$ with argument i_ℓ the root label is returned.

For F as above we define $initial(F) = i_0$ and for $0 \leq j \leq \ell$, we let $prefix(F, j)$ denote the function $root(child(i_\ell, child(i_{\ell-1}, \ldots, child(i_{j+1}, \cdot) \ldots))$. In words, from F we remove the initial application of nth and the next j applications of $child$. We let $prefixes(F) = \{prefix(F, j) \mid 0 \leq j \leq \ell\}$. For a function of the form $prefix(F, j)$, we let $head(prefix(F, j)) = i_{j+1}$ and $tail(prefix(F, j)) = prefix(F, j + 1)$ for $0 \leq j < \ell$, and $head(prefix(F, \ell)) = tail(prefix(F, \ell)) = \perp$. In words, $head$ returns the index of the next application of $child$ if there is one, and $tail$ removes the next application of $child$.

We say oracle Ω is determined by the sequence $F_1, \ldots, F_f$ of features if for every τ_1, τ_2, a_1, a_2, the equalities $F_j(\tau_1) = F_j(\tau_2)$ for every j ($1 \leq j \leq f$) and $a_1 = a_2$ together imply $\Omega(\tau_1, a_1) = \Omega(\tau_2, a_2)$. Here we have treated the lookahead (a_1 or a_2) as an implicit feature.

In order to obtain a tree congruence from a sequence $F_1, \ldots, F_f$ of simple features as above, we first define $\mathcal{F} = \cup_{1 \leq j \leq f} prefixes(F_j)$. Next we define a function $erase$, which erases from a tree t all subtrees that are outside the reach of the functions in $\mathcal{F}$, and that remain so if t becomes a subtree of a bigger tree. Erasing is done by removing subtrees or replacing them by $\perp$. Formally, for $\mathcal{G} \subseteq \mathcal{F}$, $erase(\mathcal{G}, t) = \perp$ if $\mathcal{G} = \emptyset$, and for $\mathcal{G} \neq \emptyset$ we define:

$$erase(\mathcal{G}, A(t_1 \cdots t_k)) = A(t_1' \cdots t_{k'}' t_{k''}'' \cdots t_k'')$$

where the t_i' and t_i'' are defined below. First, let $i_{max} = \max\{i \in head(F) \mid F \in \mathcal{G}, 1 \leq i \leq k\}$ and $i_{min} = \min\{i \in head(F) \mid F \in \mathcal{G}, 1 \leq -i \leq k\}$. In words, in potential next applications of $child$ in functions in $\mathcal{G}$, we consider the

indices counting from the left and those counting from the right and take the rightmost and leftmost, respectively of those indices. If i_{max} is defined then $k' = i_{max}$ and otherwise $k' = 0$. If i_{min} is defined then $k'' = k + 1 + i_{min}$ and otherwise $k'' = k + 1$. Note that k' may be greater than $k'' - 1$.

For $1 \leq i \leq k'$ we now define $t_i' = erase(\mathcal{G}_i', t_i)$ where $\mathcal{G}_i' = \{tail(F) \mid F \in \mathcal{G}, head(F) = i\}$. For $k'' \leq i \leq k$ we define $t_i'' = erase(\mathcal{G}_i'', t_i)$ where $\mathcal{G}_i'' = \{tail(F) \mid F \in \mathcal{G}, k + 1 + head(F) = i\}$. Note that the total number of nodes in (the tree representations of) the functions in $\mathcal{G}_i'$ and $\mathcal{G}_i''$ is strictly smaller than the total number of nodes in the trees in $\mathcal{G}$. It follows that, for any t, the size of tree $erase(\mathcal{F}, t)$ is bounded, that is, the set of such trees is finite.

Define $\equiv_{tr}$ by $t_1 \equiv_{tr} t_2$ if and only if $erase(\mathcal{F}, t_1) = erase(\mathcal{F}, t_2)$. By the definition of $erase$, we have $erase(\mathcal{F}, A(t_1 \cdots t_k)) = erase(\mathcal{F}, A(erase(\mathcal{F}, t_1) \cdots erase(\mathcal{F}, t_k)))$ for every tree $A(t_1 \cdots t_k)$. It follows that $\equiv_{tr}$ is a (finite) tree congruence.

As an example, consider $f = 1$ and:

$$F_1 = root(child(3, child(2, nth(-1, \cdot))))$$
$$t = A(B_1(b_1)B_2(C_1(c_1)C_2(c_2)C_3(c_3))B_3(b_3))$$

Then $\mathcal{F} = \{root(\cdot), root(child(3, \cdot)), root(child(3, child(2, \cdot)))\}$ and $erase(\mathcal{F}, t) = A(\perp B_2(\perp \perp C_3())B_3())$.

In order to obtain our (finite) stack congruence $\equiv_{st}$, we erase elements from a stack $t_1 \cdots t_k$. We now determine $i_{max} = \max\{initial(F_j) \mid 1 \leq j \leq f, 1 \leq initial(F_j) \leq k\}$ and $i_{min} = \min\{initial(F_j) \mid 1 \leq j \leq f, 1 \leq -initial(F_j) \leq k\}$. Much as before we have $k' = i_{max}$ if i_{max} is defined and $k' = 0$ otherwise and $k'' = k + 1 + i_{min}$ if i_{min} is defined and $k'' = k + 1$ otherwise. The stack after erasure is $erase(\mathcal{F}, t_1) \cdots erase(\mathcal{F}, t_{k'})erase(\mathcal{F}, t_{k''}) \cdots erase(\mathcal{F}, t_k)$. This allows definition of $\equiv_{st}$, in the same way as of $\equiv_{tr}$.

We can extend the repertoire of functions in our features. For example, we can include *first* and *last* as defined in Section 2. We can also add the function *first_intern*, which returns the internal symbol just above the leftmost leaf. Formally, $first\_intern(A(a)) = A$ and $first\_intern(A(t_1 \cdots t_k)) = first\_intern(t_1)$ if $t_1 \notin \Sigma_{leaf}$. The definition of *last_intern* is symmetric. Allowing such functions requires appropriate refinements of *erase*, such that the depth of the resulting trees remains bounded, by keeping only the relevant nodes near selected leaves.

We will now discuss the features used by the MaltParser, one of the most widely publicized transition-based dependency parsers. The descriptions will be based on Nivre et al. (2006) and Nivre et al. (2007).

All features are defined in terms of word form, part of speech or dependency relation. In our oracle automata, this information can all be encoded as parts of names of terminals and nonterminals. In the MaltParser, the word forms, parts of speech and dependency relations are attached to 'tokens' in the state of the parser. These tokens are found in the stack or in the remaining input.

Tokens can be addressed by an index, which for the stack counts from the top downward (cf. our function *nth* with negative first argument), and for the remaining input counts rightward from the first unconsumed token. One source of confusion with our automata is that in the MaltParser dependency links can be attached to the first token in the remaining input, whereas our automata would first have to transfer such a token to the stack before linking it to other tokens by means of a reduction. There can therefore be a slight mismatch in the type of addressing of tokens, relative to our formal framework above.

For presentational reasons, we have limited the size of the lookahead of our oracle automata to 1. Without causing any further complications however, this can be relaxed to lookahead of any fixed size. In this way, we can model features of the MaltParser that look a fixed distance ahead in the remaining input. As for the construction of the L-CFG, this would be modified accordingly, with latent symbols in which the third component is a string of the appropriate length.

Next to addressing tokens by index, features of the MaltParser can also refer to leftmost and rightmost dependents of indexed tokens. In our framework, such features could be expressed using functions similar to *child*, *first_intern* and *last_intern*, all allowing *erase* to return trees of bounded size as before.

Features similar to those of the MaltParser are used by Sagae and Lavie (2005), but in addition, their features also include e.g. the *number* of dependents of a token. This might suggest the number of equivalence classes is infinite after all. In practice however, the oracle would only deal with one from a bounded number of possible values, that is, those that were encountered during training, which is necessarily finite. It is not clear to us how their parser would behave if a value is encountered during testing that is larger than the maximum one encountered during training.

7 The probabilistic case

One may redefine Ω to be a probability distribution, constrained by:

- if $\Omega(A \rightarrow b \mid [\tau], a) > 0$, then $a = b$; and

- if $\Omega(A \rightarrow B_1 \cdots B_k \mid [\tau], a) > 0$, then τ can be written as $\tau' t_1 \cdots t_k$, where $root(t_i) = B_i$ for each i $(1 \leq i \leq k)$.

This is in the same spirit as the non-deterministic oracles of Goldberg and Nivre (2013).

With Ω now being a probability distribution, we can refine the semantics of our automata to assign a probability to each computation, which is the product of the probabilities of all used steps. The construction from Section 5 can be extended to produce a L-PCFG, where:

- $S^\dagger \rightarrow S^{([\varepsilon],[t],\$)}$ is assigned probability 1,

- $A^{([\tau],[A(a)],b)} \rightarrow a$ is assigned $\Omega(A \rightarrow a \mid [\tau], a)$,

- $A^{([\tau_0],[t_0],a_0)} \rightarrow B_1^{([\tau_1],[t_1],a_1)} \cdots B_k^{([\tau_k],[t_k],a_k)}$ is assigned $\Omega(A \rightarrow B_1 \cdots B_k \mid [\tau_k], a_0)$.

If desired, the L-PCFG can be normalized to become proper, i.e. so that the probabilities of all rules with given left-hand side sum to 1; see e.g. Chi (1999).

8 Conclusions

We have explored formal properties of transition-based dependency parsing, in terms of traditional automata theory. Through our formalization, an explicit link has been established between projective transition-based dependency parsing and constituent parsing, in particular latent-variable context-free parsing. Extension to the non-projective/discontinuous case will be the subject of future investigations.

Acknowledgements

Thanks go to reviewers for helpful comments.

References

A. Boyd. 2007. Discontinuity revisited: An improved conversion to context-free representations. In *Proceedings of the Linguistic Annotation Workshop, at ACL 2007*, pages 41–44, Prague, Czech Republic, June.

W.S. Brainerd. 1969. Tree generating regular systems. *Information and Control*, 14:217–231.

M. Candito, J. Nivre, P. Denis, and E. Henestroza Anguiano. 2010. Benchmarking of statistical dependency parsers for French. In *The 23rd International Conference on Computational Linguistics*, pages 108–116, Beijing, China, August.

S.A. Caraballo and E. Charniak. 1998. New figures of merit for best-first probabilistic chart parsing. *Computational Linguistics*, 24(2):275–298.

G. Carroll and E. Charniak. 1992. Two experiments on learning probabilistic dependency grammars from corpora. In *Statistically-Based NLP Techniques, Papers from the AAAI Workshop*, pages 1–13, San Jose.

D. Cer, M.-C. de Marneffe, D. Jurafsky, and C. Manning. 2010. Parsing to Stanford dependencies: Trade-offs between speed and accuracy. In *LREC 2010: Seventh International Conference on Language Resources and Evaluation, Proceedings*, pages 1628–1632, Valletta , Malta, May.

Z. Chi. 1999. Statistical properties of probabilistic context-free grammars. *Computational Linguistics*, 25(1):131–160.

M. Collins. 2003. Head-driven statistical models for natural language parsing. *Computational Linguistics*, 29(4):589–637.

M.A. Covington. 2001. A fundamental algorithm for dependency parsing. In *Proceedings of the 39th Annual ACM Southeast Conference*, pages 95–102.

J. Eisner and G. Satta. 1999. Efficient parsing for bilexical context-free grammars and head automaton grammars. In *37th Annual Meeting of the Association for Computational Linguistics, Proceedings of the Conference*, pages 457–464, Maryland, USA, June.

H. Gaifman. 1965. Dependency systems and phrase-structure systems. *Information and Control*, 8:304–337.

F. Gécseg and M. Steinby. 1997. Tree languages. In G. Rozenberg and A. Salomaa, editors, *Handbook of Formal Languages, Vol. 3*, chapter 1, pages 1–68. Springer, Berlin.

Y. Goldberg and J. Nivre. 2012. A dynamic oracle for arc-eager dependency parsing. In *The 24th International Conference on Computational Linguistics*, pages 959–976, Mumbai, India, December.

Y. Goldberg and J. Nivre. 2013. Training deterministic parsers with non-deterministic oracles. *Transactions of the Association for Computational Linguistics*, 1:403–414.

J. Goodman. 1997. Global thresholding and multiple-pass parsing. In *Proceedings of the Second Conference on Empirical Methods in Natural Language Processing*, pages 11–25, Providence, Rhode Island, USA, August.

K. Hall and V. Novák. 2005. Corrective modeling for non-projective dependency parsing. In *Proceedings of the Ninth International Workshop on Parsing Technologies*, pages 42–52, Vancouver, British Columbia, Canada, October.

M.A. Harrison. 1978. *Introduction to Formal Language Theory*. Addison-Wesley.

D.G. Hays. 1964. Dependency theory: A formalism and some observations. *Language*, 40(4):511–525.

L. Huang and K. Sagae. 2010. Dynamic programming for linear-time incremental parsing. In *Proceedings of the 48th Annual Meeting of the Association for Computational Linguistics*, pages 1077–1086, Uppsala, Sweden, July.

M. Johnson. 2007. Transforming projective bilexical dependency grammars into efficiently-parsable CFGs with Unfold-Fold. In *45th Annual Meeting of the Association for Computational Linguistics, Proceedings of the Conference*, pages 168–175, Prague, Czech Republic, June.

S. Kahane, A. Nasr, and O. Rambow. 1998. Pseudo-projectivity, a polynomially parsable non-projective dependency grammar. In *36th Annual Meeting of the Association for Computational Linguistics and 17th International Conference on Computational Linguistics*, volume 1, pages 646–652, Montreal, Quebec, Canada, August.

K. Kallmeyer and M. Kuhlmann. 2012. A formal model for plausible dependencies in lexicalized tree adjoining grammar. In *Eleventh International Workshop on Tree Adjoining Grammar and Related Formalisms*, pages 108–116.

L. Kallmeyer and W. Maier. 2010. Data-driven parsing with probabilistic linear context-free rewriting systems. In *The 23rd International Conference on Computational Linguistics*, pages 537–545, Beijing, China, August.

T. Kalt. 2004. Induction of greedy controllers for deterministic treebank parsers. In *Conference on Empirical Methods in Natural Language Processing*, pages 17–24, Barcelona, Spain, July.

D. Klein and C. Manning. 2004. Corpus-based induction of syntactic structure: Models of dependency and constituency. In *42nd Annual Meeting of the Association for Computational Linguistics, Proceedings of the Conference*, pages 478–485, Barcelona, Spain, July.

M. Kuhlmann, C. Gómez-Rodríguez, and G. Satta. 2011. Dynamic programming algorithms for transition-based dependency parsers. In *49th Annual Meeting of the Association for Computational Linguistics, Proceedings of the Conference*, pages 673–682, Portland, Oregon, June.

M. Kuhlmann. 2013. Mildly non-projective dependency grammar. *Computational Linguistics*, 39(2):355–387.

A. Lavie and M. Tomita. 1993. GLR* – an efficient noise-skipping parsing algorithm for context free grammars. In *Third International Workshop on Parsing Technologies*, pages 123–134, Tilburg (The Netherlands) and Durbuy (Belgium), August.

D. Lin. 1998. A dependency-based method for evaluating broad-coverage parsers. *Natural Language Engineering*, 4(2):97–114.

X. Ma, X. Zhang, H. Zhao, and B.-L. Lu. 2010. Dependency parser for Chinese constituent parsing. In *CIPS-SIGHAN Joint Conference on Chinese Language Processing*.

T. Matsuzaki, Y. Miyao, and J. Tsujii. 2005. Probabilistic CFG with latent annotations. In *43rd Annual Meeting of the Association for Computational Linguistics, Proceedings of the Conference*, pages 75–82, Ann Arbor, Michigan, June.

Y. Miyao, R. Sætre K. Sagae, T. Matsuzaki, and J. Tsujii. 2008. Task-oriented evaluation of syntactic parsers and their representations. In *46th Annual Meeting of the Association for Computational Linguistics: Human Language Technologies*, pages 46–54, Columbus, Ohio, June.

S. Narayan and S.B. Cohen. 2015. Diversity in spectral learning for natural language parsing. In *Conference on Empirical Methods in Natural Language Processing, Proceedings of the Conference*, pages 1868–1878, Lisbon, Portugal, September.

M.-J. Nederhof and M. McCaffery. 2014. Deterministic parsing using PCFGs. In *Proceedings of the 14th Conference of the European Chapter of the Association for Computational Linguistics*, pages 338–347, Gothenburg, Sweden.

J. Nivre and J. Nilsson. 2005. Pseudo-projective dependency parsing. In *43rd Annual Meeting of the Association for Computational Linguistics, Proceedings of the Conference*, pages 99–106, Ann Arbor, Michigan, June.

J. Nivre and M. Scholz. 2004. Deterministic dependency parsing of English text. In *The 20th International Conference on Computational Linguistics*, volume 1, pages 64–70, Geneva, Switzerland, August.

J. Nivre, J. Hall, and J. Nilsson. 2004. Memory-based dependency parsing. In *Proceedings of the Eighth Conference on Computational Natural Language Learning*, pages 49–56, Boston, Massachusetts, May.

J. Nivre, J. Hall, and J. Nilsson. 2006. MaltParser: A data-driven parser-generator for dependency parsing. In *LREC 2006: Fifth International Conference on Language Resources and Evaluation, Proceedings*, pages 2216–2219, Genoa, Italy, May.

J. Nivre, J. Hall, J. Nilsson, A. Chanev, G. Eryiğit, S. Kübler, S. Marinov, and E. Marsi. 2007. MaltParser: A language-independent system for data-driven dependency parsing. *Natural Language Engineering*, 13(2):95–135.

J. Nivre. 2003. An efficient algorithm for projective dependency parsing. In *8th International Workshop on Parsing Technologies*, pages 149–160, LORIA, Nancy, France, April.

J. Nivre. 2009. Non-projective dependency parsing in expected linear time. In *Proceedings of the Joint Conference of the 47th Annual Meeting of the ACL and the 4th International Joint Conference on Natural Language Processing of the AFNLP*, pages 351–359, Suntec, Singapore, August.

F.C.N. Pereira and R.N. Wright. 1997. Finite-state approximation of phrase-structure grammars. In E. Roche and Y. Schabes, editors, *Finite-State Language Processing*, pages 149–173. MIT Press.

S. Petrov, L. Barrett, R. Thibaux, and D. Klein. 2006. Learning accurate, compact, and interpretable tree annotation. In *Proceedings of the 21st International Conference on Computational Linguistics and 44th Annual Meeting of the Association for Computational Linguistics*, pages 433–440, Sydney, Australia, July.

O. Rambow. 2010. The simple truth about dependency and phrase structure representations: An opinion piece. In *Human Language Technologies: The 2010 Annual Conference of the North American Chapter of the Association for Computational Linguistics, Proceedings of the Main Conference*, pages 337–340, Los Angeles, California, June.

A. Ratnaparkhi. 1997. A linear observed time statistical parser based on maximum entropy models. In *Proceedings of the Second Conference on Empirical Methods in Natural Language Processing*, pages 1–10, Providence, Rhode Island, USA, August.

K. Sagae and A. Lavie. 2005. A classifier-based parser with linear run-time complexity. In *Proceedings of the Ninth International Workshop on Parsing Technologies*, pages 125–132, Vancouver, British Columbia, Canada, October.

S. Seneff. 1989. TINA: A probabilistic syntactic parser for speech understanding systems. In *ICASSP-89*, volume 2, pages 711–714, Glasgow.

S. Sippu and E. Soisalon-Soininen. 1990. *Parsing Theory, Vol. II: LR(k) and LL(k) Parsing*, volume 20 of *EATCS Monographs on Theoretical Computer Science*. Springer-Verlag.

Y. Tsuruoka and J. Tsujii. 2005. Chunk parsing revisited. In *Proceedings of the Ninth International Workshop on Parsing Technologies*, pages 133–140, Vancouver, British Columbia, Canada, October.

A. van Cranenburgh, R. Scha, and F. Sangati. 2011. Discontinuous data-oriented parsing: A mildly context-sensitive all-fragments grammar. In *Proceedings of the Second Workshop on Statistical Parsing of Morphologically Rich Languages*, pages 34–44, Dublin, Ireland.

A. Wong and D. Wu. 1999. Learning a lightweight robust deterministic parser. In *Sixth European Conference on Speech Communication and Technology*, pages 2047–2050.

H. Yamada and Y. Matsumoto. 2003. Statistical dependency analysis with support vector machines. In *8th International Workshop on Parsing Technologies*, pages 195–206, LORIA, Nancy, France, April.

Distributed representation and estimation of WFST-based n-gram models

Cyril Allauzen, Michael Riley and Brian Roark
Google, Inc.
{allauzen,riley,roark}@google.com

Abstract

We present methods for partitioning a weighted finite-state transducer (WFST) representation of an n-gram language model into multiple blocks or *shards*, each of which is a stand-alone WFST n-gram model in its own right, allowing processing with existing algorithms. After independent estimation, including normalization, smoothing and pruning on each shard, the shards can be reassembled into a single WFST that is identical to the model that would have resulted from estimation without sharding. We then present an approach that uses data partitions in conjunction with WFST sharding to estimate models on orders-of-magnitude more data than would have otherwise been feasible with a single process. We present some numbers on shard characteristics when large models are trained from a very large data set. Functionality to support distributed n-gram modeling has been added to the open-source OpenGrm library.

1 Introduction

Training n-gram language models on ever increasing amounts of text continues to yield large model improvements for tasks as diverse as machine translation (MT), automatic speech recognition (ASR) and mobile text entry. One approach to scaling n-gram model estimation to peta-byte scale data sources and beyond, is to distribute the storage, processing and serving of n-grams (Heafield, 2011). In some scenarios – most notably ASR – a very common approach is to heavily prune models trained on large resources, and then pre-compose the resulting model off-line with other models (e.g., a pronunciation lexicon) in order to optimize the model for use at time of first-pass decoding (Mohri et al., 2002). Among other things, this approach can impact the choice of smoothing for the first-pass model (Chelba et al., 2010), and the resulting model is generally stored as a weighted finite-state transducer (WFST) in order to take advantage of known operations such as determinization, minimization and weight pushing (Allauzen et al., 2007; Allauzen et al., 2009; Allauzen and Riley, 2013). Even though the resulting model in such scenarios is generally of modest size, there is a benefit to training on very large samples, since model pruning generally aims to minimize the KL divergence from the unpruned model (Stolcke, 1998).

Storing such a large n-gram model in a single WFST prior to model pruning is not feasible in many situations. For example, speech recognition first pass models may be trained as a mixture of models from many domains, each of which are trained on billions or tens of billions of sentences (Sak et al., 2013). Even with modest count thresholding, the size of such models before entropy-based pruning would be on the order of tens of billions of n-grams.

Storing this model in the WFST n-gram format of the OpenGrm library (Roark et al., 2012) allocates an arc for every n-gram (other than end-of-string n-grams) and a state for every n-gram prefix. Even using very efficient specialized n-gram representations (Sorensen and Allauzen, 2011), a single FST representing this model would require on the order of 400GB of storage, making it difficult to access and process on a single processor.

In this paper, we present methods for the distributed representation and processing of large WFST-based n-gram language models by partitioning them into multiple blocks or *shards*. Our sharding approach meets two key desiderata: 1) each sub-model shard is a stand-alone "canonical format" WFST-based model in its own right, providing correct probabilities for a particular subset of the n-grams from the full model; and 2) once n-gram counts have been sharded, downstream pro-

Proceedings of the ACL Workshop on Statistical NLP and Weighted Automata, pages 32–41,
Berlin, Germany, August 12, 2016. ©2016 Association for Computational Linguistics

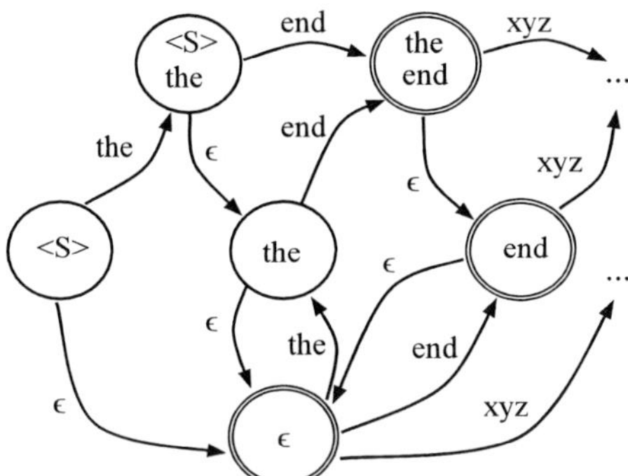

Figure 1: Schematic of canonical WFST n-gram format, unweighted for simplicity. Each state shows the history it encodes for convenience (they are actually unlabeled). Final states are denoted with double circle.

cessing such as model normalization, smoothing and pruning, can occur on each shard independently. Methods, utilities and convenience scripts have been added to the OpenGrm NGram library[1] to permit distributed processing. In addition to presenting design principles and algorithms in this paper, we will also outline the relevant library functionality.

2 Canonical WFST n-gram format

We take as our starting point the standard 'canonical' WFST n-gram model format from Open-Grm, which is presented in Roark et al. (2012) and at ngram.opengrm.org, but which we summarize briefly here. Standard n-gram language models can be presented in the following well-known backoff formulation:

$$P(w \mid h) = \begin{cases} \hat{P}(w \mid h) & \text{if } c(hw) > 0 \\ \alpha(h)\, P(w \mid h') & \text{otherwise} \end{cases} \quad (1)$$

where w is the word (or symbol) being predicted based on the previous history h, and h' is the longest proper suffix of h (or ϵ if h is a single word/symbol). The backoff weight $\alpha(h)$ ensures that this is a proper probability distribution over symbols in the vocabulary, and is easily calculated based on the estimates $\hat{P}$ for observed n-grams. Note that interpolated n-gram models also fit this formulation, if pre-interpolated.

Figure 1 presents a schematic of the WFST n-gram model format that we describe here. The WFST format represents n-gram histories h as states[2], and words w following h as arcs leaving

the state that encodes h. There is exactly one unigram state (labeled with ϵ in Figure 1), which represents the empty history. For every state h in the model other than the unigram state, there is a special backoff arc, labeled with ϵ, with destination state h', the backoff state of h. For an n-gram hw, the arc labeled with w leaving history state h will have as destination the state hw if hw is a proper prefix of another n-gram in the model; otherwise the destination will be $h'w$. The start state of the model WFST represents the start-of-string history (typically denoted <s>), and the end-of-string (</s>) probability is encoded in state final costs. Neither of these symbols labels any arcs in the model, hence they are not required to be part of the explicit vocabulary of the model. Costs in the model are generally represented as negative log counts or probabilities, and the backoff arc cost from state h is -log $\alpha(h)$.

With the exception of the start and unigram states, every state h in the model is the destination state of an n-gram transition originating from a prefix history, which we will term an 'ascending' n-gram transition. If $h = w_1 \ldots w_k$ is a state in the model ($k > 0$ and if $k = 1$ then $w_1 \neq$ <s>), then there also exists a state in the model $\bar{h} = w_1 \ldots w_{k-1}$ and a transition from $\bar{h}$ to h labeled with w_k. We will call a sequence of such ascending n-gram transitions an ascending path, and every state in the model (other than unigram and start) can be reached via a single ascending path from either the unigram state or the start state. This plus the backoff arcs make the model fully connected.

3 Sharding count n-gram WFSTs

3.1 Model partitioning

Our principal interest in breaking (or sharding) this WFST representation into smaller parts lies in enabling model estimation for very large training sets by allowing each shard to be processed (normalized, smoothed and pruned) as independently as possible. Further, we would like to simply use existing algorithms for each of these stages on the model shards. To that end, all of the arcs leaving a particular state must be included in the same shard, hence our sharding function is for states in the automaton, and arcs go with their state of origin. We shard the n-gram WFST model into a collection of n-gram WFSTs by partitioning the histories into intervals on a colexicographic ordering defined below. The model's symbol table maps from sym-

---

[1] ngram.opengrm.org

[2] For convenience, we will refer to states as encoding (or representing) a history h – or even just call the state h – though there is no labeling of states, just arcs.

bols in the model to unique indices that label the arcs in the WFST. We use indices from this symbol table to define a total order $<_V$ on our vocabulary augmented with start-of-string token which is assigned index 0.[3] We then define the colexicographic (or reverse lexicographic) order $<$ over V^* recursively on the length of the sequences as follow. For all $x, y \neq \epsilon$, we have $\epsilon < x$ and

$$x < y \text{ iff } \begin{cases} x_{|x|} <_V y_{|y|} \text{ or,} \\ x_{|x|} = y_{|y|} \text{ and } \bar{x} < \bar{y} \end{cases} \quad (2)$$

where $\bar{x}$ denotes the longest prefix of x distinct from x itself. The colexicographic interval $[x, y)$ then denotes the set of sequences z such that $x \leq z < y$.

For example, assuming symbol indices the=1 and end=2, the colexicographic ordering of the states in Figure 1 is:

Colex. Order	State histories (as words)	(as indices)
0	ϵ	ϵ
1	<s>	0
2	the	1
3	<s> the	0 1
4	end	2
5	the end	1 2

If we want, say, 4 shards of this model (at least, the visible part in the schematic in Figure 1), we can partition the state histories in 4 intervals; for example:

$$\{[\epsilon, 1), [1, 2), [2, 1\ 2), [1\ 2, 3)\} = \\ \{\{\epsilon, 0\}, \{1, 0\ 1\}, \{2\}, \{1\ 2\}\}.$$

By convention, we write the interval $[x, y)$ as $x_1 \ldots x_l : y_1 \ldots y_m$. Thus, the above partition would be written as:[4]

$$\begin{aligned} 0 \quad &: \quad 1 \\ 1 \quad &: \quad 2 \\ 2 \quad &: \quad 1\ 2 \\ 1\ 2 \quad &: \quad 3 \end{aligned}$$

While this partitions the states into subsets, it remains to turn these subsets into stand-alone, connected WFSTs with the correct topology to allow for direct use of existing language model estimation algorithms on each shard independently. For this to be the case, we need to: (1) be

---

[3] Not to be confused with the convention that ϵ has index 0 in FST symbol tables.

[4] We omit the empty history ϵ from the interval specification since it is always assigned to the first interval.

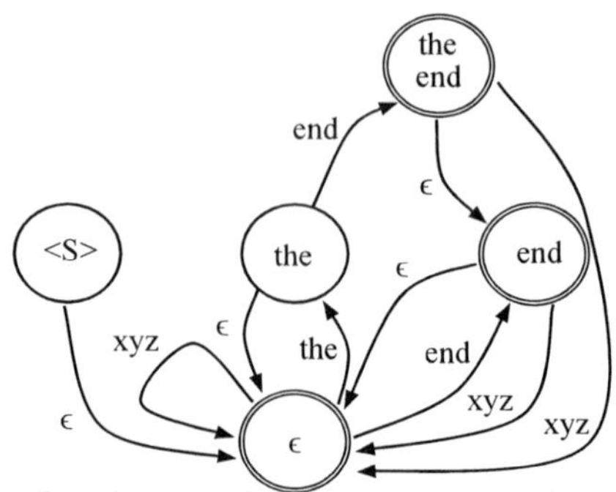

Figure 2: Schematic of a completed shard of the model in Figure 1. The state corresponding to the history 'the end' is the only state strictly in-context for this shard.

able to reach each state via the correct ascending path from the start or unigram state, with correct counts/probabilities; (2) have backoff states of all in-shard states, along with their arcs, for calculating backoff costs; and (3) correctly assign all arc destinations within each new WFST.

3.2 Model completion

Given a set of states to include in a context shard, the shard model must be 'completed' to include all of the requisite states and arcs needed to conform to the canonical n-gram topology. We step through each of the key requirements in turn. We refer to those states that fall within the context interval as 'strictly in-context'. Figure 2 shows a schematic of the shard model that results for the context 1 2 : 3, which we will refer to when illustrating particular requirements. Only the state corresponding to 'the end' is strictly in-context for this particular shard. All states that are suffixes of strictly in-context states are also referred to as in-context (though not *strictly* so), since they are needed for proper normalization – i.e., calculation of $\alpha(h)$ in the recursive n-gram model definition in equation 1. Hence, the state corresponding to 'end' in Figure 2 is in-context and is included in the shard, as is the unigram state.

The start state and all states and transitions on ascending paths from the start and unigram states to in-context states must be included, so that states that are in-context can be reached from the start state. Thus, the state corresponding to 'the' in Figure 2 must be included, along with its arc labeled with 'end', since they are on the ascending path to 'the end', which is strictly in-context.

For every state in the model, the backoff arc should allow transition to the correct backoff state. Finally, for all arcs (labeled with w) leaving states h that have been included in the shard model, their destination must be the longest suffix of hw that has been included as a state in the shard model. The arcs labeled with 'xyz' in Figure 2 all point to the unigram state, since no states representing histories ending in 'xyz' are in the shard model.

For the small schematic example in Figures 1 and 2, there is not much savings from sharding after completing the shard model: only one state and four arcs from the observed part of the model in Figure 1 were omitted in the schematic in Figure 2. And it is clear from the construction that there will be some redundancy between shards in the states and arcs included when the shard model is completed. But for large models, each shard will be a small fraction of the total model. Note that there is a tradeoff between the number of shards and the amount of redundancy across shards.

Another way to view the shard model in Figure 2 relative to the full model in Figure 1 is as a pruned model, where the arcs and states that were pruned are precisely those that are not needed within that particular shard. This perspective is useful when discussing distributed training in the next section.

4 Distributed training of n-gram models

When presenting model sharding in the previous section, we had access to the specific states in the model schematic, and defined the contexts accordingly. When training a model from data at the scale that requires distributed processing, the full model does not exist to inspect and partition. Instead, we must derive the context sharding in some fashion prior to training the model. We will thus break this section into two parts: first, deriving context intervals for model sharding; then estimating models given context intervals.

4.1 Deriving context intervals

Given a large corpus, there are a couple of ways to approach efficient calculation of effective context intervals. Effective in this case is balanced, i.e., one would like each sharded model to be of roughly the same size, so that the time for model estimation is roughly commensurate across shards and lagging shards are avoided.

The first approach is to build a smaller footprint model than the desired model, which would take a fraction of the time to train, then derive the contexts from that model. For example, if one wanted to train a 5-gram model from a billion word corpus, then one may derive context intervals based on trigram model trained by sampling one out of every hundred sentences from the corpus. Given that more compact model, it is relatively straightforward to examine the storage required for each state and choose a balanced partition accordingly. At higher orders and with the full sample, the size of each shard may ultimately differ, but we have found that estimating relative shard sizes based on lower-order sampled models is effective at providing functional context intervals. See section 5 for specific OpenGrm NGram library functionality related to context interval estimation.

Another method for deriving context intervals is to accumulate the set of n-grams into a large collection, sort it by history in the same colexicographic order as is used to define the context intervals, and then take quantiles from that sorted collection. This can lead to more balanced shards than the previous method, though efficient methods for distributed quantile extraction from collections of that sort is beyond the scope of this paper.

4.2 Estimating models given context intervals

Given a definition of k context intervals $C_1 \ldots C_k$, we can train sharded models on very large data sets as follows:

1. Partition data into m data shards $D_1 \ldots D_m$

2. For each data shard D_i
   (a) Count the n-grams from D_i and build full WFST n-gram representation T_i
   (b) Split T_i into k shard models $T_{i1} \ldots T_{ik}$

3. For each context interval C_j, merge counts $T_{\cdot j}$ from all data shards: $F_j = \text{Merge}_{i=1}^{m}(T_{ij})$

4. Perform these global operations on collection $F_1 \ldots F_k$ to prepare for model estimation:
   (a) Transfer correct counts as needed across shards (see Section 4.2.4 below).
   (b) Derive resources such as count-of-counts by aggregating across shards.

5. Normalize, smooth, prune each F_j as needed: $M_j = \text{MakeModel}(F_j)$

6. Merge model shards: $M = \text{Merge}_{j=1}^{k}(M_j)$

We now go through each of these 6 stages one by one in the following sub-sections.

4.2.1 Partition data

Given a large text corpus, this simply involves placing each string into one of m separate collections, preferably of roughly equal size.

4.2.2 Count and split data shards

For each data shard D_i, perform n-gram counting exactly as one would in a non-distributed scenario. (See Section 5 for specific commands within the OpenGrm NGram library.) This results in an n-gram count WFST T_i for each data shard. Using the context interval specifications $C_1 \ldots C_k$ we then split T_i into k shard models. Because we have the full model T_i, we can determine exactly which states and arcs need to be preserved for each context interval, and prune the rest away.

4.2.3 Merge sharded models

For each context interval C_j, there will be a shard model T_{ij} for every data shard D_i. Standard count merging will yield the correct counts for all in-context n-grams and the correct overall model topology, i.e., every state and arc that is required will be there. However, n-grams that are not in-context may not have the correct count, since they may have occurred in a data shard but were not included in the context shard due to the absence of any in-context n-grams for which it is a prefix.

To illustrate this point, consider a scenario with just two data shards, D_1 and D_2, and a context shard C_j that only includes the n-gram history 'foo bar baz' strictly in-context. Suppose 'foo bar' occurs 10 times in D_1 and also 10 times in D_2, while 'foo bar baz' occurs 3 times in D_1 but doesn't occur at all in D_2. Recall that states and ascending arcs that are not in-context are only included in the shard model as required to ascend to the in-context states. In the absence of 'foo bar baz' in T_{2j}, the n-gram arc and state corresponding to 'foo bar' will not be included in that shard, despite having occurred 10 times in D_2. When the counts in T_{1j} and T_{2j} are merged, 'foo bar' will be included in the merger, but will only have counts coming from T_{1j}. Hence, rather than the correct count of 20, that n-gram will just have a count of 10. The correct count of 'foo bar' is only guaranteed to be found in the shard for which it is in-context.

To get the correct counts in every shard that needs them, we must perform a **transfer** operation to pass correct counts from shards where n-grams are strictly in-context to shards where they are needed as prefixes of other n-grams.

4.2.4 Global operations on the collection

Transfer: As mentioned above, count merging of sharded count WFSTs across data shards yields correct counts for in-context states, as well as the correct WFST topology – i.e., all needed n-grams

are included – but is not guaranteed to have the correct counts of n-grams that are not in-context. For each shard F_i, however, we know which n-grams we *need* to get the correct count for, and can easily calculate the context shard that these n-grams fall into. Using that information, a transfer of correct counts is effected via the following three stages:

1. For each shard F_i, for each F_j ($j \neq i$), prune F_i to only those n-grams that are strictly in-context for context C_j, and send the resulting F_{ij} to shard F_j to give correct counts.
2. For every shard F_j, provide correct counts for each incoming $F_{\cdot j}$ requiring them and return to the appropriate shard F_i.
3. For every shard F_i, update counts from incoming $F_{i\cdot}$.

Only needed n-grams are processed in this transfer algorithm, which we will term the "standard" transfer algorithm in the experimental results. Let Q_i be the set of states for shard F_i. Each state is an n-gram of length less than n (where n is the order of the model) that must have its correct count requested from the shard where it is strictly in context. This leads to a complexity of $O(n \sum_{i=1}^{k} |Q_i|)$.

An alternative, which we will term the "by-order" transfer algorithm, performs transfer of a more restricted set of n-grams in multiple phases, which occur in ascending n-gram order. Note that, when transfer of correct counts for a particular n-gram is requested, the correct counts for all prefixes of that n-gram can also be collected at the same time at no extra cost, provided the prefix counts are correct in the shard where we request them, even though the prefixes may or may not be in-context. By processing in ascending n-gram order, we can guarantee that the prefixes of requested n-grams have already been updated to the correct counts. If we can update the counts of n-gram prefixes, we can defer the transfer of an out-of-context n-gram's count until an update is required. The correct count of an out-of-context n-gram of order n is thus only requested if one of the following two conditions hold: (1) its count may be requested by another context shard from the current context shard during the transfer phase of order $n+1$; or (2) its count would not be transferred at some order greater than n, hence must be transferred now to be correct at the end of transfer. The former condition holds if the n-gram arc has an origin state that is out-of-context and a destination state that is strictly in-context. The latter condition holds if the n-gram arc's origin state is out-of-context, its destination state is in-context (though not strictly in-context), and the n-gram is not a prefix of any in-context state. We will call an n-gram of order n that meets either of those conditions "needed at order n". Then, for each order n from 1 to the highest order in the model, transfer is carried out by replacing step number 1 in the standard transfer algorithm above with the following:

1. For each shard F_i, for each F_j ($j\neq i$), prune F_i to only those n-grams that are strictly in-context for context C_j, and are needed at order n, along with all prefixes of such n-grams. If the resulting F_{ij} is non-empty, send it to shard F_j to give correct counts.

The rest of transfer at order n proceeds as before. In this algorithm, a shard requests an n-gram only if the destination state of its corresponding n-gram arc is in-context. This leads to a complexity in $O(n \sum_{i=1}^{k} |Q_i^c|)$ where Q_i^c denotes the set of states in shard F_i corresponding to in-context histories for that shard. This is a complexity reduction from the standard transfer algorithm above, since $|Q_i|/n < |Q_i^c| < |Q_i|$.

Counts-of-counts: Deriving counts-of-count histograms is key for certain smoothing methods such as Katz (1987). Each shard F_i can produce a histogram from only those n-grams that are strictly in-context, then the histograms can be aggregated straightforwardly across shards to produce a global histogram, since each n-gram is strictly in-context in only one shard.

4.2.5 Process count shards

Given the correct counts in each of the count shards F_i, we can proceed to use existing, standard n-gram processing algorithms to normalize, smooth and prune each of the models independently. These algorithms are linear in the size of the model being processed. With some minor exceptions, existing WFST-based language modeling algorithms, such as those in the OpenGrm NGram library, can be applied to each shard independently. We mention two such exceptions in turn, both impacting the correct application of model pruning algorithms after the model shard has been normalized and smoothed.

First, whereas common smoothing algorithms such as Katz (1987) and absolute discounting (Ney et al., 1994) will properly discount and normalize all n-grams in the model shard, Witten-Bell smoothing (Witten and Bell, 1991) will yield correct smoothed probabilities for in-context n-grams, but for n-grams not in-context in the current shard, the smoothed probabilities will not be guaranteed to be correctly estimated. This is because Witten-Bell smoothing is defined in terms of the number of words that have been observed following a particular history, which in the WFST encoding of the n-gram model is represented by the number of arcs (other than the backoff arc) leaving the history state (plus one if the state is final). While for any in-context state h, all of the arcs leaving the state will be present, some of the other n-gram states that were included to create the model topology – notably the states along the ascending path to in-context states – will not typically have all of the arcs that they have in their own shard. Hence the denominator in Witten-Bell smoothing (the count of the state plus the number of words observed following the history) cannot be calculated locally, and the direct application of the algorithm will end up with mis-estimated n-gram probabilities along the ascending paths.

If no pruning is done, then only the in-context probabilities matter, and merging can take place with no issues (see the next section 4.2.6).

Pruning algorithms, however, such as relative entropy pruning (Stolcke, 1998), typically use the joint n-gram probability – P(hw) – when calculating the scores that are used to decide whether to prune the n-gram or not. This joint probability is calculated by taking the product of all ascending path conditional probabilities. If the ascending path probabilities are wrong, these scores will also be wrong, and pruning will proceed in error. For Katz and absolute discounting, the ascending probabilities are correct when calculated on the shard independently of the other shards (when given counts-of-counts); but Witten Bell will not be immediately ready for pruning.

To get correct pruning for a sharded Witten-Bell model, another round of the transfer algorithm outlined in Section 4.2.4 is required, to retrieve the correct probabilities of ascending arcs in each shard.

The second issue to note here arises when pruning the model to have a particular number of desired n-grams in the model. For example, in some of the trials that we run in Section 6 we prune the n-gram models to result in 100 million n-grams in the final model. To establish a pruning threshold that will result in a given total number of n-grams across all shards, the shrinking score must be calculated for every n-gram in the collection and then these scores sorted to derive the right threshold. This requires a process not unlike the counts-of-counts aggregation presented in Section 4.2.4, yet with a sorting of the collection rather than compilation into a histogram.

Once all of the model shards have been normalized, smoothed and pruned using standard WFST-based n-gram algorithms, the shards can be reassembled to produce a single WFST.

4.2.6 Merge model shards

Merging the shard models into a single WFST n-gram model is a straightforward special case of general model merging, whereby two models are merged into one. In general, model merging algorithms of two WFST models with canonical n-gram topology will: (a) result in a new model with canonical n-gram topology; and (b) the n-gram costs in the new model are some function of the n-gram costs in the two models. If the models are being linearly interpolated, then the n-gram probability will be calculated as $\lambda p_1 + (1 - \lambda)p_2$, where p_k comes from the kth model, and the n-gram cost will be the negative log of that probability.[5]

To merge model shards M_1 and M_2, we must know, for each state h, whether h is in-context for M_1 or M_2. The n-gram cost in the merged model is c_2 if h is in-context for M_2; and c_1 otherwise, where c_k is the cost of the n-gram in M_k. If we start with an arbitrary model shard and designate that as M_1, then we can merge each other shard into the merged model in turn, and designate the resulting merged model as M_1 for a subsequent merge. By the end of merging in every context, all of the n-grams in the final model will have been merged in, so they will all have received their correct probabilities. The resulting WFST will have the same probabilities as it would if the model had been trained in a single process.

5 OpenGrm distributed functionality

While most of these distributed functions will likely be implemented in some kind of large, data-parallel processing system[6], such as MapReduce (Dean and Ghemawat, 2008), these pipelines will rely upon core OpenGrm NGram library functions to count, make, prune and merge models. The OpenGrm NGram library now includes some distributed functionality, along with a convenience script to illustrate the sort of approach we have described in this paper.

Recall that the basic approach involves sharding the data, counting n-grams on each data shard separately, and then splitting the counts from each data shard into context shards. Two command-line utilities in OpenGrm provide functionality for (1) defining context shards; and (2) splitting an n-gram WFST based on given context shards. One method described in Section 4.1 for deriving context shards is to train a smaller model (e.g., lower order and/or sampled from the full target training scenario) and then derive balanced context shards from that smaller model. For example, if we want to train a 5-gram model on 1B words of text, we might count[7] trigrams from every 100th sentence, yielding the n-gram count WFST `3g.fst`. Then the command line binary `ngramcontext` can make use of the sampled counts to derive a balanced sharding of the requested size:

```
ngramcontext --contexts=10 3g.fst >ctx.txt
```

The resulting text file (`ctx.txt`) will look something like this:

```
        0 : 18
       18 : 307 35
  307 35 : 70
      70 : 147
        . . .
```

as discussed in Section 3.1. Given these context definitions, we can now use `ngramsplit` to partition full count WFSTs derived from particular data shards. For example, suppose that we counted 5-grams from data shard k, yielding `DS-k.5g-counts.fst`. Then we can produce 10 count shards as follows:

```
ngramsplit --contexts=ctx.txt --complete \
   DS-k.5g-counts.fst DS-k.5g-counts
```

which would result in 10 count shard WFSTs `DS-k.5g-counts.0000i` for $0 \leq i < 10$. The `--complete` flag ensures that all required n-grams are included in the shard, not just those strictly in-context. Once this has been done for all data shards, the counts for each context shard can be merged across the data shards, i.e., `ngrammerge` using the `count_merge` method on `DS-*.5g-counts.0000i` for all i.

As discussed in Section 4.2.4, once we have the merged counts for each model shard, we must perform a transfer of the correct counts. This involves

---

[5]Backoff arc costs can then be calculated in closed form.

[6]We have implemented an end-to-end pipeline, which makes use of the OpenGrm NGram library, in Flume (Chambers et al., 2010). Results in Section 6 were generated with this pipeline.

[7]See Roark et al. (2012) for details on n-gram counting in the OpenGrm library.

| Corpus (words; sents) | order | n-grams | | time (hours) to | | model shards | pct. in-context ngrams | largest to smallest shard ratio |
		total	target per shard	preproc. + count	make, prune +			
Billion word benchmark (BWB) (769M; 30.3M)	3	238M	4M	1.5	1.2	59	56.0	1.20
			40M	1.6	1.6	5	84.8	1.07
	5	1.14B	4M	4.1	2.0	285	36.8	2.07
			40M	4.7	3.5	28	50.5	1.26
Search queries (SQ) (70B; 13.2B)	5	16.6B	4M	23.4	8.9	5090	38.8	1.93
			40M	10.2	7.1	502	64.4	1.77

Table 1: Sharding characteristics and time to estimate under different training scenarios. As noted in Section 6, times are not comparable if n-gram order or size of corpus are different, and times should be interpreted as a relatively coarse measure of work. The last two columns (100*in-context/total n-ngrams and the ratio of sizes in ngrams) indicate shard redundancy.

splitting again and using the command line binary `ngramtransfer` twice: once to extract the correct counts from the correct shards; and once to return the extracted counts to the shards requesting them. We refer the reader to Section 4.2.4 for high level detail, and the convenience script `ngram.sh` in the OpenGrm NGram library for specifics.

Several new functions have been added via options to existing command line binaries in the OpenGrm NGram library. For example, `ngramcount` can now produce counts of counts (`--method=count_of_counts`) and produce them only for a specified context shard. Further, `ngrammerge` has a `context_merge` method, which uses a derived class of OpenGrm's NGramMerge class to correctly reassemble count or language model sharded WFSTs into a single WFST. See the script `ngram.sh` in the OpenGrm NGram library for details.

In the next section, we provide some data on the characteristics of n-gram models of different orders and sizes when they are trained via sharding.

6 Shard size versus redundancy

As stated earlier, we use Flume (Chambers et al., 2010) in C++ to distribute our OpenGrm NGram model training. This system is not currently publicly available, but within it we use methods generally very similar to what is available in Open-Grm, just pipelined together in a different way. One difference between the Flume version and `ngram.sh` is the method for deriving contexts, which in Flume is based on efficient quantiles extracted from the set of n-grams. While this is also a sampling method for deriving the contexts, the ordering constraints of quantiles do often lead to better (though not perfect) estimates of balanced shards. Additionally, the Flume system that was used to generate these numbers uses a smart distributed processing framework, which allocates processors based on estimated size of the process. This impacts the interpretability of timing results, as noted below.

Table 1 presents some characteristics of language model training under several conditions which demonstrate some of the tradeoffs in distributing the model in slightly different ways. From the Billion Word Benchmark (BWB) corpus (Chelba et al., 2014), we train trigram and 5-gram language models with different parameterizations for determining the model sharding. We also report results on a proprietary 70 billion word collection of search queries (SQ), also with different sharding parameterizations. For the BWB trials, no symbol or n-gram frequency cutoffs were used, but for the search queries, as part of the pre-processing and counting, we selected the 4 million most common words from the collection to include in the vocabulary (all others mapped to an out-of-vocabulary token) and limited 4-grams and 5-grams to those occurring at least twice or 4 times, respectively. All trigram models were pruned to 50 million n-grams prior to shard merging (reassembling into a single WFST), and 5-gram models were pruned to 100 million n-grams. For these trials, the standard transfer algorithm in Section 4.2.4 was used. Run times are averaged over five independent runs.

Note that, due to the smart distributed processing framework, the times are not comparable if n-gram order or size of corpus are different. Further, due to distributed processing with resource contention, etc., the times should be interpreted as a coarse measure of work. That said, we note that in the largest scenario, parameterizing for relatively small shards (4M n-grams in-context per shard) yields over 5000 shards, which results in extra time in transfer (hence higher count times) and in final merging of the contexts (hence higher make,

Task	target per shard	trans. by order	time (hours) to count		
			before trans.	trans. to end	total
BWB	4M	N	2.4	1.7	4.1
		Y	2.1	3.5	5.5
	40M	N	2.6	2.1	4.7
		Y	3.1	5.9	9.0
SQ	4M	N	4.7	18.7	23.4
		Y	4.5	7.6	12.1
	40M	N	5.7	4.4	10.2
		Y	5.9	6.7	12.6

Table 2: Counting time broken down between stages occurring before transfer and those occurring from transfer to the end of counting, using either the original transfer algorithm or transferring by order.

prune, etc. times). With larger shard sizes (and hence fewer shards), the percentage of n-grams in each shard that are in-context (rather than ascending or backoff n-grams) is higher, and the size of the largest shard (in terms of total n-grams in the shard, both in-context and not) is much closer in size to the smallest shard, leading to better load balancing. Smaller shards, however, will generally distribute more effectively for many of the estimation tasks, leading to some speedups relative to fewer, larger shards.

Table 2 presents counting times for the 5-gram trials using both the standard transfer algorithm reported in Table 1 and the alternate "by order" transfer algorithm outlined in Section 4.2.4. The times are broken down into the part of counting before transfer and the part including transfer until the end. From these we can see that in scenarios with a very large number of shards – e.g., SQ with 4M target per shard, which yields more than 5000 shards – the "by order" transfer algorithm is much faster than the standard algorithm, leading to a factor of 2 speedup overall. However, increasing the target number of n-grams per shard, thus yielding fewer shards, is overall a more effective way to speedup processing. For much larger training scenarios, when even 40M n-grams per shard would yield a large number of shards, one would expect this alternative transfer algorithm to be useful. Otherwise, the additional overhead of the additional stages simply adds to the processing time.

7   Related work

Brants et al. (2007) presented work on distributed language model training that has been very influential. In that work, n-grams were sharded based on a hash function of the first words of the n-gram, so that prefix n-grams, which carry normalization counts, end up in the same shard as those requiring the normalization. Because suffix n-grams do not end up in the same shard, smoothing methods that need access to backoff histories, such as Katz, require additional processing.

In contrast, our sharding is on the suffix of the history, which ensures that all n-grams with the same history fall together, and very often the backoff histories also fall in the same shard without having to be added. Since normalization values can be derived by summing the counts of all n-grams with the same history, the prefix is not strictly speaking required for normalization, though, as described in Section 3.2, we do add them when 'completing' a model shard to canonical WFST n-gram format.

Sharding with individual n-grams as the unit rather than working with the more complex WFST topologies does have its benefits, particularly when it comes to relatively easy balancing of shards. The primary benefit of using WFSTs in such a distributed setting lies in making use of WFST functionality, such as modeling with expected frequencies derived from word lattices (Kuznetsov et al., 2016). Additionally, sharding on the suffix of the history does allow for scaling to much longer n-gram histories, such as would arise in character language modeling. If we train a 15-gram character language model from standard English corpora, then a significant number of those n-grams will begin with the space character, so creating a shard from a two character prefix may lead to extremely unbalanced sharding. In contrast, intervals of histories allow for balance even in such an extreme setting.

8   Summary and Future Directions

We have presented methods for distributing the estimation of WFST-based n-gram language models. We presented a model sharding approach that allows for much of the model estimation to be carried out on shards independently. We presented some pipeline algorithms that yield models identical with what would be trained on a single processor, and provided some data on what the resulting sharding looks like in real processing scenarios. We intend to create a full open-source distributed setup that makes use of the building blocks outlined here.

References

Cyril Allauzen and Michael Riley. 2013. Pre-initialized composition for large-vocabulary speech recognition. In *Proceedings of Interspeech*, pages 666–670.

Cyril Allauzen, Michael Riley, Johan Schalkwyk, Wojciech Skut, and Mehryar Mohri. 2007. OpenFst: A general and efficient weighted finite-state transducer library. In *Implementation and Application of Automata*, pages 11–23. Springer.

Cyril Allauzen, Michael Riley, and Johan Schalkwyk. 2009. A generalized composition algorithm for weighted finite-state transducers. In *Proceedings of Interspeech*, pages 1203–1206.

Thorsten Brants, Ashok C Popat, Peng Xu, Franz J Och, and Jeffrey Dean. 2007. Large language models in machine translation. In *Proceedings of the Joint Conference on Empirical Methods in Natural Language Processing (EMNLP) and Computational Natural Language Learning (CoNLL)*.

Craig Chambers, Ashish Raniwala, Frances Perry, Stephen Adams, Robert R Henry, Robert Bradshaw, and Nathan Weizenbaum. 2010. Flumejava: easy, efficient data-parallel pipelines. In *ACM Sigplan Notices*, volume 45-6, pages 363–375.

Ciprian Chelba, Thorsten Brants, Will Neveitt, and Peng Xu. 2010. Study on interaction between entropy pruning and Kneser-Ney smoothing. In *Proceedings of Interspeech*, pages 2422–2425.

Ciprian Chelba, Tomas Mikolov, Mike Schuster, Qi Ge, Thorsten Brants, Phillipp Koehn, and Tony Robinson. 2014. One billion word benchmark for measuring progress in statistical language modeling. In *Proceedings of Interspeech*, pages 2635–2639.

Jeffrey Dean and Sanjay Ghemawat. 2008. Mapreduce: simplified data processing on large clusters. *Communications of the ACM*, 51(1):107–113.

Kenneth Heafield. 2011. Kenlm: Faster and smaller language model queries. In *Proceedings of the Sixth Workshop on Statistical Machine Translation*, pages 187–197. Association for Computational Linguistics.

Slava M. Katz. 1987. Estimation of probabilities from sparse data for the language model component of a speech recognizer. *IEEE Transactions on Acoustics, Speech and Signal Processing*, 35(3):400–401.

Vitaly Kuznetsov, Hank Liao, Mehryar Mohri, Michael Riley, and Brian Roark. 2016. Learning n-gram language models from uncertain data. In *Proceedings of Interspeech (to appear)*.

Mehryar Mohri, Fernando Pereira, and Michael Riley. 2002. Weighted finite-state transducers in speech recognition. *Computer Speech & Language*, 16(1):69–88.

Hermann Ney, Ute Essen, and Reinhard Kneser. 1994. On structuring probabilistic dependences in stochastic language modeling. *Computer Speech and Language*, 8:1–38.

Brian Roark, Richard Sproat, Cyril Allauzen, Michael Riley, Jeffrey Sorensen, and Terry Tai. 2012. The OpenGrm open-source finite-state grammar software libraries. In *Proceedings of the ACL 2012 System Demonstrations*, pages 61–66.

Hasim Sak, Yun-hsuan Sung, Françoise Beaufays, and Cyril Allauzen. 2013. Written-domain language modeling for automatic speech recognition. In *Proceedings of Interspeech*, pages 675–679.

Jeffrey Sorensen and Cyril Allauzen. 2011. Unary data structures for language models. In *Proceedings of Interspeech*, pages 1425–1428.

Andreas Stolcke. 1998. Entropy-based pruning of backoff language models. In *Proceedings of the DARPA Broadcast News Transcription and Understanding Workshop*, pages 270–274.

Ian H. Witten and Timothy C. Bell. 1991. The zero-frequency problem: Estimating the probabilities of novel events in adaptive text compression. *IEEE Transactions on Information Theory*, 37(4):1085–1094.

Learning Transducer Models for Morphological Analysis from Example Inflections

Markus Forsberg
Språkbanken
University of Gothenburg
markus.forsberg@gu.se

Mans Hulden
Department of Linguistics
University of Colorado
mans.hulden@colorado.edu

Abstract

In this paper, we present a method to convert morphological inflection tables into unweighted and weighted finite transducers that perform parsing and generation. These transducers model the inflectional behavior of morphological paradigms induced from examples and can map inflected forms of previously unseen word forms into their lemmas and give morphosyntactic descriptions of them. The system is evaluated on several languages with data collected from the Wiktionary.

1 Introduction

Wide-coverage morphological parsers that return lemmas and morphosyntactic descriptions (MSDs) of arbitrary word forms are fundamental for achieving strong performance of many downstream tasks in NLP (Tseng et al., 2005; Spoustová et al., 2007; Avramidis and Koehn, 2008; Zeman, 2008; Hulden and Francom, 2012). This is particularly true for languages that exhibit rich inflectional and derivational morphology. Finite-state transducers are the standard technology for addressing this issue, but constructing them often requires not only significant commitment of resources but also demands linguistic expertise from the developers (Maxwell, 2015). Access to large numbers of example inflections organized into inflection tables in resources such as the Wiktionary promises to offer a less laborious route to constructing robust large-scale analyzers. Learning morphological generalizations from such example data has been the focus of much recent research, particularly in the domain of morphologically complex languages (Cotterell et al., 2016).

In this paper we present a tool for automatic generation of both probabilistic and non-probabilistic morphological analyzers that can be represented as unweighted and weighted transducers. The assumption is that we have access to a collection of example word forms together with corresponding MSDs. We present two systems: one that is designed to be high-recall and operates with unweighted automata, the purpose of which is to return all linguistically plausible analyses for an unknown word form; the second is an addition to the first in that the word shapes are modeled with a generative probabilistic model that can be implemented as a weighted transducer that produces a ranking of the plausible analyses. The analyzers are constructed with standard finite state tools and are designed to operate similarly to a hand-constructed morphophonological analyzer extended with a 'guesser' module to handle unknown word forms.

The system takes as input sets of lemmatized words annotated with an MSD, all grouped into inflection tables—such as can be found in, for example, the *Wiktionary*. The output is a morphological analyzer either as an unweighted (in the non-probabilistic case) or a weighted model (in the probabilistic case). For the non-probabilistic case we use the Xerox regular expression formalism (Karttunen et al., 1996), which we compile into a transducer with the open-source finite-state toolkit *foma* (Hulden, 2009) and for the weighted case we have used the *Kleene* toolkit (Beesley, 2012).[1]

2 Paradigm Learning

The starting point for the research in this paper is the notion that inflections and derivations of related word forms can be expressed as functions—this idea is often filed under the rubric of 'functional morphology' and is strongly related to word-and-paradigm models of morphology (Hockett, 1954;

---

[1]Our code and data are available at: https://github.com/marfors/paradigmextract

Proceedings of the ACL Workshop on Statistical NLP and Weighted Automata, pages 42–50,
Berlin, Germany, August 12, 2016. ©2016 Association for Computational Linguistics

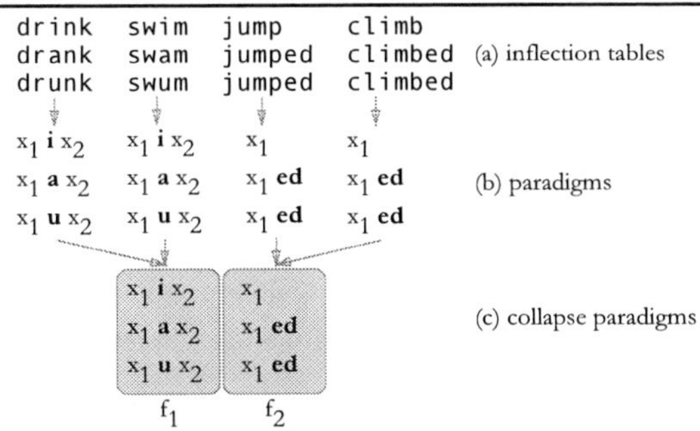

Figure 1: Generalizing inflection tables into paradigm functions: (1) a number of complete inflection tables are given; (2) the aligned Longest Common Subsequence is extracted; (3) resulting identical paradigms are merged. If the resulting paradigm f_1 is interpreted as a function, $f_1(shr, nk)$ produces **shrink, shrank, shrunk**.

Robins, 1959; Matthews, 1972; Stump, 2001). In particular, we assume a model where a single function generates all the possible inflected forms of a group of lemmas that behave alike. This approach has earlier been seen as an alternative to finite-state morphology, and the functions that model inflectional behavior have been hand-built in much previous work (Forsberg and Ranta, 2004; Forsberg et al., 2006; Détrez and Ranta, 2012). Here, we assume the recent model of Ahlberg et al. (2014) and Ahlberg et al. (2015), which work with a system that automatically learns these functions that model inflection tables from labeled data.

The purpose of modeling inflection types as functions is to be able to generalize concrete manifestations of word inflection for specific lemmas, and to apply those generalizations to unseen word forms. The generalization in question is performed by extracting the Longest Common Subsequence (LCS) from all word forms related to some specific lemma and then expressing each word form in terms of the LCS (Hulden, 2014). The LCS in turn is broken down into possibly discontiguous sequences that express parts of word forms that are variable in nature. Figure 1 shows a toy example of four inflection tables generalized into variable- and non-variable parts by first extracting the LCS, expressing the original word forms in terms of this LCS, and then collapsing the resulting functions that are identical. The resulting representation, which is essentially a set of strings which have variable parts $(x_1, \ldots, x_n)$, and fixed parts (such as **i, a, u**) that

can be used to generate an unbounded number of new inflection tables by instantiating the variable parts in new ways and concatenating the variables and the fixed parts.

This learning method often produces a very small number of functions compared with the number of complete inflection tables that have been input—obviously, because many lemmas behave alike and result in identical functions. We note that the output of this procedure is human-readable, i.e. it can be inspected (even in real-world scenarios) for correctness and also hand-corrected in case of noise in the learning data. In the current work, we use these functions as the backbone of a generative model and implement them as transducers that can be run in the inverse direction to map fully inflected forms into their lemmas and morphosyntactic descriptions.

2.1 Paradigm functions

The variables $x_1, \ldots, x_n$ that are used in the paradigm function representation capture possible inter-word variation. This means that each lemma that gives rise to an inflection table can be directly represented as simply an instantiation of the variables, together with the inflection function. As seen in Figure 1, the function f_1 learned from the inflection tables *swim* and *drink* can be used to represent some other word, e.g. *sing* by instantiating x_1 as **s** and x_2 as **ng**.

As we collect a large number of inflection tables, many of which result in identical paradigms, we can also collect statistics about the variables involved and how they were assumed to be instantiated in the original table. For example, from the truncated tables in Figure 1, we can gather that f_1 has witnessed x_1 as both **dr** and **sw**, and x_2 as **nk** and **m**. These statistics can be used to turn the learned functions into a restricted generative model that produces entire inflection tables, but also taking advantage of how variables tend to be instantiated in that paradigm function.

Additionally, since each possible inflected form consists of the same variables, we can also define a string-to-string mapping between any two related forms, where the content of the variable parts stay fixed, and the non-variable parts change. For example, in Figure 1, we know that we can, for some verbs, go from the *past participle* (e.g. **drunk**) to the *past* (e.g. **drank**) by a string transformation x_1 u $x_2 \rightarrow x_1$ a x_2, with some constraints on the nature of x_1 and x_2. This information can then be encoded in transducer form where the variable parts can be modeled as a probabilistic language model (for weighted transducers) or a non-probabilistic, constrained model (for unweighted transducers).

Figure 2 illustrates this idea. We have learned a paradigm in Spanish—we call the paradigm **avenir** (arbitrarily), since that is one of the verbs out of 12 that behaved the same way and gave rise to the same function. A natural mapping to learn from the data is how to go from any inflected form to the dictionary or 'citation' form. For example, going from the *present participle* to the *infinitive* would involve changing the fixed **i** occurring between the two variables x_1 and x_2 into **e** and then changing the fixed suffix after x_2 from **iendo** to **ir**. The figure also shows how the different variables were instantiated in the training data: x_1 showed up in variable shapes (but always ending in **v**), while x_2 was always **n**.

Although the learning model in principle states nothing about the nature of the variables, morphophonological restrictions will constrain their appearance and the key to producing a transducer that can inflect unseen words without undue overgeneration is to take these restrictions into account. We do so in two ways: (1) for the unweighted case, we collect statistics on the seen variables and constrain their possible shapes in an absolute manner, and (2) for the weighted case, we induce a language model over the shapes of the variables, which can later be used to rank parses produced by the system.

3 The unweighted case: constraining variables

Different generalized inflection tables naturally give rise to different variable instantiations for $x_1, \ldots, x_n$. However, many of the seen variables will not differ arbitrarily in a paradigm. This is something we can take advantage of when designing a parsing mechanism; in particular, we can express preferences to the effect that such parses where variables resemble already seen instantiations should be preferred.

Figure 3 is a case in point. Here, we show the implicit string-to-string rule in the paradigm which derives the lemma form from the present participle and the first person singular present forms in Spanish. In both the paradigms learned, the variables x_1 and x_2 show a somewhat repetitive pattern. In the paradigm **avenir**, x_1 ends in the letter **v** for all the inflection tables seen that produced that paradigm, while x_2 always consists of the single letter **n**. Likewise, in the other paradigm (**negar**), x_2 is consistently the string **eg** across all forms seen (the inflected forms of **cegar**, **denegar**, etc.). The only variable that does not show such a regular pattern is the x_1 variable for the paradigm called **negar**.

3.1 Estimating probabilities of new variable instantiations

That the parts of paradigms that vary from lemma to lemma, i.e. the 'variables', are not subject to arbitrary variation can be used to constrain their shape. To model the unweighted transducers, we begin by formalizing our belief in not seeing novel variable shapes in the future. To quantify this, we assume we have seen n concrete instantiations of t different types of variables, and subsequently ask: if there were in fact $t + 1$ types, all of which are drawn from a uniform distribution, how likely are we to have witnessed only the t types we did? This quantity can be expressed as

$$p_{\text{unseen}} = (1 - \frac{1}{t+1})^n \tag{1}$$

For example, the measure for the x_2 variable in Figure 3 (**avenir**) becomes $(1 - \frac{1}{2})^{12} \approx 0.0002$. We can use this as a cutoff parameter that defines how much evidence we require to declare a variable not subject to further variation apart from the types we have already seen. With this, we assume that if $p_{\text{unseen}} \leq 0.05$ for some variable, that variable in the paradigm will not exhibit new types.[2]

3.2 Expressing constraints through regular expressions

We also expand this measure to cover variables that show variation only in non-edge positions. For example, x_2 in the **avenir**-paradigm in Table 3 is always **n** and can be assumed to not be subject to variation by the calculation above. The paradigm's x_1-variable, however, cannot. That variable seems to vary much more, with the exception of the last letter, which is always **v**. To capture this, we extend the method to apply not only to the whole

---

[2]Estimating the probability of the existence of unseen types is a classical problem (Good, 1953); see Ogino (1999) and Kageura and Sekine (1999) for linguistics-related discussions and Chen and Goodman (1996) for the relationship to smoothing in language models.

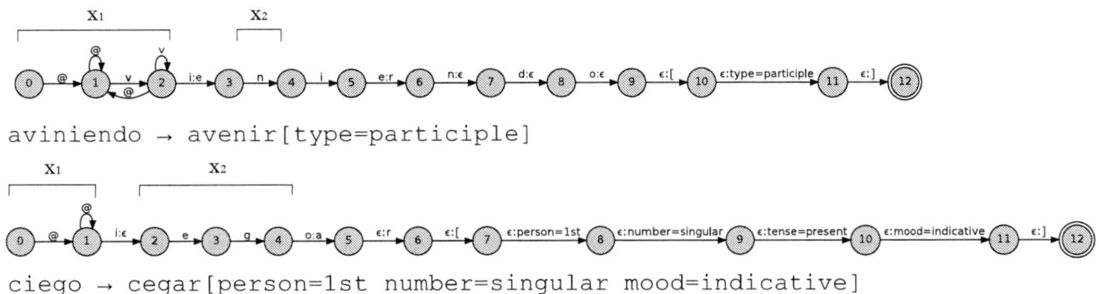

```
aviniendo → avenir[type=participle]
```

```
ciego → cegar[person=1st number=singular mood=indicative]
```

Figure 2: Examples of two single generalized word forms mapped to lemmas followed by morphosyntactic description. The parts that correspond to constraints of the variables x_1 and x_2 are marked. Transitions marked @ are identity transduction 'elsewhere' cases, matching any symbol not explicitly mentioned in the state.

Inflection table	Paradigm	MSD	Inflection table	Paradigm	MSD
avenir	x_1+e+x_2+ir	infinitive	**neg**ar	x_1+x_2+ar	infinitive
aveniendo	x_1+i+x_2+iendo	pres part	**neg**ando	x_1+x_2+ando	pres part
avenido	x_1+e+x_2+ido	past part	**neg**ado	x_1+x_2+ado	past part
avengo	x_1+e+x_2+go	1sg pres ind	**nieg**o	x_1+i+x_2+o	1sg pres ind
avienes	x_1+ie+x_2+es	2sg pres ind	**nieg**as	x_1+i+x_2+as	2sg pres ind

Table 1: Two partial Spanish verb inflection tables generalized into paradigm functions. The segments that are part of the longest common subsequence, which are cast as variables in the generalization, are shown in boldface in the inflection tables.

string, but also edge positions of the string. First, we examine the whole string, and if that fails to yield the conclusion that the variable is 'fixed', we find the longest prefix and suffix which can be assumed to be fixed by the same measure. With this we construct a regular expression that models the variables as follows:

1. $(w_1 \cup w_2 \cup \ldots \cup w_n)$ if the variable is assumed to be fixed, where the w_is are the complete strings seen as instantiations.

2. $(p_1 \cup \ldots \cup p_n)\Sigma^* \cap \Sigma^*(s_1 \cup \ldots \cup s_n)$, if both prefixes and suffixes can be constrained; here the p_is correspond to the prefixes of the maximal length that can be assumed to be drawn from a fixed set of types, and the s_is the suffixes.

3. $(p_1 \cup \ldots \cup p_n)\Sigma^*$ if only prefixes appear fixed.

4. $\Sigma^*(s_1 \cup \ldots \cup s_n)$ if only suffixes appear fixed.

5. Σ^+ otherwise.

In the above, Σ represents all the symbols seen in the training data. Under this formulation, the variables in the **avenir** paradigm in Figure 3 yield the following regular expressions:

$$x_1 = (\Sigma^* v) \quad x_2 = n \qquad (2)$$

4 Deriving morphological analyzers

Once we have the constraints in place, they can be used to construct larger regular expressions that reflect mappings from a specific word form to a lemma together with the MSD. We convert each inflection form in a paradigm to a regular expression that permits the above variable values in place of $x_1, \ldots, x_n$, and that maps the remaining fixed strings to other fixed strings, depending on what kind of application is needed.

For example, to create a regular expression for mapping the *1p pres ind*-form (exemplified by **niego**) to the lemma form in Table 1, we proceed as follows: we construct a transducer that repeats the x_1 and x_2-variables, possibly subject to the constraints on their shape, and maps an **i** to the empty string and **o** to **ar**. Since x_1 is not constrained in the paradigm, while x_2 is constrained to always be the string **eg**, this produces the following regular expression:

Paradigm *avenir*
Rule: pres part → inf

x_1 + i→e + x_2 + iendo→ir

av	n
circunv	n
contrav	n
conv	n
dev	n
entrev	n
interv	n
prev	n
prov	n
rev	n
v	n
adv	n

Paradigm *negar*
Rule: 1p sg pres → inf

x_1 + i→0 + x_2 + o→ar

c	eg
den	eg
desasos	eg
despl	eg
fr	eg
n	eg
pl	eg
r	eg
ren	eg
repl	eg
restr	eg
s	eg
sos	eg
an	eg

Figure 3: Paradigm functions generalized from inflection tables provide a mechanism for mapping an inflected form to any other inflected form. Illustrated here are two rules extracted from different Spanish verb paradigms showing a string-to-string mapping from the participle to the infinitive, and from the first person singular present form to the infinitive. Also shown are the variable parts of the paradigms x_1 and x_2 and how they have been instantiated in the training data.

$$\underbrace{(\Sigma^+)}_{x_1} \; (i{:}\epsilon) \; \underbrace{e\,g}_{x_2} \; (o{:}ar[\text{1sg pres ind}]) \qquad (3)$$

The transducer corresponding to the expression is seen in Figure 2, and will generalize to words that fit the variable pattern, e.g. **ciego → cegar**.

Each inflection form of every paradigm is converted in such a manner to a transducer that maps that single inflection to its lemma and morphosyntactic description. All such individual transducers can then be unioned together for every form in every paradigm:

$$f_1 \cup f_2 \cup \ldots \cup f_1 \cup \ldots \cup f_m \qquad (4)$$

5 Prioritizing analyses

The above formulation, though it already produces a working transducer that generalizes to unseen forms, can be refined further. First, if a word form matches the original variables seen exactly, it may be superfluous to return extra analyses from other paradigms that the word form might also fit. Secondly, it may be the case that we have overconstrained some variable with the heuristic described

Analysis: **peleaste**		
O	**pelear**	**[pers=2 number=sg tense=past mood=ind]**
C	peleastar	[pers=1 num=sg tense=pres mood=subj]
	peleastar	[pers=3 num=sg tense=pres mood=subj]
	peleastir	[pers=3 num=sg tense=pres mood=ind]
	pelear	**[pers=2 num=sg tense=past mood=ind]**
U	peleaster	[pers=3 num=sg tense=pres mood=ind]
	peleastar	[pers=1 num=sg tense=pres mood=subj]
	peleastar	[pers=3 num=sg tense=pres mood=subj]
	peleastir	[pers=3 num=sg tense=pres mood=ind]
	pelear	**[pers=2 num=sg tense=past mood=ind]**
	pelastir	[pers=3 num=sg tense=pres mood=ind]
	pleastir	[pers=3 num=sg tense=pres mood=ind]
Analysis: **aceleran**		
O	???	???
C	**acelerar**	**[pers=3 num=pl tense=pres mood=ind]**
	acelerir	[pers=3 num=pl tense=pres mood=subj]
U	**acelerar**	**[pers=3 num=pl tense=pres mood=ind]**
	aceler	[pers=3 num=pl tense=imp-ra mood=subj]
	acelerir	[pers=3 num=pl tense=pres mood=subj]
	acelerer	[pers=3 num=pl tense=pres mood=subj]
	acelrir	[pers=3 num=pl tense=pres mood=subj]
	acelir	[pers=3 num=pl tense=imp-ra mood=subj]
	aclerir	[pers=3 num=pl tense=pres mood=subj]

Table 2: Example of the tri-level analyses produced by the unweighted system: here the three sub-grammars (**Original = O, Constrained = C, Unconstrained = U**) each allow for successively more analyses. The word **peleaste** 'quarrel' has been seen in the training data and thus receives an analysis from the constrained analyzer, whereas **aceleran** 'accelerate' has not and only receives parses from **C** and **U**.

earlier, and so return no analyses at all, motivating a potential relaxation of the constraints on variable shapes.

To provide a ranking of the analyses in the unweighted analyzer, we actually generate a layered approach with three different models:

- **Original**: an analyzer where each x_i must match exactly some shape seen in training data.

- **Constrained**: an analyzer where variables are constrained as described above.

- **Unconstrained**: an analyzer where there are no constraints on variables, except that they must be at least one symbol long, i.e. match Σ^+.

The three analyzers can be joined by a "priority union" operation (Kaplan, 1987), in effect producing a single analyzer that prioritizes more constrained analyses, if such are possible: **Original** $\cup_P$ **Constrained** $\cup_P$ **Unconstrained**.

This in effect leads to an analyzer that can be thought of as first consulting **Original**, and that failing to produce an analysis, consults **Constrained**, and if that also fails, consults **Unconstrained**. The same effect can also be modeled in runtime code by keeping the three transducers separate for potential savings of space. Table 2 illustrates this priority effect with two Spanish words being analyzed.

6 The weighted case: language models over variables

The above unweighted model provides a hierarchical system by which to return plausible analyses, while curbing implausible ones. However, it lacks the power to provide a ranking of analyses within each layer of ever laxer constraints on the variables. An alternative to that model is to directly use the statistics over the variable parts to generate a weighted transducer that performs the same type of parsing, but with a (hopefully) strict ranking of candidate parses. We address this by inducing an n-gram model over each variable in each paradigm. We calculate these individual n-gram models in the usual way for a single variable $\mathbf{v}$, consisting of the letters $v_1, \ldots, v_n$:

$$P(v_1, \ldots, v_n) = \prod_{i=1}^{n} P(v_i | v_{i-(n-1)}, \ldots, v_{i-1})$$
(5)

For each variable and function, we perform a standard maximum likelihood estimate of the n-grams by

$$\begin{aligned}
&P(v_i | v_{i-(n-1)}, \ldots, v_{i-1}) \\
&= \frac{\#(v_{i-(n-1)}, \ldots, v_{i-1}, v_i)}{\#(v_{i-(n-1)}, \ldots, v_{i-1})}
\end{aligned}$$
(6)

with some additional add-δ smoothing to prevent zero counts. The resulting variable models can then (after taking negative logs) replace the variable portions of each individual transducer that maps a word form to its citation form. The fixed parts of the inflection mappings retain the weight 0.

These language models are then concatenated with the same model as used for the unweighted case in place of the variables. This is illustrated in Figure 4.

We tune the model for each language evaluated by doing a grid search on (1) the order of the n-gram (1–5), (2) the prior on the n-grams (0.01–3.0),

(3) the prior of picking a paradigm (we include a paradigm weight for each individual paradigm).

Similarly to the unweighted case, the final model is a union of all the individual inflection models for each paradigm and word, with the language models for the variables interleaved.

7 Evaluation

To evaluate the systems, we used the data set published by Durrett and DeNero (2013) (D&DN13), which includes full inflection tables for a large number of lemmas in German (nouns and verbs), Spanish (verbs), and Finnish (nouns+adjectives and verbs). That source also provides a division into train/dev/test splits, with 200 tables in dev and test, respectively. We then evaluated the ability of our systems to provide a correct lemmatization and MSD of each word form in the held-out tables, testing separately on each part of speech. For the unweighted analyzer, we use the three-part setup as described above. For the weighted case, we produce a single highest scoring analysis. The train/dev/test sets are entirely disjoint and share no tables.

We trained the models by inspecting all the word forms and corresponding MSDs, organizing them into tables, learning the paradigms, and the generating weighted and unweighted transducers as described above. These transducers were then run on the test data to provide lemmatization and analyses of the unseen word forms. Table 4 summarizes the number of inflection tables seen during training, together with the final number of paradigms learned. Table 5 shows the statistics in the held-out data.

Because we focus on the recall figures of the analyzers, we also calculated an "inherent ambiguity" measure of the test data. This is the average number of different MSDs that are given for each word form. This ambiguity may arise as follows: the Spanish verb **tenga**, for example, can be either the first person singular present subjunctive of **tener** 'to have' or the third person singular present subjunctive. Such ambiguity shows that there exist cases where returning multiple analyses is warranted, given that we do not have any sentence context to determine the correct choice.

For the weighted case, sometimes the system returns multiple equally scoring parses. This is due to the fact that the language model only operates over the variables, and, in many languages multi-

Language		L-recall	L+M-recall	L/W	L+M/W
German	nouns	95.30	95.06	2.08	9.52
	verbs	91.18	92.44	4.16	9.57
	nouns+verbs	92.11	93.04	4.91	14.10
Spanish	verbs	98.06	97.98	1.93	2.20
Finnish	nounadj	88.69	88.48	4.10	5.30
	verbs	94.52	94.47	3.77	4.60
	nounadj+verbs	92.63	92.43	12.56	16.40

Table 3: The result of the unweighted evaluation, where we report separately on the recall of just the lemma (L-recall), and the recall of the lemma and corresponding MSD (L+M-recall). Also shown are the average number of unique lemmas returned per word form to be analyzed (L/W), and the average number of lemmas and MSDs returned (L+M/W).

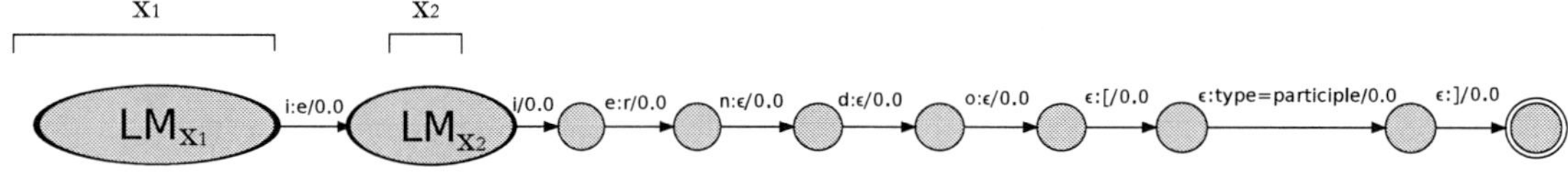

Figure 4: Illustration of the coupling of language models for variables x_1 and x_2 to create the weighted analyzer. Here, LM_{x_1} and LM_{x_2} illustrate a collection of states representing the language models for the variables, inferred from variable instantiations seen in the training data.

Language		Tables	Paradigms
German	nouns	2564	70
	verbs	1827	139
	nouns+verbs	4391	209
Spanish	verbs	3855	96
Finnish	nounadj	6200	259
	verbs	7049	276
	nounadj+verbs	13249	535

Table 4: Statistics on the D&DN13 train+dev sets. **Paradigms** is the corresponding number of induced paradigm functions.

Language		Tables	Unique wf's	Amb.
German	nouns	200	553	2.89
	verbs	200	2324	2.32
	nouns+verbs	400	2877	2.43
Spanish	verbs	200	10003	1.14
Finnish	nounadj	200	5198	1.08
	verbs	200	10466	1.03
	nounadj+verbs	400	15664	1.05

Table 5: Statistics on the D&DN13 test set. **Amb.** is the average number of lemma-MSD pairs per unique word form (wf).

Language		Lemma	L+MSD	MSD
German	nouns	77.06	69.44	79.50
	verbs	90.02	89.76	92.78
Spanish	verbs	96.92	96.92	97.43
Finnish	nounadj	70.29	69.68	91.59
	verbs	90.44	90.44	98.02

Table 6: Evaluation of the weighted model (all figures represent the recall).

ple MSDs often have the same surface form. For example, Spanish **compraba** 'bought 1P/3P' (and **-aba** suffix-bearing verbs in general) are always ambiguous between 1st/3rd past tense. For this reason, we calculate the recall (as opposed to accuracy) of all the top scoring parses. The weighted system always returns a single lemma in the evaluation. It can, of course, produce a number of ranked analyses if needed—an example of extracting the top-10 ranked analyses of a word form is given in Table 7.

7.1 Results

Table 3 shows the main results of the evaluation of the unweighted model and Table 6 the results of the weighted model. For the unweighted case,

rank	w	paradigm	vars	lemma	analyses
1	14.10	p1_abadernar	(1=compr)	**comprar**	**[pers=2 num=sg tense=past mood=ind]**
2	18.22	p1_abadernar	(1=comprast)	comprastar comprastar	[pers=1 **num=sg** tense=pres mood=sub] [pers=3 **num=sg** tense=pres mood=sub]
3	23.57	p5_abogar	(1=compr)	**comprar**	**[pers=2 num=sg tense=past mood=ind]**
4	24.58	p4_abolir	(1=comprast)	comprastir	[pers=3 **num=sg** tense=pres **mood=ind**]
5	24.58	p8_acrecentar	(1=com,2=pr)	**comprar**	**[pers=2 num=sg tense=past mood=ind]**
6	25.51	p37_colgar	(1=c,2=mpr)	**comprar**	**[pers=2 num=sg tense=past mood=ind]**
7	26.20	p10_acostar	(1=c,2=mpr)	**comprar**	**[pers=2 num=sg tense=past mood=ind]**
8	26.61	p7_acceder	(1=comprast)	compraster	[pers=3 **num=sg** tense=pres **mood=ind**]
9	26.87	p8_acrecentar	(1=comp,2=r)	**comprar**	**[pers=2 num=sg tense=past mood=ind]**
10	29.98	p20_cegar	(1=c,2=ompr)	**comprar**	**[pers=2 num=sg tense=past mood=ind]**

Table 7: Weighted parsing example: top-10 ranked parses for the word form **compraste** 'buy PAST' in Spanish with weights (in effect the negative log probability), the inferred variable division, the lemmatization, and MSDs. Lemmas and parts of the analysis that are correct are given in boldface. Note that several paradigms can produce an entirely correct parse for a single form such as this one, even though the paradigms would differ in other forms.

we consider the lemma-recall and lemma+MSD recall, and also document the average number of unique parses returned (lemma or lemma+MSD). For the weighted model, we give the recall for all combinations of lemma+MSD.

The weighted recall is—for obvious reasons—consistently below the unweighted version as the unweighted case uses the hierarchical model to potentially return a much larger number of analyses. The weighted version always returns a single lemma, and possibly several equally ranked MSDs, as discussed above. Still, for some languages (Spanish and Finnish verbs in particular), despite returning only a single analysis, performance is on par with the unweighted model, which returns 1.93 analyses on average (Spanish) and 3.77 (Finnish). We emphasize that the test set for our experiments is entirely disjoint from the training set, and that the figures therefore reflect potential performance on unseen word forms, not standard per-token performance in running text, which is presumably much higher. The reported figures can thus be interpreted to correspond to a per-type performance for OOV items.

8 Conclusion and future work

We have described two supervised methods for producing finite-state models morphological analyzers and guessers from labeled word forms, organized into inflection tables. The method can be used to quickly produce high-recall morphological analysis from labeled data with little or no linguistic development effort.

These tools can be used as is and can also be modified to exploit unlabeled data in the form of raw text corpora in a semi-supervised lexicon expansion setting. Some potential extensions could be of immediate value: the generative weighted model could be combined and evaluated on a task of tagging/disambiguating running text where contextual features could be used and seamlessly combined with the morphological language model. The weighted model also offers paths for further experimentation—for example, it is not immediately obvious that an n-gram model is the best choice. It seems reasonable to assume that those parts of the variables modeled that stand closer to the fixed parts, i.e. at the edges, would be more important in judging similarity to previously seen inflected forms. Table 2 hints at this being the case since, for example, the Spanish variables seem far more constrained at edge positions than in the middle of the variable string. Which parts to weight as more important in judging similarity could also be inferred from data. Another potential extension is to also constrain the analysis form by integrating a word-level language model instead of only a variable-level one, either replacing the variable-level model or working in conjunction with it.

Acknowledgements

This work has been partly funded by the Swedish Research Council under grant number 2012-5738, *Towards a knowledge-based culturomics* and the University of Gothenburg through its support of the Centre for Language Technology and its support of Språkbanken.

References

Malin Ahlberg, Markus Forsberg, and Mans Hulden. 2014. Semi-supervised learning of morphological paradigms and lexicons. In *Proceedings of the 14th EACL*, pages 569–578, Gothenburg, Sweden. Association for Computational Linguistics.

Malin Ahlberg, Markus Forsberg, and Mans Hulden. 2015. Paradigm classification in supervised learning of morphology. In *Proceedings of the NAACL-HLT 2015*, pages 1024–1029, Denver, Colorado, May–June. Association for Computational Linguistics.

Eleftherios Avramidis and Philipp Koehn. 2008. Enriching morphologically poor languages for statistical machine translation. *NAACL-HLT 2008*, pages 763–770.

Kenneth R. Beesley. 2012. Kleene, a free and open-source language for finite-state programming. In *10th International Workshop on Finite State Methods and Natural Language Processing*, page 50.

Stanley F. Chen and Joshua Goodman. 1996. An empirical study of smoothing techniques for language modeling. In *Proceedings of the 34th ACL*, pages 310–318. Association for Computational Linguistics.

Ryan Cotterell, Christo Kirov, John Sylak-Glassman, David Yarowsky, Jason Eisner, and Mans Hulden. 2016. The SIGMORPHON 2016 shared task—morphological reinflection. In *Proceedings of the 2016 Meeting of SIGMORPHON*, Berlin, Germany, August. Association for Computational Linguistics.

Grégoire Détrez and Aarne Ranta. 2012. Smart paradigms and the predictability and complexity of inflectional morphology. In *Proceedings of the 13th EACL*, pages 645–653.

Greg Durrett and John DeNero. 2013. Supervised learning of complete morphological paradigms. In *Proceedings of NAACL-HLT*, pages 1185–1195.

Markus Forsberg and Aarne Ranta. 2004. Functional morphology. *ACM SIGPLAN Notices*, 39(9):213–223.

Markus Forsberg, Harald Hammarström, and Aarne Ranta. 2006. Morphological lexicon extraction from raw text data. In *Advances in Natural Language Processing*, pages 488–499. Springer.

Irving J. Good. 1953. The population frequencies of species and the estimation of population parameters. *Biometrika*, 40(3-4):237–264.

Charles F Hockett. 1954. Two models of grammatical description. *Morphology: Critical Concepts in Linguistics*, 1:110–138.

Mans Hulden and Jerid Francom. 2012. Boosting statistical tagger accuracy with simple rule-based grammars. In *Proceedings of the Language Resources and Evaluation Conference (LREC 2012)*, pages 2114–2117.

Mans Hulden. 2009. Foma: a finite-state compiler and library. In *Proceedings of the 12th EACL*, pages 29–32, Athens, Greece. Association for Computational Linguistics.

Mans Hulden. 2014. Generalizing inflection tables into paradigms with finite state operations. In *Proceedings of the 2014 Joint Meeting of SIGMORPHON and SIGFSM*, pages 29–36. Association for Computational Linguistics.

Kyo Kageura and Satoshi Sekine. 1999. A note on Ogino's "method to estimate probability of new appearance". *Journal of Mathematical Linguistics*, 22(3).

Ronald M. Kaplan. 1987. Three seductions of computational psycholinguistics. In P. Whitelock, M. M. Wood, H. L. Somers, R. Johnson, and P. Bennett, editors, *Linguistic Theory and Computer Applications*, London. Academic Press.

Lauri Karttunen, Jean-Pierre Chanod, Gregory Grefenstette, and Anne Schiller. 1996. Regular expressions for language engineering. *Natural Language Engineering*, 2(4):305–328.

Peter H. Matthews. 1972. *Inflectional morphology: A theoretical study based on aspects of Latin verb conjugation*. Cambridge University Press.

Michael Maxwell. 2015. Grammar debugging. In *Systems and Frameworks for Computational Morphology*, pages 166–183. Springer.

T. Ogino. 1999. How many examples are required in language research—a proposal of a method to estimate probability of new appearance. *Mathematical Linguistics*, 22(1):11–17.

Robert H Robins. 1959. In defence of WP. *Transactions of the Philological Society*, 58(1):116–144.

Drahomíra Spoustová, Jan Hajič, Jan Votrubec, Pavel Krbec, and Pavel Květoň. 2007. The best of two worlds: Cooperation of statistical and rule-based taggers for Czech. In *Proceedings of the Workshop on Balto-Slavonic Natural Language Processing*, pages 67–74.

Gregory T. Stump. 2001. *A theory of paradigm structure*. Cambridge University Press.

Huihsin Tseng, Daniel Jurafsky, and Christopher Manning. 2005. Morphological features help POS tagging of unknown words across language varieties. In *Proceedings of the fourth SIGHAN workshop on Chinese language processing*, pages 32–39.

Daniel Zeman. 2008. Reusable tagset conversion using tagset drivers. In *Proceedings of the Language Resources and Evaluation Conference (LREC 2008)*.

Data-Driven Spelling Correction using Weighted Finite-State Methods

Miikka Silfverberg[a] **Pekka Kauppinen**[b] **Krister Lindén**[b]
Department of Modern Languages, University of Helsinki
[a]mpsilfve@iki.fi, [b]firstname.lastname@helsinki.fi

Abstract

This paper presents two systems for spelling correction formulated as a sequence labeling task. One of the systems is an unstructured classifier and the other one is structured. Both systems are implemented using weighted finite-state methods. The structured system delivers state-of-the-art results on the task of tweet normalization when compared with the recent AliSeTra system introduced by Eger et al. (2016) even though the system presented in the paper is simpler than AliSeTra because it does not include a model for input segmentation. In addition to experiments on tweet normalization, we present experiments on OCR post-processing using an Early Modern Finnish corpus of OCR processed newspaper text.

1 Introduction

Spelling correction is one of the most widely applied language technological utilities. The most obvious application of spelling correction is as a writer's aid. However, many natural language processing applications can also benefit from a spelling correction component. For example, many existing NLP systems are trained on newswire which tends to closely adhere to orthographical and grammatical norms. These systems may incur a substantial hit in performance when they are applied to noisy domains like social media. When spelling correction is applied as a pre-processing step, performance can be better. Digitization of documents is another domain where spelling correction is useful. Digitization often aims to transform physical documents into digital representations which support free text search. This requires the use of an optical character recog-

input	A	m	.	c
output	A	nn	ε	e

Figure 1: Post-editing as sequence labeling. The input to the post-editor is "Am.c" and the correct output is "Anne". This representation corresponds to the 1-to-n alignment of Bisani and Ney (2008) because each input symbol is associated with a possibly empty sequence of outputs.

nition (OCR) engine. Depending on the quality of the engine and source documents, this can succeed to varying degrees. Spelling correction can be applied as a post-processing step in order to improve quality.

Spelling correction is an instance of the more general task of string-to-string translation. In spelling correction, the objective is to transform a possibly erroneous input string, for example a misspelling or OCR error, into a correct output string. Like many string-to-string translation tasks, spelling correction can be formulated as sequence labeling: the correction system receives a string of input symbols and associates each input symbol with a (possibly empty) sequence of output symbols as shown in Figure 1. The input to the correction system can represent a line of text or an isolated word. We will only consider the case of isolated word correction in the present work.

This paper presents two models for supervised spelling correction. Both treat the task as sequence labeling but one of the models is structured and the other one is unstructured. Both systems are implemented as finite-state machines and are trained on data consisting of word pairs aligned at character level.

Our unstructured model is a finite-state transducer compiled from a set of weighted context-sensitive replace rules that are used to generate

51

Proceedings of the ACL Workshop on Statistical NLP and Weighted Automata, pages 51–59,
Berlin, Germany, August 12, 2016. ©2016 Association for Computational Linguistics

correction candidates from input strings. These substitutions and their contexts are extracted from training data. This approach was first presented by Lindén (2006) for generating multilingual spelling variants of scientific and medical terms originating from Latin and Greek, but it also suitable for other tasks involving probabilistic string-to-string translation.

Our structured model is an averaged perceptron tagger. We represent the classifier as a composition of two weighted finite-state machines which incorporate the unstructured and structured features and parameters of the tagger. When these are combined with an input string, the resulting finite-state machine encodes all correction candidates with their respective weights assigned by the tagger. The finite-state implementation allows us to extract a given amount of the best scoring correction candidates using well-known and efficient algorithms that are widely available. The finite-state implementation also allows for restricting candidates to those found in a dictionary.

The paper is structured in the following way. Section 2 presents earlier approaches to spelling correction and the more general task of string-to-string translation. In Section 3, we present the unstructured and structured models used for spelling correction. In Section 4, we present the features utilized by the correction systems and in Section 5, we show how the systems can be implemented using finite-state methods. In Section 6, we present the data sets used in the experiments and in Section 7, we present the experimental setup of the paper and the results of the experiments. Finally, we discuss the results in Section 8 and conclude the paper in Section 9.

2   Related Work

Spelling correction is an old NLP task. The earliest approaches used plain edit distance combined with a lexicon. The edit distance approach was refined by Brill and Moore (2000) who added weights for edit operations. These systems ignored the context of the edit operation, which can nevertheless be quite useful.

Dreyer et al. (2008) investigate string-to-string translation which is a more general task than spelling correction. In order to incorporate symbol contexts into their models, they formulate string-to-string translation as a sequence labeling task. Their sequence labeling model is discriminative

and the alignment between the input and output string is a latent variable. Dreyer et al. (2008) implement their model as a finite-state machine. This model is similar to ours but we do not treat the alignment between input and output strings as a latent variable. Instead, the training data for our model is aligned in advance.

Another interesting approach is presented by Xu et al. (2014) who learn a number of weighted rewrite rules from data. They use a log linear model to combine the rules and treat the alignment of the input and output forms as a latent variable like Dreyer et al. (2008). This system is reminiscent of ours because we also implement our two systems using rewrite rules. However, again, we do not treat the alignment of the input and output strings as a hidden variable.

Hulden and Francom (2013) compare two FST based methods for Spanish-language tweet normalization. The first method relies on a hierarchically arranged set of unweighted context-sensitive replace rules, while their other approach utilizes a noisy-channel FST model on the input string. These operations and their weights are extracted from the training data set. The authors report a somewhat better performance for the unweighted rule-based method, with a final accuracy of 60 %, but note that there is no theoretical obstacle that would prevent the inclusion of contexts in the weighted model.

Han and Baldwin (2011) present a method for recognizing and correcting out-of-vocabulary words in tweets and SMSs. They perform a set of normalization processes to the input word to make the relationship between the incorrect form and the correct form more transparent and generate a set of candidates within a certain edit distance. In addition to comparing orthographic forms, they also consider the phonetic realization of the input word and find correction candidates whose pronunciation is within a certain edit distance from the pronunciation of the input word.

In recent work, Eger et al. (2016) survey four systems for string-to-string translation on spelling correction of Tweets and normalization of historical Latin text. (1) The Sequitur system (Bisani and Ney, 2008) implements a joint generative model on input and output strings using *graphones*, which are units consisting of one input symbol and a possibly empty sequence of output symbols. (2) The DirecTL+ (Jiampojamarn et al.,

2010) represents the translation task as a pipeline of a string segmentation system, which splits the input string into character sequences, and a discriminative sequence labeling system which translates the character sequences into output symbols. DirecTL+ utilizes joint character n-grams in the discriminative sequence labeling system. (3) The AliSeTra system is based on the work of Eger (2012). Like DirecTL+, it also views string-to-string translation as a pipeline of segmentation and sequence labeling. (4) The final system surveyed by Eger et al. (2016) represents the string-to-string translation task as a series of contextual edit operations on the input string (Cotterell et al., 2015). The operations are compiled into a weighted finite-state machine. The edit operations are weighted using a probabilistic model which resembles the maximum entropy Markov model (MEMM) (McCallum et al., 2000). This system is similar to our structured system but we use a different feature set and estimate weights using the average perceptron algorithm. This avoids the well-known label bias problem (Lafferty et al., 2001) associated with MEMMs.

Systems 1, 2 and 3 surveyed by Eger et al. (2016) form an interesting contrast to our systems because we do not use segmentation of the input string. In this sense, our system is simpler.

Eger et al. (2016) present experiments on spelling correction both for the individual systems discussed in the paper and also various combinations of the systems. The AliSeTra system is shown to give the best performance of all individual surveyed systems on both Twitter data and historical Latin. We also present experiments on the Twitter data used by Eger et al. (2016) and show that our structured system delivers at least the same level of performance as the AliSeTra system.

3   Models

In the following, we present the unstructured and structured models used for spelling correction. Both models express the probability $p(y|x)$ of a normalization sequence $y = (y_1, ..., y_T)$ given an input sequence $x = (x_1, ..., x_T)$.

The input sequence x and output sequence y are formally required to have the same length. In practice, each element of y can, however, consist of a number of characters. This allows modeling of insertions and deletions. For example in Figure 1,

the input sequence is $(A, m, ., c)$ and the output sequence is (A, nn, ε, e). This corresponds to a deletion $. \to \varepsilon$ and a substitution $m \to nn$. The model cannot directly express the substitution of two consecutive input symbols with one output, for example $nn \to m$. This can, however, be expressed indirectly using a deletion and subsequent substitution as in $n \to \varepsilon$ and $n \to m$.

The parameters of the models are estimated in a supervised manner using training data consisting of pairs of input and output strings. In order to accelerate training, we use aligned training data (consisting of symbol pairs) instead of treating the alignment of input and output strings as a latent variable.

3.1   Unstructured Classifier

This classifier represents the conditional probability $p(y|x)$ of a normalization $y = (y_1, ..., y_T)$ given an input $x = (x_1, ..., x_T)$ in an unstructured manner, that is

$$p(y|x) = \prod_{t=1}^{T} p(y_t|x, t)$$

This corresponds to making the assumption that output symbols y_t and y_u ($t \neq u$) are independent given the input x.

To determine the probabilities $p(y_t, |x, t)$, we first map each input position (x, t) to a context $L \diamond x_t \diamond R$, where L and R are regular languages, and the input position (x, t) matches $L \diamond x_t \diamond R$, that is

$$x_1 \ ... \ x_{t-1} \diamond x_t \diamond x_{t+1} \ ... \ x_T \in L \diamond x_t \diamond R.$$

The $\diamond$ symbol is a special symbol which does not occur in any input string or output string.

We then define

$$p(y_t|x, t) = p(y_t|L \diamond x_t \diamond R)$$

where the probability $p(y_t|L \diamond x_t \diamond R)$ is estimated from the training data simply by counting occurrences of output symbols z in positions which match $L \diamond x_t \diamond R$. More precisely,

$$p(z|L \diamond x_t \diamond R) =$$

$$\frac{|\{(x, t) \text{ matches } L \diamond x_t \diamond R \text{ and } y_t = z\}|}{|\{(x, t) \text{ matches } L \diamond x_t \diamond R\}|}$$

Every input position encountered during test time should be mapped to a unique context. Therefore, the collection of contexts $L \diamond x_t \diamond R$ is chosen in such a way that it forms a partition of $\Sigma^* \diamond \Sigma \diamond \Sigma^*$, where Σ is the set of all input symbols. In Section 4, we give a more detailed explanation of how these contexts are chosen.

3.2 Peceptron Tagger

Our structured spelling correction system is formulated as a traditional averaged perceptron tagger (Collins, 2002) as shown in Equation 1. Given an input sequence x of length T, the model assigns a score $s(\cdot)$ for each output sequence y of length T as determined by the model parameters w and a vector valued feature extraction function ϕ. The n best normalization candidates given by the system can be extracted by finding the n highest scoring outputs y.

$$s(x, y; w) = \sum_{t=1}^{T} w \cdot \phi(y_{t-2}, y_{t-1}, y_t, x, t) \quad (1)$$

The labels y_{-1} and y_0 required for Equation 1 are word boundary symbols.

4 System Specification

This section presents the contexts used for the unstructured correction system and the features used by the structured correction system.

4.1 Contexts for the Unstructured Classifier

As explained in Section 3.1, the unstructured normalization model maps each input position (x, t) to a context $L \diamond x_t \diamond R$. These contexts form a partition of $\Sigma^* \diamond \Sigma \diamond \Sigma^*$.

The inventory of contexts is controlled by hyper-parameters which are determined using held-out data: n_{TH} which is a minimum number of context occurrences in the training data. Another parameter is l_C which is the length of the maximal right-hand context. We have set the value of l_C as 2 based on preliminary experiments.

If $x_{t-1} x_t x_{t+1} ... x_{t+l_C}$ occurs at least n_{TH} times in the training data,

$$\Sigma^* x_{t-1} \diamond x_t \diamond x_{t+1} ... x_{t+l_C} \Sigma^*$$

is chosen as context. If it occurs fewer times, each of the sub-strings $x_{t-1} x_t x_{t+1} ... x_{t+k}$, where $0 \leq k < n_C$ is considered in turn. The longest one that occurs at least n_{TH} times in the training data is used to define a context. If none of them occur more than n_{TH} times, the single symbol x_t is used to define the context.

For each context $L \diamond x_t \diamond R$, we include a number of back-off contexts. For example, let $\Sigma^* a \diamond x_t \diamond b\, c\, \Sigma^*$ be a context, then back-off contexts are the following contexts.

$$\Sigma^* a \diamond x_t \diamond b\, \Sigma^*$$
$$\Sigma^* a \diamond x_t \diamond \Sigma^*$$
$$\Sigma^* \diamond x_t \diamond \Sigma^*$$

In order to ensure that no two contexts overlap, we need to modify the contexts slightly:

$$\Sigma^* a \diamond x_t \diamond b\, [\Sigma - c]\, \Sigma^*$$
$$\Sigma^* a \diamond x_t \diamond [\Sigma - b]\, \Sigma^*$$
$$\Sigma^* [\Sigma - a] \diamond x_t \diamond \Sigma^*$$

4.2 Features for the Perceptron Tagger

The structured correction system extracts unstructured and structured features from the input and output context of letters. Unstructured features associate the output in a single position with letters in the input. In contrast, structured features associate output letters with each other. Given an input string $x = (x_1, ..., x_T)$ and an output string $y = (y_1, ..., y_T)$, the unstructured features extracted at position t are

1. (x_t, y_t)

2. (x_{t-1}, x_t, y_t) and (x_t, x_{t+1}, y_t)

3. $(x_{t-3}, x_{t-2}, x_{t-1}, y_t)$, $(x_{t-2}, x_{t-1}, x_t, y_t)$, $(x_{t-1}, x_t, x_{t+1}, y_t)$, $(x_t, x_{t+1}, x_{t+1}, y_t)$ and $(x_{t+1}, x_{t+2}, x_{t+3}, y_t)$

In addition, we extract the structured features

1. (y_t)

2. (y_{t-1}, y_t)

3. (y_{t-2}, y_{t-1}, y_t)

The unstructured features are aimed at capturing the context of edit operations. Meanwhile, the structured features act as a language model.

5 Implementation

This section describes the finite-state implementation of our correction systems as weighted replace rules (Mohri and Sproat, 1996). Formally, the systems can be seen as sets of weighted *parallel* replace rules. As explained below, we however implement them using a *cascade* of weighted rules for efficiency reasons. This section will also describe the combination of replace rules and lexicon which is used in some of the experiments.

5.1 Weighted Parallel Replace Rules

Consider the following rule in XFST syntax (Beesley and Karttunen, 2003)

$$\text{u} \rightarrow \varepsilon\text{::}0.05 \quad \| \quad \text{u} \,\_$$

The rule matches in a context where the input contains two consecutive symbols u, deletes the second of them and assigns a penalty weight of $0.05 \approx -\log(0.95)$. The HFST library (Lindén et al., 2011) implements these weighted rules.

The unstructured system described in Section 3.1 uses a set of mutually exclusive features as explained in Section 4.1. Conceptually, the system can therefore be seen as a set of parallel replace rules (Kempe and Karttunen, 1996) acting on the same input strings. Although this formulation is theoretically pleasing and weighted parallel replace rules are available through the HFST interface (Lindén et al., 2011), preliminary experiments revealed that compilation of the system represented using parallel replace rules is slow in presence of training data of realistic scope. However, the subset of parallel replace rules needed in our two systems can be reformulated as normal replace rules to take advantage of a sequence of compose operations eliminating the speed issue in practice, see Section 5.3.

5.2 Unstructured Rules

The formulation of the substitutions and the contexts as explained in 4.1 as parallel replace rules is fairly straightforward. For instance, the substitution x_t with z in the context $\Sigma^* a \diamond x_t \diamond b\, c\, \Sigma^*$ is accomplished by the rule

$$x_t \rightarrow z\text{::}w \quad \| \quad a \,\_\, b\, c$$

Rules are assigned log weights which correspond to the probabilities p of the substitutions they express, i.e. $w = -log(p)$.

As explained in 5.1, rules are formulated as mutually exclusive by supplementing the contexts of the backoff rules with a negative expression containing the non-overlapping parts from the higher-order rule. This expression effectively blocks the lower-order rule if a higher-order rule can be applied instead. For instance, if the rule set contains the higher-order rule

$$x \rightarrow z\text{::}0.4 \quad \| \quad x \,\_\, y\, z$$

and a backoff rule

$$a \rightarrow b\text{::}0.2 \quad \| \quad x \,\_\, y$$

the latter is rewritten as

$$a \rightarrow b\text{::}0.2 \quad \| \quad x \,\_\, y\, [\,? \,-\, z\,]$$

Note that deletions and insertions are treated here as ordinary substitutions, and the empty string ε is thus treated like any other symbol. The weights for insertions such as $\varepsilon \rightarrow$ a and non-insertions ($\varepsilon \rightarrow \varepsilon$) are estimated accordingly. The sole exception to this are context-free insertions that, unlike other context-free substitutions, are disallowed altogether.

5.3 Cascaded Weighted Rewrite Rules

In order to avoid the slow compilation of general parallel replace rules, we can reformulate the problem using a cascade of replace rules. In order to maintain the correct semantics of the system in a cascaded setting, we formulate the input and output in such a way that rules no longer perform translation of the input string. Instead the input already encodes all possible outputs and rules simply assign weights to alternative output candidates. In practice, we represent inputs as sequences of pairs separated[1] by a special symbol • which is neither an input nor a potential output symbol. Let us look at the following regular expression in Xerox syntax:

$$\bullet\, \#\, \#\, \bullet\, \text{t}\, [\text{t}|\text{th}|\mathbb{O}]\, \bullet\, \text{e}\, [\text{e}|\text{c}|\mathbb{O}]\, \bullet\, \#\, \#\, \bullet$$

The • symbol unambiguously outlines the sequence of input and output symbol pairs. The first pair of the sequence contains the word boundary symbols #. Before feature extraction, we pad the aligned strings with this auxiliary symbol in order to formulate correspondences occurring in string-inital and and string-final positions.The second pair of the sequence contains an input symbol t and a set of potential output symbols, of which the $\mathbb{O}$ symbol denotes a deletion.

Using this representation, rules can be reformulated as weighting expressions. For example, the rule

$$\mathbb{O} \rightarrow \mathbb{O}\text{::}0.05 \quad \| \quad \text{t}\, ?\, \bullet\, e \,\_\, \bullet$$

assigns a penalty of 0.05 to a deletion of the second of the input symbols in our example above.

Features are composed into a weighted transducer W. Given an input I in the format presented above, an n-best algorithm (Allauzen et al., 2007) can extract the best scoring paths of $I \circ W$, from which the output strings are extracted.

---

[1]The inventory of pairs is extracted from the training data

5.4 Structured Rules

The structured classifier uses both unstructured and structured features. As seen above, unstructured features can be compiled into replace rules. Structured features can also be formulated as rules. For example, the following rule assigns a penalty to the output sequence "thh":

$$h \rightarrow h{::} -33126 \quad || \quad ? t \bullet ? h \bullet ? \_ \bullet$$

Both the unstructured and the structured systems apply rules in the same way. Unstructured and structured features are composed respectively giving us two weighted transducers U and S. Given an input I in the format presented above, we extract the best scoring paths from $I \circ U \circ S$.

5.5 Minimization of Transducers with Weights in the Tropical Semiring

We use finite-state machines with weights in the tropical weight semiring as defined by Allauzen et al. (2007). Because we use a series of compositions spanning several thousands of rule transducers for compiling the unstructured and structured feature transducers U and S, efficient determinization and minimization algorithms are crucial.

The minimization algorithm presented by Mohri and Sproat (1996) is available through the HFST interface and applicable to transducers with tropical weights where the weights are non-negative. Unfortunately, the structured correction system incorporates both positive and negative weights.

One solution to this problem is provided by Eisner (2003) who introduces a more general formulation of transducer minimization which is applicable to transducers with tropical weights in the entire range $\mathbb{R} \cup \{\infty, -\infty\}$ and many other weight classes as well. We have, however, resorted to a simpler approach which is applicable in the special case of tropical weights. After epsilon removal and determinization but before minimization, we traverse the transitions and the final state of the transducer M once and find the minimal weight w_{min}. Subsequently, we increment all transition and final weights in transducer M by $|w_{min}|$ which results in a transducer M^+ with non-negative weights.

Let $w_{M(p)}$ be the weight assigned by transducer M to path p. It is easy to see that $w_{M^+(p)} = w_{M(p)} + |p| \cdot |w_{min}|$, where $|p|$ is the length of p.

We then apply conventional minimization resulting in a machine N^+. Subsequently, we subtract the weight $|w_{min}|$ from each transition in N^+ resulting in a machine N. As long as M does not contain any epsilon transitions, the length of each path p must be preserved by minimization. Therefore the total weight of each path p

$$\begin{aligned} w_N(p) &= w_M(p) + |p| \cdot |w_{min}| - |p| \cdot |w_{min}| \\ &= w_M(p) \end{aligned}$$

is also preserved. Consequently, the minimized machine accepts the same weighted relation as the original machine.

5.6 Using a Lexicon

Some of our experiments utilize a lexicon. Preliminary experiments indicated that the lexicon should be combined in different ways with the unstructured and structured system.

When using a lexicon, the unstructured system returns the highest scoring correction candidate which is found in the lexicon. If none of the candidates are found in the lexicon, the system returns the input form. In the unstructured system, the task of an ouput language model is carried by the lexicon alone.

The structured system extracts the N highest scoring correction candidates and returns the highest scoring one of these that is found in the lexicon. If none of the candidates are found in the lexicon, the system returns the highest scoring candidate, which is plausible when part of the ouput language model is encoded by the structured features assuming that the lexicon is incomplete. This setup was also used by Eger et al. (2016).

6 Data and Resources

We perform experiments on two data sets: a collection of twitter spelling errors[2] used by Eger et al. (2016) and a corpus of Early Modern Finnish scanned texts that have been processed using an OCR engine. The data sets differ in the sense that the Twitter data contains only spelling errors but the Early Modern Finnish corpus contains a large number of correctly recognized forms in addition to OCR errors. Following Eger et al. (2016), we use only the first 5000 word pairs from the Twitter data set.

Both data sets consist of word pairs where the first word is the original word and the second one

---

[2] Available from http://luululu.com/tweet/.

is its normalization. As our systems are trained on aligned data, we used the grapheme to phoneme translation system Phonetisaurus (Novak et al., 2016) to align input and output strings used for training.

The Finnish data used in our experiments constitutes a part of a larger corpus of historical newspapers and magazines (KLK) that has been digitized by the National Library of Finland. Some of this digitized material has been manually corrected and edited at the Institute for the Languages of Finland. Further correction has been carried out via crowd-sourcing. Our data set consists of running text extracted from the OCR processed 19th-century publications for which manually edited material is available and comprises roughly 40 000 OCR processed word pairs.

We perform tenfold cross-validation on both data sets. We divide the data sets into ten non-overlapping parts $D_1, ..., D_{10}$ in the following way. For each consecutive ten word pairs (starting with the first), we assign the pair at position i to set D_i. We then form ten training, development and test sets. The test set E_i is D_i. The development set U_i is T_{i-1} when $i > 1$ and T_{10} when $i = 1$. The training set T_i consists of the remaining partitions D_j. Hence training set T_i, development set U_i and test set E_i never overlap.

A lexicon is required for some of the experiments. For Twitter data, we use the lexicon ColLex.EN (Brück et al., 2014) following Eger et al. (2016), and for the Finnish OCR data, we use the OMorFi open-source Finnish morphological analyzer (Pirinen, 2008).

For the task of correcting text written in Early Modern Finnish, the OMorFi analyzer had to be modified slightly to recognize capitalized variants of all word forms as well as to accept some of the more archaic spelling variants and vocabulary found in Early Modern Finnish. We did this by supplementing the acceptor with word forms extracted from the KLK corpus whose frequency equals or exceeds 100. Word forms already accepted by OMorFi were given precedence.

7 Experiments

We perform experiments on the Twitter data and Early Modern Finnish OCR data in the same manner. For each data set, we measure the performance of the unstructured and structured correction system using tenfold cross-validation on the

tp	Number of erroneous inputs which are corrected.
fp	Number of correct inputs which are changed to an incorrect output.
fn	Number of erroneous input which are not corrected.

Table 1: Definition of edit types.

data splits presented in Section 6. Our data sets and code are available online.[3]

Both of the models presented in the paper incorporate hyper-parameters. We first set the hyper-parameters using development data, then combined the development and training data and use the combination to train the final system which is used to process the test data.

The FinnPos tagger toolkit (Silfverberg et al., 2015) is used to train the models for the structured system and the HFST Python interface (Lindén et al., 2011) is used for constructing and operating finite-state machines. When training FinnPos models, we used default settings for most hyper-parameters. Only the number of training epochs is determined using development data. For experiments using a lexicon, we additionally use development data to set the number of top correction candidates N which are looked up in the lexicon as explained in Section 5.6. For tweet normalization, we use $N = 80$ and for Finnish OCR post processing, we use $N = 5$.

As an evaluation metrics, we use *correction rate* (CR) defined as

$$\text{CR} = \frac{tp - fp}{tp + fn}$$

where tp, fp and fn are defined in Table 1. Note that when all input forms are incorrect (as in the case of the Twitter data), CR corresponds exactly to the evaluation metric word accuracy (WACC) used by Eger et al. (2016) because the count fp is 0.

$$\text{WACC} = \frac{tp}{tp + fn}$$

7.1 Results

Tables 2 and 3 show the results of the experiments on the Finnish OCR data and Twitter data. We perform tenfold cross-validation and provide t-based confidence intervals at the 95% level.

---

[3]https://github.com/mpsilfve/ocrpp

	No lexicon (%)	Lexicon (%)
UC	48.56 ± 2.00	57.80 ± 1.82
AliSeTra	68.38 ± 1.52	72.98 ± 2.01
PT	$\mathbf{70.14 \pm 1.43}$	$\mathbf{74.66 \pm 1.38}$

Table 2: Results for tweet normalization. UC refers to the unstructured classifier presented in Section 3.1, PT to the perceptron tagger presented in Section 3.2 and AliSeTra to the system presented by Eger et al. (2016).

	No lexicon (%)	Lexicon (%)
UC	20.02 ± 1.29	21.58 ± 2.11
PT	$\mathbf{32.05 \pm 1.97}$	$\mathbf{35.09 \pm 2.08}$

Table 3: Results for Finnish historical OCR.

For the Finnish OCR data, the structured perceptron correction system clearly outperforms the unstructured system both without using a lexicon and when using a lexicon. The difference in performance is statistically significant in both cases at the 95% confidence level. Because the AliSeTra system is not freely available, we do not have results for that system on the Finnish OCR data.

For the Twitter data, both AliSeTra and the perceptron tagger deliver superior accuracy when compared with the unstructured system. The average performance of the perceptron tagger in this experiment is superior to the performance of the AliSeTra system as reported by Eger et al. (2016). The difference in performance is, however, not statistically significant. It should be noted that the data splits used in this work differ from the splits used by Eger et al. (2016).

8 Discussion

The advantage of the unstructured approach is that relatively little time is required for training the error model (on the league of ten minutes for our data sets). The drawback of the unstructured models used is that they accommodate a very limited set of features which manifests as comparably low normalization performance.

The performance of our structured system is at least equal to recent work of Eger et al. (2016) on tweet normalization even though our system is simpler in the sense that we use a 1-to-n mapping from inputs to outputs whereas Eger et al. (2016) use an n-to-n alignment between the input and output. The n-to-n alignment, however, requires segmentation of the input as a preprocessing step. This may induce errors which cannot be corrected later. Treating the segmentation as a latent variable following (Cotterell et al., 2015) could be a solution but it carries the disadvantage of slow estimation and inference.

It should be noted that we use some additional unstructured features compared with Eger et al. (2016) which may explain our slight performance advantage.

9 Conclusions

We have presented two systems for word based spelling correction using finite-state methods. We have shown that we reach state-of-the-art results when compared with a recent system presented by Eger et al. (2016) on the task of tweet normalization. Additionally, we have presented experiments on the task of OCR post-processing on a corpus consisting of Early Modern Finnish newspaper text.

10 Acknowledgments

We wish to thank the anonymous reviewers for their valuable suggestions.

References

Cyril Allauzen, Michael Riley, Johan Schalkwyk, Wojciech Skut, and Mehryar Mohri. 2007. Openfst: A general and efficient weighted finite-state transducer library. In *Proceedings of the 12th International Conference on Implementation and Application of Automata*, CIAA'07, pages 11–23, Berlin, Heidelberg. Springer-Verlag.

Kenneth R. Beesley and Lauri Karttunen. 2003. *Finite State Morphology*, volume 3 of *CSLI Studies in Computational Linguistics*. CSLI Publications.

Maximilian Bisani and Hermann Ney. 2008. Joint-sequence models for grapheme-to-phoneme conversion. *Speech Commun.*, 50(5):434–451, May.

Eric Brill and Robert C. Moore. 2000. An improved error model for noisy channel spelling correction. In *Proceedings of the 38th Annual Meeting on Association for Computational Linguistics*, ACL '00, pages 286–293, Stroudsburg, PA, USA. Association for Computational Linguistics.

Tim Vor Der Brück, Alexander Mehler, and Zahurul Islam. 2014. Collex.en: Automatically generating and evaluating a full-form lexicon for english. In Nicoletta Calzolari (Conference Chair), Khalid Choukri, Thierry Declerck, Hrafn Loftsson, Bente

Maegaard, Joseph Mariani, Asuncion Moreno, Jan Odijk, and Stelios Piperidis, editors, *Proceedings of the Ninth International Conference on Language Resources and Evaluation (LREC'14)*, Reykjavik, Iceland, may. European Language Resources Association (ELRA).

Michael Collins. 2002. Discriminative training methods for hidden markov models: Theory and experiments with perceptron algorithms. In *Proceedings of the ACL-02 Conference on Empirical Methods in Natural Language Processing - Volume 10*, EMNLP '02, pages 1–8, Stroudsburg, PA, USA. Association for Computational Linguistics.

Ryan Cotterell, Nanyun Peng, and Jason Eisner. 2015. Modeling word forms using latent underlying morphs and phonology. *Transactions of the Association for Computational Linguistics*, 3:433–447.

Markus Dreyer, Jason R. Smith, and Jason Eisner. 2008. Latent-variable modeling of string transductions with finite-state methods. In *Proceedings of the Conference on Empirical Methods in Natural Language Processing*, EMNLP '08, pages 1080–1089, Stroudsburg, PA, USA. Association for Computational Linguistics.

Steffen Eger, Tim vor der Brck, and Alexander Mehler. 2016. A comparison of four character-level string-to-string translation models for (ocr) spelling error correction. *The Prague Bulletin of Mathematical Linguistics*, 105:77–99.

Steffen Eger. 2012. S-restricted monotone alignments: Algorithm, search space, and applications. In *Proceedings of COLING 2012*, pages 781–798, Mumbai, India, December. The COLING 2012 Organizing Committee.

Jason Eisner. 2003. Simpler and more general minimization for weighted finite-state automata. In *HLT-NAACL*.

Bo Han and Timothy Baldwin. 2011. Lexical normalisation of short text messages: Makn sens a# twitter. In *Proceedings of the 49th Annual Meeting of the Association for Computational Linguistics: Human Language Technologies-Volume 1*, pages 368–378. Association for Computational Linguistics.

Mans Hulden and Jerid Francom. 2013. Weighted and unweighted transducers for tweet normalization. In *Tweet-Norm@ SEPLN*, pages 69–72. Citeseer.

Sittichai Jiampojamarn, Colin Cherry, and Grzegorz Kondrak. 2010. Integrating joint n-gram features into a discriminative training framework. In *Human Language Technologies: Conference of the North American Chapter of the Association of Computational Linguistics, Proceedings, June 2-4, 2010, Los Angeles, California, USA*, pages 697–700.

André Kempe and Lauri Karttunen. 1996. Parallel replacement in finite state calculus. In *Proceedings of the 16th Conference on Computational Linguistics - Volume 2*, COLING '96, pages 622–627, Stroudsburg, PA, USA. Association for Computational Linguistics.

John D. Lafferty, Andrew McCallum, and Fernando C. N. Pereira. 2001. Conditional random fields: Probabilistic models for segmenting and labeling sequence data. In *Proceedings of the Eighteenth International Conference on Machine Learning*, ICML '01, pages 282–289, San Francisco, CA, USA. Morgan Kaufmann Publishers Inc.

Krister Lindén, Erik Axelson, Sam Hardwick, Tommi A Pirinen, and Miikka Silfverberg. 2011. HFSTFramework for Compiling and Applying Morphologies. In Cerstin Mahlow and Michael Piotrowski, editors, *Systems and Frameworks for Computational Morphology*, volume 100 of *Communications in Computer and Information Science*, pages 67–85. Springer Berlin Heidelberg.

Krister Lindén. 2006. Multilingual modeling of cross-lingual spelling variants. *Inf. Retr.*, 9(3):295–310, June.

Andrew McCallum, Dayne Freitag, and Fernando C. N. Pereira. 2000. Maximum entropy markov models for information extraction and segmentation. In *Proceedings of the Seventeenth International Conference on Machine Learning*, ICML '00, pages 591–598, San Francisco, CA, USA. Morgan Kaufmann Publishers Inc.

Mehryar Mohri and Richard Sproat. 1996. An efficient compiler for weighted rewrite rules. In *Proceedings of the 34th Annual Meeting of the Association for Computational Linguistics*, pages 231–238, Santa Cruz, California, USA, June. Association for Computational Linguistics.

Josef Robert Novak, Nobuaki Minematsu, and Keikichi Hirose. 2016. Phonetisaurus: Exploring grapheme-to-phoneme conversion with joint n-gram models in the wfst framework. *Natural Language Engineering*, FirstView:1–32, 4.

Tommi Pirinen. 2008. Automatic finite state morphological analysis of Finnish language using open source resources (in Finnish). Master's thesis, University of Helsinki.

Miikka Silfverberg, Teemu Ruokolainen, Krister Lindn, and Mikko Kurimo. 2015. Finnpos: an open-source morphological tagging and lemmatization toolkit for finnish. *Language Resources and Evaluation*, pages 1–16.

Gu Xu, Hang Li, Ming Zhang, and Ziqi Wang. 2014. A probabilistic approach to string transformation. *IEEE Transactions on Knowledge and Data Engineering*, 26(5):1–1.

EM-Training for Weighted Aligned Hypergraph Bimorphisms

Frank Drewes
Department of Computing Science
Umeå University
S-901 87 Umeå, Sweden
drewes@cs.umu.se

Kilian Gebhardt and **Heiko Vogler**
Department of Computer Science
Technische Universität Dresden
D-01062 Dresden, Germany
kilian.gebhardt@tu-dresden.de
heiko.vogler@tu-dresden.de

Abstract

We develop the concept of weighted aligned hypergraph bimorphism where the weights may, in particular, represent probabilities. Such a bimorphism consists of an $\mathbb{R}_{\geq 0}$-weighted regular tree grammar, two hypergraph algebras that interpret the generated trees, and a family of alignments between the two interpretations. Semantically, this yields a set of bihypergraphs each consisting of two hypergraphs and an explicit alignment between them; e.g., discontinuous phrase structures and non-projective dependency structures are bihypergraphs. We present an EM-training algorithm which takes a corpus of bihypergraphs and an aligned hypergraph bimorphism as input and generates a sequence of weight assignments which converges to a local maximum or saddle point of the likelihood function of the corpus.

1 Introduction

In natural language processing alignments play an important role. For instance, in machine translation they show up as hidden information when training probabilities of dictionaries (Brown et al., 1993) or when considering pairs of input/output sentences derived by a synchronous grammar (Lewis and Stearns, 1968; Chiang, 2007; Shieber and Schabes, 1990; Nederhof and Vogler, 2012). As another example, in language models for discontinuous phrase structures and non-projective dependency structures they can be used to capture the connection between the words in a natural language sentence and the corresponding nodes of the parse tree or dependency structure of that sentence.

In (Nederhof and Vogler, 2014) the generation of discontinuous phrase structures has been for-

malized by the new concept of hybrid grammar. Much as in the mentioned synchronous grammars, a hybrid grammar synchronizes the derivations of nonterminals of a string grammar, e.g., a linear context-free rewriting system (LCFRS) (Vijay-Shanker et al., 1987), and of nonterminals of a tree grammar, e.g., regular tree grammar (Brainerd, 1969) or simple definite-clause programs (sDCP) (Deransart and Małuszynski, 1985). Additionally it synchronizes terminal symbols, thereby establishing an explicit alignment between the positions of the string and the nodes of the tree. We note that LCFRS/sDCP hybrid grammars can also generate non-projective dependency structures.

In this paper we focus on the task of training an LCFRS/sDCP hybrid grammar, that is, assigning probabilities to its rules given a corpus of discontinuous phrase structures or non-projective dependency structures. Since the alignments are first class citizens, we develop our approach in the general framework of hypergraphs and hyperedge replacement (HR) (Habel, 1992). We define the concepts of *bihypergraph* (for short: bigraph) and *aligned HR bimorphism*. A bigraph consists of hypergraphs H_1, λ, and H_2, where λ represents the alignment between H_1 and H_2. A bimorphism $\mathcal{B} = (g, \mathcal{A}_1, \Lambda, \mathcal{A}_2)$ consists of a regular tree grammar g generating trees over some ranked alphabet Σ, two Σ-algebras $\mathcal{A}_1$ and $\mathcal{A}_2$ which interpret each symbol in Σ as an HR operation (thus evaluating every tree to two hypergraphs), and a Σ-indexed family Λ of alignments between the two interpretations of each $\sigma \in \Sigma$. The semantics of $\mathcal{B}$ is a set of bigraphs.

For instance, each discontinuous phrase structure or non-projective dependency structure can be represented as a bigraph (H_1, λ, H_2) where H_1 and H_2 correspond to the string component and the tree component, respectively. Fig. 1 shows an example of a bigraph representing a non-projective depen-

Proceedings of the ACL Workshop on Statistical NLP and Weighted Automata, pages 60–69,
Berlin, Germany, August 12, 2016. ©2016 Association for Computational Linguistics

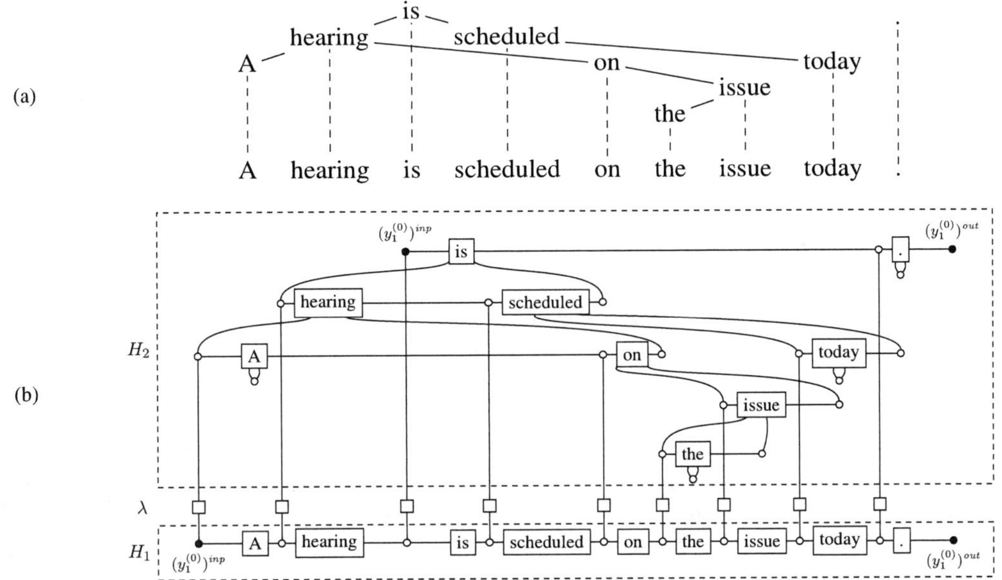

Figure 1: (a) A sentence with non-projective dependencies is represented in (b) by a bigraph (H_1, λ, H_2). Both hypergraphs H_1 and H_2 contain a distinct hyperedge (box) for each word of the sentence. H_1 specifies the linear order on the words. H_2 describes parent-child relationships between the words, where children form a list to whose start and end the parent has a tentacle. The alignment λ establishes a one-to-one correspondence between the (input vertices of the) hyperedges in H_1 and H_2.

dency structure. We present each LCFRS/sDCP hybrid grammar as a particular aligned HR bimorphism; this establishes an initial algebra semantics (Goguen et al., 1977) for hybrid grammars.

The flexibility of aligned HR bimorphisms goes well beyond hybrid grammars as they generalize the synchronous HR grammars of (Jones et al., 2012), making it possible to synchronously generate two graphs connected by explicit alignment structures. Thus, they can for instance model alignments involving directed acyclic graphs like Abstract Meaning Representations (Banarescu et al., 2013) or Millstream systems (Bensch et al., 2014).

Our training algorithm takes as input an aligned HR bimorphism $\mathcal{B} = (g, \mathcal{A}_1, \Lambda, \mathcal{A}_2)$ and a corpus c of bigraphs. It is based on the dynamic programming variant (Baker, 1979; Lari and Young, 1990; Prescher, 2001) of the EM-algorithm (Dempster et al., 1977) and thus approximates a local maximum or saddle point of the likelihood function of c.

In order to calculate the significance of each rule of g for the generation of a single bigraph (H_1, λ, H_2) occurring in c, we proceed as usual, constructing the reduct $\mathcal{B} \rhd (H_1, \lambda, H_2)$ which generates the singleton (H_1, λ, H_2) via the same derivation trees as $\mathcal{B}$ and preserves the probabil-

ities. We show that the complexity of constructing the reduct is polynomial in the size of g and (H_1, λ, H_2) if $\mathcal{B}$ is an LCFRS/sDCP hybrid grammar. However, as the algorithm itself is not limited to this situation, we expect it to be useful in other cases as well.

2 Preliminaries

Basic mathematical notation We denote the set of natural numbers (including 0) by $\mathbb{N}$ and the set $\mathbb{N} \setminus \{0\}$ by $\mathbb{N}_+$. For $n \in \mathbb{N}$, we denote $\{1, \ldots, n\}$ by $[n]$. An alphabet A is a finite set of symbols. We denote the set of all strings over A by A^*, the empty string by ε, and $A^* \setminus \{\varepsilon\}$ by A^+. We denote the length of $s \in A^*$ by $|s|$ and, for each $i \in [|s|]$, the ith item in s by $s(i)$, i.e., s is identified with the function $s \colon [|s|] \to A$ such that $s = s(1) \cdots s(|s|)$. We denote the range $\{s(1), \ldots, s(|s|)\}$ of s by $[s]$. The powerset of a set A is denoted by $\mathcal{P}(A)$. The canonical extension of a function $f \colon A \to B$ to $f \colon \mathcal{P}(A) \to \mathcal{P}(B)$ and to $f \colon A^* \to B^*$ are defined as usual and denoted by f as well. We denote the restriction of $f \colon A \to B$ to $A' \subseteq A$ by $f|_{A'}$.

For an equivalence relation $\sim$ on B we denote the equivalence class of $b \in B$ by $[b]_\sim$ and the quotient of B modulo $\sim$ by $B/\sim$. For $f \colon A \to$

B we define the function $f/\sim\colon A \to B/\sim$ by $f/\sim(a) = [f(a)]_\sim$. In particular, for a string $s \in B^*$ we let $s/\sim = [s(1)]_\sim \cdots [s(|s|)]_\sim$.

Terms, regular tree grammars, and algebras
A *ranked alphabet* is a pair (Σ, rk) where Σ is an alphabet and $\mathrm{rk}\colon \Sigma \to \mathbb{N}$ is a mapping associating a rank with each symbol of Σ. Often we just write Σ instead of (Σ, rk). We abbreviate $\mathrm{rk}^{-1}(k)$ by Σ_k. In the following let Σ be a ranked alphabet.

Let A be an arbitrary set. We let $\Sigma(A)$ denote the set of strings $\{\sigma(a_1, \ldots, a_k) \mid k \in \mathbb{N}, \sigma \in \Sigma_k, a_1, \ldots, a_k \in A\}$ (where the parentheses and commas are special symbols not in Σ). The *set of well-formed terms over Σ indexed by A*, denoted by $\mathrm{T}_\Sigma(A)$, is defined to be the smallest set T such that $A \subseteq T$ and $\Sigma(T) \subseteq T$. We abbreviate $\mathrm{T}_\Sigma(\emptyset)$ by T_Σ and write σ instead of $\sigma()$ for $\sigma \in \Sigma_0$.

A *regular tree grammar* (RTG)[1] (Gécseg and Steinby, 1984) is a tuple $g = (\Xi, \Sigma, \xi_0, R)$ where Ξ is an alphabet (nonterminals), $\Xi \cap \Sigma = \emptyset$, elements in Σ are called terminals, $\xi_0 \in \Xi$ (initial nonterminal), R is a ranked alphabet (rules); each rule in R_k has the form $\xi \to \sigma(\xi_1, \ldots, \xi_k)$ where $\xi, \xi_1, \ldots, \xi_k \in \Xi$, $\sigma \in \Sigma_k$. We denote the set of all rules with left-hand side ξ by R_ξ for each $\xi \in \Xi$.

Since RTGs are particular context-free grammars, the concepts of derivation relation and generated language are inherited. The *language of the RTG g* is the set of all well-formed terms in T_Σ generated by g; this language is denoted by $\mathcal{L}(g)$.

We define the Ξ-indexed family $(D_g^\xi \mid \xi \in \Xi)$ of mappings $D_g^\xi\colon \mathrm{T}_\Sigma \to \mathcal{P}(\mathrm{T}_R)$; for each term $t \in \mathrm{T}_\Sigma$, $D_g^\xi(t)$ is the set of t's *derivation trees* in T_R which start with ξ and yield t. Formally, for each $\xi \in \Xi$ and $\sigma(t_1, \ldots, t_k) \in \mathrm{T}_\Sigma$, the set $D_g^\xi(\sigma(t_1, \ldots, t_k))$ contains each term $\varrho(d_1, \ldots, d_k)$ where $\varrho = (\xi \to \sigma(\xi_1, \ldots, \xi_k))$ is in R and $d_i \in D_g^{\xi_i}(t_i)$ for each $i \in [k]$. We define $D_g(t) = \bigcup_{\xi \in \Xi} D_g^\xi(t)$ and $D_g^\xi(\mathrm{T}_\Sigma) = \bigcup_{t \in \mathrm{T}_\Sigma} D_g^\xi(t)$. Finally, $D_g^{\xi_0}(\mathrm{T}_\Sigma, \xi)$ is the set of all $\zeta \in \mathrm{T}_R(\{\xi\})$ such that there is a $\zeta' \in D_g^{\xi_0}(\mathrm{T}_\Sigma)$ which has a subtree whose root is in R_ξ, and ζ is obtained from ζ' by replacing exactly one of these subtrees by ξ.

Example 2.1. Let $\Sigma = \Sigma_0 \cup \Sigma_2$ where $\Sigma_0 = \{\sigma_2, \sigma_4, \sigma_5\}$ and $\Sigma_2 = \{\sigma_1, \sigma_3\}$. Let g be an RTG

with initial nonterminal S and the following rules:

$$S \to \sigma_1(A, B) \qquad A \to \sigma_2$$
$$B \to \sigma_3(C, D) \qquad C \to \sigma_4 \qquad D \to \sigma_5$$

We observe that $S \Rightarrow_g^* \sigma_1(\sigma_2, \sigma_3(\sigma_4, \sigma_5))$. Let η, ζ, and ζ' be the following trees (in order):

$$
\begin{array}{ccc}
B \to \sigma_3(C, D) & S \to \sigma_1(A, B) & S \to \sigma_1(A, B) \\
\swarrow \quad \searrow & \swarrow \quad \searrow & \swarrow \quad \searrow \\
C \to \sigma_4 \quad D \to \sigma_5 & A \to \sigma_2 \quad B & A \to \sigma_2 \quad \eta
\end{array}
$$

Then $\zeta \in D_g^S(\mathrm{T}_\Sigma, B)$ because $\zeta' \in D_g^S(\mathrm{T}_\Sigma)$ and the left-hand side of the root of η is B. $\qquad\square$

A *Σ-algebra* is a pair $\mathcal{A} = (A, (\sigma_\mathcal{A} \mid \sigma \in \Sigma))$ where A is a set and $\sigma_\mathcal{A}$ is a k-ary operation on A for every $k \in \mathbb{N}$ and $\sigma \in \Sigma_k$. As usual, we will sometimes use $\mathcal{A}$ to refer to its carrier set A or, conversely, denote $\mathcal{A}$ by A (and thus $\sigma_\mathcal{A}$ by σ_A) if there is no risk of confusion. The *Σ-term algebra* is the Σ-algebra T_Σ with $\sigma_{\mathrm{T}_\Sigma}(t_1, \ldots, t_k) = \sigma(t_1, \ldots, t_k)$ for every $k \in \mathbb{N}$, $\sigma \in \Sigma_k$, and $t_1, \ldots, t_k \in \mathrm{T}_\Sigma$. For each Σ-algebra $\mathcal{A}$ there is exactly one Σ-homomorphism, denoted by $[\![.]\!]_\mathcal{A}$, from the Σ-term algebra to $\mathcal{A}$ (Wechler, 1992).

Hypergraphs and hyperedge replacement In the following let Γ be a finite set of *labels*. A *Γ-hypergraph* is a tuple $H = (V, E, \mathrm{att}, \mathrm{lab}, \mathrm{ports})$, where V is a finite set of *vertices*, E is a finite set of *hyperedges*, $\mathrm{att}\colon E \to V^* \setminus \{\varepsilon\}$ is the *attachment* of hyperedges to vertices, $\mathrm{lab}\colon E \to \Gamma$ is the *labeling* of hyperedges, and $\mathrm{ports} \in V^*$ is a sequence of (not necessarily distinct) *ports*. The set of all Γ-hypergraphs is denoted by $\mathcal{H}_\Gamma$. The vertices in $V \setminus [\mathrm{ports}]$ are also called *internal vertices* and denoted by $\mathrm{int}(H)$.

For the sake of brevity, we shall in the following simply call Γ-hypergraphs and hyperedges *graphs* and *edges*, respectively. We illustrate a graph in figures as follows (cf., e.g., $\mathrm{graph}((\sigma_2)_\mathcal{A})$ in Fig. 2a). A vertex v is illustrated by a circle, which is filled and labeled by i in case that $\mathrm{ports}(i) = v$. An edge e with label γ and $\mathrm{att}(e) = v_1 \ldots v_n$ is depicted as a γ-labeled rectangle with n *tentacles*, lines pointing to $v_1, \ldots, v_n$ which are annotated by $1, \ldots, n$. (We sometimes drop these annotations.)

If we are not interested in the particular set of labels Γ, then we also call a Γ-graph simply *graph* and write $\mathcal{H}$ instead of $\mathcal{H}_\Gamma$. In the following, we will refer to the components of a graph H by indexing them with H unless they are explicitly named.

Let H and H' be graphs. H and H' are *disjoint* if $V_H \cap V_{H'} = \emptyset$ and $E_H \cap E_{H'} = \emptyset$.

---

[1] in this context we use "tree" and "term" as synonyms

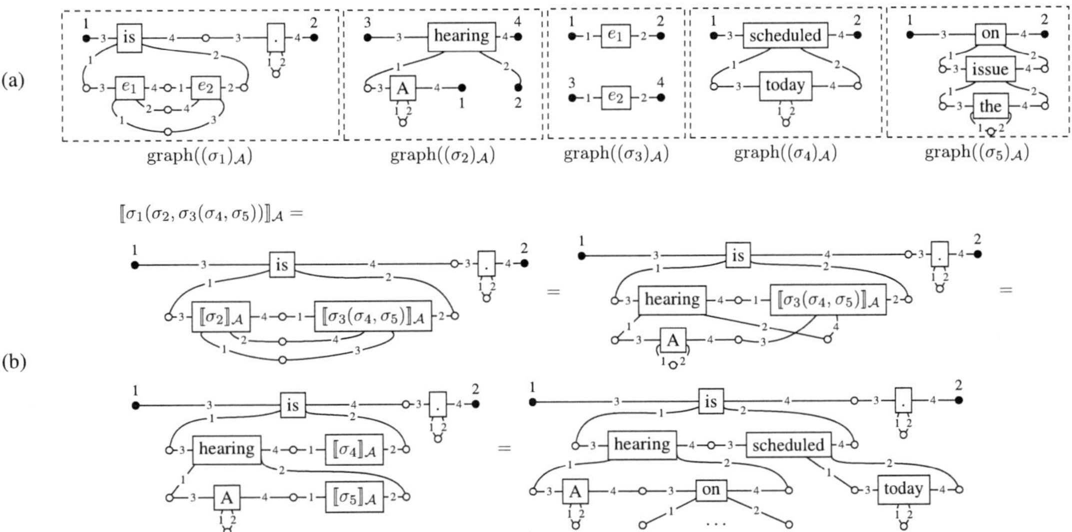

Figure 2: (a) The (Σ, Γ)-HR algebra $\mathcal{A}$ and (b) the evaluation of the term $\sigma_1(\sigma_2, \sigma_3(\sigma_4, \sigma_5))$ in $\mathcal{A}$.

Let $E = E_H \cap E_{H'}$. If $\mathrm{att}_H|_E = \mathrm{att}_{H'}|_E$ and $\mathrm{lab}_H|_E = \mathrm{lab}_{H'}|_E$, then the *union* of the graphs H and H' is the graph $H \cup H' = (V_H \cup V_{H'}, E_H \cup E_{H'}, \mathrm{att}_H \cup \mathrm{att}_{H'}, \mathrm{lab}_H \cup \mathrm{lab}_{H'}, \mathrm{ports}_H \mathrm{ports}_{H'})$.

For every $F \subseteq E_H$ let $H \setminus F = (V_H, E, \mathrm{att}_H|_E, \mathrm{lab}_H|_E, \mathrm{ports}_H)$ where $E = E_H \setminus F$.

Let $k \in \mathbb{N}_+$ and $H, H_1, \ldots, H_k \in \mathcal{H}$ be pairwise disjoint. Let $e_1, \ldots, e_k \in E_H$ be pairwise distinct edges, called *variables*. Let I be the graph $H \setminus \{e_1, \ldots, e_k\} \cup H_1 \cup \cdots \cup H_k$. The *hyperedge replacement* (HR) of e_1 by $H_1, \ldots,$ and e_k by H_k in H (Bauderon and Courcelle, 1987; Habel and Kreowski, 1987) yields the graph

$$H[e_1/H_1, \ldots, e_k/H_k]$$
$$= (V_I/\!\sim, E_I, \mathrm{att}_I/\!\sim, \mathrm{lab}_I, \mathrm{ports}_H/\!\sim)$$

where $\sim$ is the least equivalence relation on V_I such that $\mathrm{att}_H(e_i, j) \sim \mathrm{ports}_{H_i}(j)$ for every $i \in [k]$ and $j \in [\min(|\mathrm{att}_H(e_i)|, |\mathrm{ports}_{H_i}|)]$. In the following, we call $\sim$ the *equivalence relation involved in the HR that yields* $H[e_1/H_1, \ldots, e_k/H_k]$.

We assume that each variable e_i is labeled by a distinguished symbol $\bot \in \Sigma$ and depict e_i by $\boxed{e_i}$ instead of $\boxed{\bot}$. Throughout this paper, we will not distinguish between isomorphic graphs, i.e., graphs that are identical up to a bijective renaming of vertices and edges. However, since hyperedge replacement is defined on concrete graphs and requires that $H, H_1, \ldots, H_k$ are pairwise disjoint, we may choose isomorphic copies of the involved graphs, i.e., rename edges or vertices. To avoid the cumbersome conversion between abstract and concrete

graphs, we assume that this renaming is *opaque*. In this sense, we may define an HR operation as a total function from $\mathcal{H}^k$ to $\mathcal{H}$ as follows.

Let H be a graph. For pairwise distinct edges $e_1, \ldots, e_k \in E_H$, the *HR operation* $H_{\langle e_1 \ldots e_k \rangle} \colon \mathcal{H}^k \to \mathcal{H}$ is given by

$$H_{\langle e_1 \ldots e_k \rangle}(H_1, \ldots, H_k) = H[e_1/H_1, \ldots, e_k/H_k]$$

for all graphs $H_1, \ldots, H_k \in \mathcal{H}$.

A (Σ, Γ)-*HR algebra* (Courcelle, 1991) is a Σ-algebra $\mathcal{A} = (\mathcal{H}_\Gamma, (\sigma_\mathcal{A})_{\sigma \in \Sigma})$ where, for every $k \in \mathbb{N}$ and $\sigma \in \Sigma_k$, we have $\sigma_\mathcal{A} = H_{\langle e_1 \ldots e_k \rangle}$ for some $H \in \mathcal{H}_\Gamma$ and pairwise distinct $e_1, \ldots, e_k \in E_H$. Then we denote H by $\mathrm{graph}(\sigma_\mathcal{A})$. An *HR algebra* is a (Σ, Γ)-HR algebra for some Σ and Γ.

An example of a (Σ, Γ)-HR algebra $\mathcal{A}$ and the application of $[\![.]\!]_\mathcal{A}$ to a term are given in Fig. 2.

3 Bigraphs and Aligned HR Bimorphisms

Now we formally introduce our central notions of bigraph and aligned HR bimorphism. A case study with examples follows in the next section. Throughout this section let Δ and Ω be alphabets.

Definition 3.1. A *bigraph of type* (Δ, Ω) is a triple $B = (H_1, \lambda, H_2)$ where $H_1 \in \mathcal{H}_\Delta$ and $H_2 \in \mathcal{H}_\Omega$ are disjoint, and λ is an *alignment of* H_1 *and* H_2, i.e., a graph with $V_\lambda = V_{H_1} \cup V_{H_2}$, $E_\lambda \cap E_{H_1} = E_\lambda \cap E_{H_2} = \emptyset$, $\mathrm{att}(e) \in (V_{H_1})^+ \cdot (V_{H_2})^+$ for each $e \in E_\lambda$, and $\mathrm{ports}_\lambda = \varepsilon$. $\qquad\square$

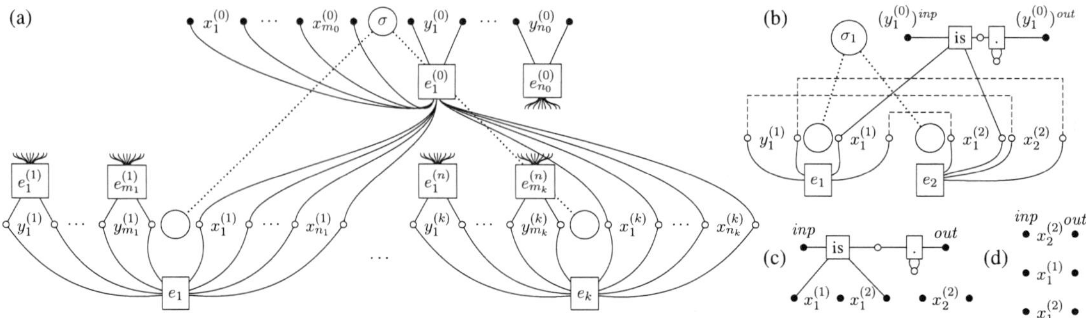

Figure 3: The graphs (a) H_{IO}^{σ}, (b) H^{σ_1}, (c) $(\!|s_1^{(0)}|\!)$, and (d) $(\!|s_1^{(1)}|\!)$. The large circles and the dotted lines in (a) and (b) visualize the underlying term structure; e.g., in (b) σ_1 has two children because $\sigma_1 \in \Sigma_2$.

Definition 3.2. An *aligned HR bimorphism of type* (Σ, Δ, Ω) is a tuple $\mathcal{B} = (g, \mathcal{A}_1, \Lambda, \mathcal{A}_2)$, where g is an RTG over Σ and $\mathcal{A}_1, \mathcal{A}_2$ are a (Σ, Δ)-HR algebra and a (Σ, Ω)-HR algebra, resp., such that $\mathrm{graph}(\sigma_{\mathcal{A}_1})$ and $\mathrm{graph}(\sigma_{\mathcal{A}_2})$ are disjoint for each $\sigma \in \Sigma$. Further, Λ is a Σ-indexed family $(\Lambda_\sigma \mid \sigma \in \Sigma)$, each Λ_σ being an alignment of $\mathrm{graph}(\sigma_{\mathcal{A}_1})$ and $\mathrm{graph}(\sigma_{\mathcal{A}_2})$. $\square$

In the following, for each term $t \in T_\Sigma$, we assume (w.l.o.g.) that $[\![t]\!]_{\mathcal{A}_1}$ and $[\![t]\!]_{\mathcal{A}_2}$ are disjoint.

Definition 3.3. Let $\mathcal{B} = (g, \mathcal{A}_1, \Lambda, \mathcal{A}_2)$ be an aligned HR bimorphism. The *semantics of $\mathcal{B}$*, denoted by $\mathcal{L}(\mathcal{B})$, is the set of bigraphs defined as follows.

First, let the $\mathcal{B}$-alignment be the T_Σ-indexed family $\Lambda_\mathcal{B} = (\Lambda_\mathcal{B}(t) \mid t \in T_\Sigma)$ where $\Lambda_\mathcal{B}(t)$ is the alignment of $[\![t]\!]_{\mathcal{A}_1}$ and $[\![t]\!]_{\mathcal{A}_2}$ defined inductively on t as follows. Let $t = \sigma(t_1, \ldots, t_k) \in T_\Sigma$. For $j \in [2]$, suppose that $\sim_j$ is the equivalence relation involved in the hyperedge replacement that yields $\mathrm{graph}(\sigma_{\mathcal{A}_j})[e_1/[\![t_1]\!]_{\mathcal{A}_j}, \ldots, e_k/[\![t_k]\!]_{\mathcal{A}_j}]$. We assume that $\Lambda_\sigma, \Lambda_\mathcal{B}(t_1), \ldots, \Lambda_\mathcal{B}(t_k)$ have pairwise disjoint sets of edges. Then we define the $\mathcal{B}$-alignment of $[\![t]\!]_{\mathcal{A}_1}$ and $[\![t]\!]_{\mathcal{A}_2}$ to be the graph

$$\Lambda_\mathcal{B}(t) = (\Lambda_\sigma \cup \Lambda_\mathcal{B}(t_1) \cup \cdots \cup \Lambda_\mathcal{B}(t_k))/(\sim_1 \cup \sim_2)$$

and we let $[\![t]\!]_\mathcal{B} = ([\![t]\!]_{\mathcal{A}_1}, \Lambda_\mathcal{B}(t), [\![t]\!]_{\mathcal{A}_2})$. Finally, we define $\mathcal{L}(\mathcal{B}) = \{[\![t]\!]_\mathcal{B} \mid t \in \mathcal{L}(g)\}$. $\square$

4 Case Study: Hybrid Grammars

We show how an LCFRS/sDCP hybrid grammar (Nederhof and Vogler, 2014) can be represented as an aligned HR bimorphism. These grammars deal with sequence terms; hence, we first recall their definition and show how to view sequence terms as particular graphs.

4.1 A Graph View on Sequence Terms

Let Γ be a ranked alphabet and Y be a set disjoint from Γ. The sets of *terms* and *sequence-terms* (*s-terms*) over Γ indexed by Y (Seki and Kato, 2008) are denoted by $T_\Gamma(Y)$ and $T_\Gamma^*(Y)$, respectively, and defined inductively as follows:

1. $Y \subseteq T_\Gamma(Y)$,

2. if $k \in \mathbb{N}$, $\gamma \in \Gamma_k$ and $s_i \in T_\Gamma^*(Y)$ for each $i \in [k]$, then $\gamma(s_1, \ldots, s_k) \in T_\Gamma(Y)$, and

3. if $n \in \mathbb{N}$ and $t_i \in T_\Gamma(Y)$ for each $i \in [n]$, then $\langle t_1, \ldots, t_n \rangle \in T_\Gamma^*(Y)$.

Let $s \in T_\Gamma^*(Y)$. We say that s is *linear* if every $y \in Y$ occurs at most once in s. *In the following we only consider linear s-terms.* We note that, if $\Gamma = \Gamma_0$, then s is essentially a string over Γ_0 and Y. If $\Gamma = \Gamma_1$, then s corresponds to a sequence of ordinary (unranked) terms over Γ_1 indexed by Y.

Every linear s-term s can be represented as a graph $(\!|s|\!)$: it has two distinct ports inp and out, representing the start and end of s, resp. For each variable $y \in Y$, $(\!|s|\!)$ has two distinct ports y^{inp} and y^{out}. For each occurrence of a symbol $\gamma \in \Gamma_k$ in s, there is a γ-labeled edge with $2k + 2$ tentacles in $(\!|s|\!)$. The $(2i - 1)$-th and $2i$-th tentacle ($i \in [k]$) point to the start and end vertex, respectively, of the i-th child sequence of γ. The last two tentacles point towards the predecessor and the successor of γ, respectively: this may be a vertex separating two symbols, the start or end vertex of a (sub-)sequence, or the port realizing y^{inp} or y^{out} for some $y \in Y$.

For instance, the s-term

$$s_1^{(0)} = \langle \mathrm{is}(\langle x_1^{(1)}, x_1^{(2)} \rangle), \, . \, (\langle \rangle) \rangle$$

in $T_\Gamma^*(\{x_1^{(1)}, x_1^{(2)}, x_2^{(2)}\})$ is represented by $(\!|s_1^{(0)}|\!)$ in Fig. 3c. The ports $(x_2^{(2)})^{inp}$ and $(x_2^{(2)})^{out}$ for $x_2^{(2)}$

are depicted as filled circles to the left and the right of $x_2^{(2)}$, and similarly for the other variables. Note that $(x_1^{(1)})^{out}$ and $(x_1^{(2)})^{inp}$ coincide because $x_1^{(1)}$ is succeeded by $x_1^{(2)}$ in $s_1^{(0)}$.

4.2 LCFRS, sDCP, and LCFRS/sDCP Hybrid Grammars

Here we formalize LCFRS/sDCP hybrid grammars as particular aligned HR bimorphisms, where the algebras $\mathcal{A}_1$ and $\mathcal{A}_2$ are an LCFRS algebra and an sDCP algebra, resp. Since both LCFRS and sDCP can be viewed as particular types of attribute grammars (AG), we first define the concept of AG algebra and, in a second step, instantiate it to LCFRS algebra and sDCP algebra.

For each $\sigma \in \Sigma_k$, let $\mathrm{syn}_{\mathcal{A}}^{\sigma} = (n_0, \ldots, n_k) \in \mathbb{N}_+^{k+1}$ and $\mathrm{inh}_{\mathcal{A}}^{\sigma} = (m_0, \ldots, m_k) \in \mathbb{N}^{k+1}$ be tuples defining the sets $I = \{y_j^{(0)} \mid j \in [n_0]\} \cup \{y_j^{(i)} \mid i \in [k], j \in [m_i]\}$ and $O = \{x_r^{(0)} \mid r \in [m_0]\} \cup \{x_r^{(\ell)} \mid \ell \in [k], r \in [n_\ell]\}$ of *inside* and *outside attributes*, resp. (The abbreviations stem from the AG notions *synthesized attributes* and *inherited attributes*.) The definition of an AG algebra $\mathcal{A}$ follows the two-phase approach in (Engelfriet and Heyker, 1992). In the first phase, for each symbol σ in Σ_k, we define a graph H_{IO}^{σ} of type $\mathrm{syn}_{\mathcal{A}}^{\sigma}, \mathrm{inh}_{\mathcal{A}}^{\sigma}$ as shown in Fig. 3a: there is a pair of vertices for each inside attribute $y_j^{(i)}$ and each outside attribute $x_r^{(\ell)}$. For each inside attribute $y_j^{(i)}$ there is a edge $e_j^{(i)}$ which connects $y_j^{(i)}$ with all outside attributes. For the edge $e_1^{(0)}$ the tentacles are shown completely in Fig. 3a; for the other edges the tentacles to outside attributes are abridged for clarity. The edges $e_1, \ldots, e_k$ correspond to the k successors of σ.

In the second phase, we choose an I-indexed family of s-terms $(s_j^{(i)} \in T_\Gamma^*(O) \mid y_j^{(i)} \in I)$ such that each $x_r^{(\ell)}$ in O occurs exactly once in all $s_j^{(i)}$ together (single syntactic use restriction). Then we replace each edge $e_j^{(i)}$ by the graph $(\!|s_j^{(i)}|\!)$; this specifies a particular information flow. Formally, we set $\sigma_{\mathcal{A}} = H_{\langle e_1 \ldots e_k \rangle}^{\sigma}$ where

$$H^{\sigma} = H_{IO}^{\sigma}[e_j^{(i)} / (\!|s_j^{(i)}|\!) \mid y_j^{(i)} \in I] \ .$$

For instance, for $\sigma_1 \in \Sigma_2$ we have $\mathrm{syn}_{\mathcal{A}}^{\sigma_1} = (1, 1, 2)$ and $\mathrm{inh}_{\mathcal{A}}^{\sigma_1} = (0, 1, 0)$, and so we construct $H_{IO}^{\sigma_1}$ accordingly. Next, we choose $(\!|s_1^{(0)}|\!)$ and $(\!|s_1^{(1)}|\!)$ as depicted in Fig. 3c and 3d, respec-

tively. Then $H^{\sigma_1} = H_{IO}^{\sigma_1}[e_1^{(0)}/(\!|s_1^{(0)}|\!), e_1^{(1)}/(\!|s_1^{(1)}|\!)]$ is the graph in Fig. 3b where dashed lines indicate the identification of vertices. Note that H^{σ_1} equals $\mathrm{graph}((\sigma_1)_{\mathcal{A}})$ in Fig. 2a.

A (Σ, Γ)-HR algebra $\mathcal{A}$ is a (Σ, Γ)-*attribute grammar algebra* $((\Sigma, \Gamma)$-*AG algebra*), if each symbol σ in Σ is interpreted as described above. For instance, $\mathcal{A}$ of Fig. 2a is a (Σ, Γ)-AG algebra.

We observe that (Σ, Γ)-AG algebras have the following property: for every edge $e \in E_{H^\sigma}$, if $\mathrm{lab}_{H^\sigma}(e) \in \Gamma_k$ then e has $2k + 2$ tentacles. We call the vertex $\mathrm{att}_{H_\sigma}(e)(k + 1)$ the *input vertex of* e and denote it by $\mathrm{inp}(e)$. Note that no two terminal edges in H^σ have the same input vertex. This *single-input property* will be crucial for an efficient representation of subgraphs during the reduct construction (cf. Sec. 5.2).

Next we instantiate the concept of AG-algebra to LCFRS algebras and to sDCP algebras. An LCFRS does not have inherited attributes:

Definition 4.1. Let $\Delta = \Delta_0$ be a ranked alphabet. A (Σ, Δ)-AG algebra $\mathcal{A}$ is a (Σ, Δ)-*LCFRS algebra*, if $\mathrm{inh}_{\mathcal{A}}^{\sigma} = (0, \ldots, 0)$ for all $\sigma \in \Sigma$. $\square$

Definition 4.2. Let $\Omega = \Omega_1$ be a ranked alphabet and let $\mathcal{A}$ be a (Σ, Ω)-AG algebra. We say that $\mathcal{A}$ is a (Σ, Ω)-*sDCP algebra*. $\square$

Then the graph view on an LCFRS/sDCP hybrid grammar is an HR bimorphism $\mathcal{B} = (g, \mathcal{A}_1, \Lambda, \mathcal{A}_2)$, where

- $g = (\Xi, \Sigma, \xi_0, R)$ is an RTG,
- $\mathcal{A}_1$ is a (Σ, Δ)-LCFRS algebra,
- $\mathcal{A}_2$ is a (Σ, Ω)-sDCP algebra, $\Delta = \Omega$ (regarding Δ and Ω as sets of symbols), and
- there are functions $\mathrm{fan} \colon \Xi \to \mathbb{N}_+$, $\mathrm{inh} \colon \Xi \to \mathbb{N}$, and $\mathrm{syn} \colon \Xi \to \mathbb{N}_+$ such that $\mathrm{fan}(\xi_0) = 1$, $\mathrm{inh}(\xi_0) = 0$, $\mathrm{syn}(\xi_0) = 1$, and for every $(\xi \to \sigma(\xi_1, \ldots, \xi_k)) \in R$, it holds that
  - $(\mathrm{fan}(\xi), \mathrm{fan}(\xi_1), \ldots, \mathrm{fan}(\xi_k)) = \mathrm{syn}_{\mathcal{A}_1}^{\sigma}$ and
  - $(\mathrm{inh}(\xi), \mathrm{inh}(\xi_1), \ldots, \mathrm{inh}(\xi_k)) = \mathrm{inh}_{\mathcal{A}_2}^{\sigma}$ and $(\mathrm{syn}(\xi), \mathrm{syn}(\xi_1), \ldots, \mathrm{syn}(\xi_k)) = \mathrm{syn}_{\mathcal{A}_2}^{\sigma}$.

Moreover, we require the following: Let $\sigma \in \Sigma$ and $H_j = \mathrm{graph}(\sigma_{\mathcal{A}_j})$ for $j \in [2]$. For each $e \in E_{\Lambda_\sigma}$ we have $\mathrm{att}_{\Lambda_\sigma}(e) = \mathrm{inp}(e_1)\,\mathrm{inp}(e_2)$ where $e_1 \in E_{H_1}$, $e_2 \in E_{H_2}$, and $\mathrm{lab}_{H_1}(e_1) = \mathrm{lab}_{H_2}(e_2)$.

Example 4.3. Let g be as in Ex. 2.1 and consider the LCFRS/sDCP hybrid grammar $\mathcal{B} = (g, \mathcal{A}_1, \Lambda, \mathcal{A}_2)$, where $\mathcal{A}_1, \Lambda$, and $\mathcal{A}_2$ are as specified in Fig. 4. Then the bigraph in Fig. 1b equals $[\![\sigma_1(\sigma_2, \sigma_3(\sigma_4, \sigma_5))]\!]_{\mathcal{B}}$ and is thus in $\mathcal{L}(\mathcal{B})$. $\square$

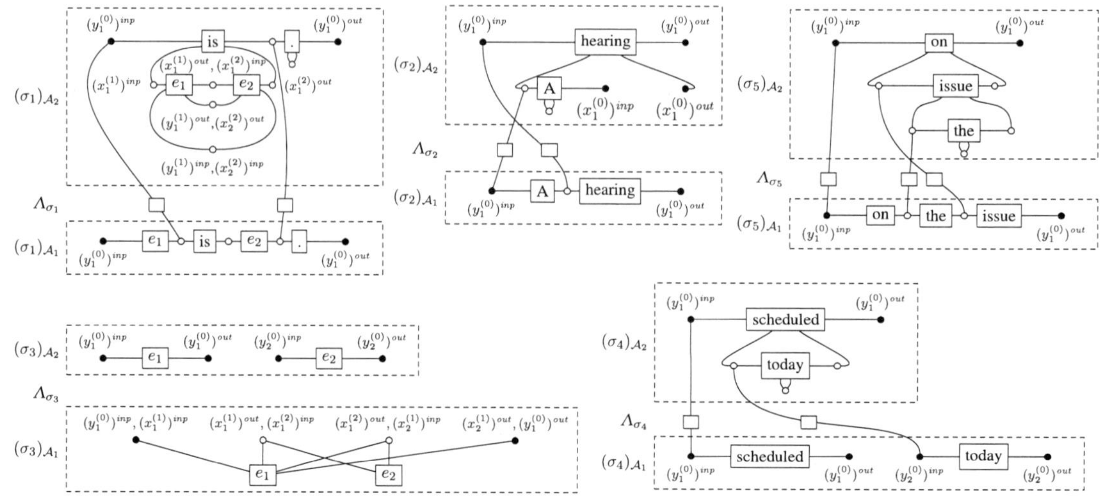

Figure 4: The interpretation of $\sigma_1, \ldots, \sigma_5$ in $\mathcal{A}_1$, Λ, and $\mathcal{A}_2$.

5 EM Training

We present a training algorithm which takes as input a weighted aligned HR bimorphism and a finite, non-empty corpus c of bigraphs. It is essentially the same as the training algorithm for probabilistic context-free grammars (PCFG) (Baker, 1979; Lari and Young, 1990; Nederhof and Satta, 2008). As shown in (Prescher, 2001), this algorithm is a dynamic programming variant of the EM-algorithm (Dempster et al., 1977). Thus, our algorithm generates a sequence of probability assignments which converges to a probability assignment $\hat{p}$; the likelihood of c under $\hat{p}$ is a local maximum or saddle point of the likelihood function of c.

5.1 Weighted Aligned HR Bimorphisms

We define weighted RTG in a similar way as PCFG was defined in (Nederhof and Satta, 2006).

A *weighted regular tree grammar (WRTG)* is a pair (g, p) where $g = (\Xi, \Sigma, \xi_0, R)$ is an RTG and $p \colon R \to \mathbb{R}_{\geq 0}$ is the *weight assignment*. A weight assignment p is a *probability assignment* if $\sum_{\rho \in R_\xi} p(\rho) = 1$ for each $\xi \in \Xi$. We extend p to the mapping $p' \colon D_g(\mathrm{T}_\Sigma) \to \mathbb{R}_{\geq 0}$ on derivations as follows: for each $d = \varrho(d_1, \ldots, d_k)$ in $D_g(\mathrm{T}_\Sigma)$ we define $p'(d) = p(\varrho) \cdot \prod_{i=1}^{k} p'(d_i)$. For each $t \in T_\Sigma$ we define $p''(t) = \sum_{d \in D_g^\xi(t)} p'(d)$. We define the mappings in$\colon \Xi \to \mathbb{R}_{\geq 0} \cup \{\infty\}$ (*inside weight*) and out$\colon \Xi \to \mathbb{R}_{\geq 0} \cup \{\infty\}$ (*outside weight*) for each $\xi \in \Xi$ by

$$\mathrm{in}(\xi) = \sum_{d \in D_g^\xi(\mathrm{T}_\Sigma)} p'(d) \qquad \mathrm{out}(\xi) = \sum_{d \in D_g^{\xi_0}(\mathrm{T}_\Sigma, \xi)} p'''(d)$$

where $p''' \colon D_g^{\xi_0}(\mathrm{T}_\Sigma, \xi) \to \mathbb{R}_{\geq 0}$ is defined in the same way as p', with the addition that $p'''(\xi) = 1$. As usual, we will drop the primes from p', p'', and p'''.

Definition 5.1. A *weighted aligned HR bimorphism* is a pair $(\mathcal{B}, p) = ((g, \mathcal{A}_1, \Lambda, \mathcal{A}_2), p)$ where $(g, \mathcal{A}_1, \Lambda, \mathcal{A}_2)$ is an aligned HR bimorphism and (g, p) is a WRTG. $\qquad\square$

5.2 Reduct Construction

Given a weighted aligned HR bimorphism $(\mathcal{B}, p) = ((g, \mathcal{A}_1, \Lambda, \mathcal{A}_2), p)$ and a bigraph (H_1, λ, H_2), we restrict g to an RTG g' such that only trees $t \in \mathcal{L}(g)$ satisfying $[\![t]\!]_\mathcal{B} = (H_1, \lambda, H_2)$ are in $\mathcal{L}(g')$. Also, we show that if $\mathcal{B}$ is an LCFRS/sDCP hybrid grammar, then g' can be constructed in time polynomial in the size of $\mathcal{B}$ and (H_1, λ, H_2).

Definition 5.2. Let $m \in \mathbb{N}$ and $H \in \mathcal{H}$. A graph H' is an *m-subgraph* of H if int$(H') \subseteq$ int(H), $E_{H'} \subseteq E_H$, lab$_{H'} = $ lab$_H|_{E_{H'}}$, and $|\mathrm{ports}_{H'}| \leq m$. Moreover, we require that there is a mapping $\varphi \colon V_{H'} \to V_H$, called *vertex mapping*, such that $\varphi(\mathrm{att}_{H'}(e)) = \mathrm{att}_H(e)$ for each $e \in E_{H'}$, $\varphi(v) = v$ for each $v \in \mathrm{int}(H')$, and $\varphi(\mathrm{int}(H')) \cap \varphi([\mathrm{ports}_{H'}]) = \emptyset$. Moreover, for each $v \in \mathrm{int}(H')$, if $v \in [\mathrm{att}_H(e)]$ for some $e \in E_H$, then $e \in E_{H'}$. The set of all *m-subgraphs* of H is denoted by $\mathcal{H}_S^m(H)$. $\qquad\square$

For instance, graph$((\sigma_4)_\mathcal{A})$ in Fig. 2a is a 2-subgraph of the last graph in Fig. 2b. If a graph H is the result of applying an HR operation to graphs $H_1, \ldots, H_k$, then each H_i is a $|\mathrm{ports}_{H_i}|$-subgraph of H. (For this, the mapping φ in Definition 5.2 is needed, because some of the ports of H_i may be identified with each other in H.) Hence, for the reduct we consider only m-subgraphs of H, where m is the maximal port length of HR operations in $\mathcal{A}_1$ or $\mathcal{A}_2$. We observe that $\mathcal{H}_S^m(H)$ is finite because we identify isomorphic graphs.

Definition 5.3. Let $(\mathcal{B}, p) = ((g, \mathcal{A}_1, \Lambda, \mathcal{A}_2), p)$ be a weighted aligned HR bimorphism with $g = (\Xi, \Sigma, \xi_0, R)$ and let (H_1, λ, H_2) be a bigraph.

We define $(\mathcal{B}, p) \triangleright (H_1, \lambda, H_2)$, the *reduct of* $(\mathcal{B}, p)$ *with respect to* (H_1, λ, H_2), to be the weighted aligned HR bimorphism $((g', \mathcal{A}_1, \Lambda, \mathcal{A}_2), p')$ where g' and p' are defined as follows.

If $[\![.]\!]_\mathcal{B}^{-1}(H_1, \lambda, H_2) = \emptyset$, then $g' = (\{\xi_0'\}, \Sigma, \xi_0', \emptyset)$ and $p' = \emptyset$. Otherwise, let $m \in \mathbb{N}$ be the maximum of all $|\mathrm{ports}_{\mathrm{graph}(\sigma_{\mathcal{A}_1})}|$ and $|\mathrm{ports}_{\mathrm{graph}(\sigma_{\mathcal{A}_2})}|$ where $\sigma \in \Sigma$. Now, we construct $g' = (\Xi', \Sigma, \xi_0', R')$ where we abbreviate $\mathcal{H}_S^m(H_1) \times \mathcal{H}_S^m(\lambda) \times \mathcal{H}_S^m(H_2)$ by $\mathcal{H}_S^m(H_1, \lambda, H_2)$:

- $\Xi' = \Xi \times (\mathcal{H}_S^m(H_1, \lambda, H_2) \cap [\![T_\Sigma]\!]_\mathcal{B})$,

- $\xi_0' = (\xi_0, H_1, \lambda, H_2)$, and

- for every rule $\varrho = (\xi \to \sigma(\xi_1, \dots, \xi_k)) \in R$ and $(s, \eta, r), (s_1, \eta_1, r_1), \dots, (s_k, \eta_k, r_k)$ in $\mathcal{H}_S^m(H_1, \lambda, H_2) \cap [\![T_\Sigma]\!]_\mathcal{B}$ we have

$$\varrho' = \big((\xi, s, \eta, r) \to \sigma((\xi_1, s_1, \eta_1, r_1), \dots,$$
$$(\xi_k, s_k, \eta_k, r_k))\big) \in R'$$

if $s = \sigma_{\mathcal{A}_1}(s_1, \dots, s_k)$, $\eta = \Lambda_\sigma \cup \eta_1 \cup \dots \cup \eta_k$, and $r = \sigma_{\mathcal{A}_2}(r_1, \dots, r_k)$.

We define $p'(\varrho') = p(\varrho)$. $\qquad\square$

Theorem 5.4. In Def. 5.3 the following hold:

1. $\mathcal{L}(g') = [\![.]\!]_\mathcal{B}^{-1}(H_1, \lambda, H_2) \cap \mathcal{L}(g)$.

2. There is a deterministic tree relabeling ϕ from $D_{g'}$ to D_g such that for all $t \in \mathcal{L}(g')$ and $d' \in D_{g'}(t)$, $\phi|_{D_{g'}(t)}$ is a bijection between $D_{g'}(t)$ and $D_g(t)$, and $p'(d') = p(\phi(d'))$.

Proof. If $[\![.]\!]_\mathcal{B}^{-1}(H_1, \lambda, H_2) = \emptyset$, then $\mathcal{L}(g') = \emptyset$ by construction, and thus, both statements of the theorem hold. Otherwise, the first statement follows from the following claim.

Claim (*) For every $n \in \mathbb{N}$, $\xi \in \Xi$, $t \in T_\Sigma$, and $(s, \eta, r) \in (\mathcal{H}_S^m(H_1, \lambda, H_2)) \cap [\![T_\Sigma]\!]_\mathcal{B}$ it holds that $(\xi, s, \eta, r) \Rightarrow_{g'}^n t$ iff $\xi \Rightarrow_g^n t$ and $[\![t]\!]_{\mathcal{A}_1} = s$ and $\Lambda_\mathcal{B}(t) = \eta$ and $[\![t]\!]_{\mathcal{A}_2} = r$.

For the proof of the second statement we define $\phi((\xi, s, \eta, r)) = \xi$ for each $(\xi, s, \eta, r) \in \Xi'$, and extend ϕ in the canonical way to derivation trees.

Then the statement is an immediate consequence of the constructions of R' and ϕ and Claim (*). $\qquad\blacksquare$

Complexity We determine the complexity of the reduct construction for the special case of LCFRS/sDCP hybrid grammars. We assume that the maximal length m of ports in the HR operations is fixed and is not part of the input. In preparation, we determine an upper bound on $|\Xi'|$.

Let $H \in \mathcal{H}$ be such that from each vertex there is an (undirected) path to a port. Given H each $H' \in \mathcal{H}_S^m(H) \cap [\![T_\Sigma]\!]_\mathcal{A}$ is uniquely determined by its *boundary representation* (Lautemann, 1990; Chiang et al., 2013; Groschwitz et al., 2015), which consists of (a) the pair $(\mathrm{ports}_{H'}, \varphi(\mathrm{ports}_{H'}))$, (b) the set of *boundary edges* $E_{H'}^B$ of H' consisting of all $e \in E_{H'}$ such that $\mathrm{att}_{H'}(e) \cap [\mathrm{ports}_{H'}] \neq \emptyset$, and (c) a function $\mathrm{att}' : E_{H'}^B \to ([\mathrm{ports}_{H'}] \cup \{\bot\})^*$ such that $\mathrm{att}'(e)(i) = \mathrm{att}_{H'}(e)(i)$ if $\mathrm{att}_{H'}(e)(i) \in [\mathrm{ports}_{H'}]$, and $\bot$ otherwise. Note that (c) is necessary because $\varphi|_{[\mathrm{ports}_{H'}]}$ might not be injective.

Now, for an arbitrary (Σ, Γ)-AG algebra $\mathcal{A}$ and $H \in (\!|T_\Gamma^*(\emptyset)|\!)$ the following holds. Due to the single-input property of H and of the involved HR operations, for each m-subgraph H' the information (b) and (c) can be inferred from (a). There are $S_{m,k}$ port sequences of length m with k distinct vertices, where $S_{m,k}$ is the *Stirling number of the second kind*. For each port we choose a vertex in V_H. Thus, we obtain that $|\mathcal{H}_S^m(H) \cap [\![T_\Sigma]\!]_\mathcal{A}| \leq \sum_{k=0}^m S_{m,k} \cdot |V_H|^k \leq m^m \cdot |V_H|^m$.

Next, we analyze the $\mathcal{B}$-alignments of an LCFRS/sDCP hybrid grammar $\mathcal{B}$. Let $(s, \eta, r) \in \mathcal{H}_S^m(H_1, \lambda, H_2)$ and $t \in T_\Sigma$ with $[\![t]\!]_\mathcal{B} = (s, \eta, r)$. Then $V_\eta = V_s \cup V_r$. Let $e \in E_\lambda$ and $e_1 \in E_{H_1}$ and $e_2 \in E_{H_2}$ with $\mathrm{att}_\lambda(e) = \mathrm{inp}(e_1)\,\mathrm{inp}(e_2)$. (i) Assume that there is $t' \in T_\Sigma$ with $[\![t']\!]_\mathcal{B} = (H_1, \lambda, H_2)$ and t is a subtree of t'. Then e_1 and e_2 are unique by the single input property. Hence, $e_1 \in E_s$ iff $e_2 \in E_r$ iff $e \in E_\eta$ because t is a subtree of t' and by the structure of Λ_σ. (ii) If there is no such t', then the equivalences under (i) may be violated, in which case (s, η, r) can safely be pruned.

Thus, for each LCFRS/sDCP hybrid grammar $\mathcal{B}$ and each (H_1, λ, H_2) with $H_1 \in (\!|T_\Lambda^*(\emptyset)|\!)$ and $H_2 \in (\!|T_\Omega^*(\emptyset)|\!)$ we obtain the upper bound $|\Xi| \cdot m^{2m} \cdot |V_{H_1}|^m \cdot |V_{H_2}|^m$ on $|\Xi'|$. This bound can be refined to $|\Xi| \cdot m^{2m} \cdot |V_{H_1}|^{2 \cdot \mathrm{fan}^*} \cdot |V_{H_2}|^{2 \cdot (\mathrm{syn}^* + \mathrm{inh}^*)}$, where $f^* = \max_{\xi \in \Xi} f(\xi)$ for $f \in \{\mathrm{fan}, \mathrm{syn}, \mathrm{inh}\}$. Constructing Ξ' and R' simultaneously with a deductive parsing algorithm (Shieber et al., 1995) has a worst-case time complexity in $\mathcal{O}(|\varXi'|^k)$ where k is the maximum rank of Σ.

5.3   EM Training Algorithm

In the first step of our training algorithm, a corpus $c' : R \to \mathbb{R}_{\geq 0}$ is computed as follows. After initialization (line 3), each bigraph B occurring in c is considered (line 4), the reduct $(\mathcal{B}, p_i) \triangleright B$ is built (line 5), the inside/outside weights of the new WRTG (g', p') are calculated (line 6), and according to these weights and the current weight assignment p_i the count $c'(\varrho)$ of each rule is incremented (lines 8–9). In the second step, the corpus c' is normalized (lines 10–14) and the result is the next probability assignment p_{i+1} (line 15).

Algorithm 5.1   EM-training algorithms for weighted aligned HR bimorphisms.

Input: weighted aligned HR bimorphism
$(\mathcal{B}, p_0) = ((g, \mathcal{A}_1, \Lambda, \mathcal{A}_2), p_0)$
with $g = (\varXi, \Sigma, \xi_0, R)$, and a finite,
non-empty corpus c of bigraphs.

Output: sequence $p_1, p_2, p_3, \ldots$ of improved
probability assignments for R.

1:   $i \leftarrow 0$
2:   **while** true **do**
3:     initialize counts $c' : R \to \mathbb{R}_{\geq 0}$: $c'(\varrho) \leftarrow 0$
4:     **for** $B = (H_1, \lambda, H_2)$ s.t. $c(B) > 0$ **do**
5:       $((g', \mathcal{A}_1, \Lambda, \mathcal{A}_2), p') \leftarrow (\mathcal{B}, p_i) \triangleright B$
        with RTG $g' = (\varXi', \Sigma, \xi_0', R')$ and
        det. tree rel. ϕ // cf. Thm 5.4
6:     compute out and in for the WRTG
        (g', p')
7:     **if** $\mathrm{in}(\xi_0') \neq 0$ **then**
8:       **for** $\varrho = (\xi \to \sigma(\xi_1, \ldots, \xi_k)) \in R$ **do**
9:         $c'(\varrho) \leftarrow c'(\varrho) + c(B) \cdot \mathrm{in}(\xi_0')^{-1} \cdot$
$$\sum_{\substack{\varrho' \in R': \\ \phi(\varrho')=\varrho \,\wedge\, \varrho'=(\xi' \to \sigma(\xi_1', \ldots, \xi_k'))}} \mathrm{out}(\xi') \cdot p_i(\varrho) \cdot \prod_{j=1}^{k} \mathrm{in}(\xi_j')$$
10:     **for** $\xi \in \varXi$ **do**
11:       $s \leftarrow \sum_{\varrho \in R_\xi} c'(\varrho)$
12:     **for** $\varrho \in R_\xi$ **do**
13:       **if** $s = 0$ **then** $p_{i+1}(\varrho) \leftarrow p_i(\varrho) \cdot |R_\xi|^{-1}$
14:       **else** $p_{i+1}(\varrho) \leftarrow s^{-1} \cdot c'(\varrho)$
15:     output p_{i+1} and $i \leftarrow i + 1$

Acknowledgment

We thank the referees for their careful reading of the manuscript.

References

James K. Baker. 1979. Trainable grammars for speech recognition. In *Speech Communication Papers for the 97th Meeting of the Acoustical Society of America*, pages 547–550.

Laura Banarescu, Claire Bonial, Shu Cai, Madalina Georgescu, Kira Griffitt, Ulf Hermjakob, Kevin Knight, Philipp Koehn, Martha Palmer, and Nathan Schneider. 2013. Abstract meaning representation for sembanking. In *Proc. 7th Linguistic Annotation Workshop, ACL 2013 Workshop*.

Michel Bauderon and Bruno Courcelle. 1987. Graph expressions and graph rewriting. *Mathematical Systems Theory*, 20:83–127.

Suna Bensch, Frank Drewes, Helmut Jürgensen, and Brink van der Merwe. 2014. Graph transformation for incremental natural language analysis. *Theoretical Computer Science*, 531:1–25.

Walter S. Brainerd. 1969. Tree generating regular systems. *Inform. and Control*, 14:217–231.

Peter F. Brown, Vincent J. Della Pietra, Stephen A. Della Pietra, and Robert L. Mercer. 1993. The mathematics of statistical machine translation: parameter estimation. *Computational Linguistics*, 19(2):263–311.

David Chiang, Jacob Andreas, Daniel Bauer, Karl Moritz Hermann, Bevan Jones, and Kevin Knight. 2013. Parsing graphs with hyperedge replacement grammars. In *Proc. of the 51st Annual Meeting of the Association for Computational Linguistics*, pages 924–932.

David Chiang. 2007. Hierarchical phrase-based translation. *Computational Linguistics*, 33(2):201–228.

Bruno Courcelle. 1991. The monadic second-order logic of graphs V: on closing the gap between definability and recognizability. *Theoretical Computer Science*, 80:153–202.

Arthur P. Dempster, Nan M. Laird, and Donald B. Rubin. 1977. Maximum likelihood from incomplete data via the EM algorithm. *Journal of the Royal Statistical Society, Series B*, 39:1–38.

Pierre Deransart and Jan Małuszynski. 1985. Relating logic programs and attribute grammars. *J. Logic Programming*, 2:119–155.

Joost Engelfriet and Linda Heyker. 1992. Context-free hypergraph grammars have the same term-generating power as attribute grammars. *Acta Informatica*, 29(2):161–210.

Ferenc Gécseg and Magnus Steinby. 1984. *Tree Automata*. Akadémiai Kiadó, Budapest. (See also arXiv:1509.06233, 2015).

Joseph A. Goguen, James W. Thatcher, Eric G. Wagner, and Jesse B. Wright. 1977. Initial algebra semantics and continuous algebras. *J. ACM*, 24:68–95.

Jonas Groschwitz, Alexander Koller, and Christoph Teichmann. 2015. Graph parsing with s-graph grammars. In *Proc. of the 53rd Annual Meeting of the Association for Computational Linguistics and the 7th International Joint Conference on Natural Language Processing*, pages 1481–1490.

Annegret Habel and Hans-Jörg Kreowski. 1987. May we introduce to you: Hyperedge replacement. In *Proc. of the Third Intl. Workshop on Graph Grammars and Their Application to Computer Science*, pages 15–26.

Annegret Habel. 1992. *Hyperedge Replacement: Grammars and Languages*, volume 643 of *Lecture Notes in Computer Science*. Springer.

Bevan Jones, Jacob Andreas, Daniel Bauer, Karl Moritz Hermann, and Kevin Knight. 2012. Semantics-based machine translation with hyperedge replacement grammars. In M. Kay and C. Boitet, editors, *Proc. 24th Intl. Conf. on Computational Linguistics (COLING 2012): Technical Papers*, pages 1359–1376.

Karim Lari and Steve J. Young. 1990. The estimation of stochastic context-free grammars using the Inside-Outside algorithm. *Computer Speech and Language*, 4:35–56.

Clemens Lautemann. 1990. The complexity of graph languages generated by hyperedge replacement. *Acta Inf.*, 27(5):399–421.

Philip M. Lewis and Richard E. Stearns. 1968. Syntax-directed transduction. *J. ACM*, 15(3):465–488.

Mark-Jan Nederhof and Giorgio Satta. 2006. Probabilistic parsing strategies. *J. ACM*, 53(3):406–436.

Mark-Jan Nederhof and Giorgio Satta. 2008. Probabilistic parsing. In Gemma Bel-Enguix, M. Dolores Jiménez-López, and Carlos Martín-Vide, editors, *New Developments in Formal Languages and Applications*, volume 113 of *Studies in Computational Intelligence*, pages 229–258. Springer.

Mark-Jan Nederhof and Heiko Vogler. 2012. Synchronous context-free tree grammars. In *Proc. of the 11th International Workshop on Tree Adjoining Grammars and Related Formalisms (TAG+11)*, pages 55–63.

Mark-Jan Nederhof and Heiko Vogler. 2014. Hybrid grammars for discontinuous parsing. In *Proc. of 25th International Conference on Computational Linguistics (COLING 2014)*, pages 1370–1381.

Detlef Prescher. 2001. Inside-outside estimation meets dynamic EM. In *Proc. of the 7th International Workshop on Parsing Technologies*, pages 241–244.

Hiroyuki Seki and Yuki Kato. 2008. On the generative power of multiple context-free grammars and macro grammars. *IEICE - Transactions on Information and Systems*, E91-D(2):209–221.

Stuart M. Shieber and Yves Schabes. 1990. Synchronous tree-adjoining grammars. In *Proc. of the 13th International Conference on Computational Linguistics*, volume 3, pages 253–258.

Stuart M. Shieber, Yves Schabes, and Fernando C. N. Pereira. 1995. Principles and implementation of deductive parsing. *J. Logic Programming*, 24(1–2):3 – 36.

Krishnamurti Vijay-Shanker, David J. Weir, and Aravind K. Joshi. 1987. Characterizing structural descriptions produced by various grammatical formalisms. In *Proc. of the 25th Annual Meeting of the Association for Computational Linguistics*, pages 104–111.

Wolfgang Wechler. 1992. *Universal Algebra for Computer Scientists*, volume 25 of *EATCS Monographs on Theoretical Computer Science*. Springer.

On the Correspondence between Compositional Matrix-Space Models of Language and Weighted Automata

Shima Asaadi[*] and **Sebastian Rudolph**
Faculty of Computer Science
Technische Universität Dresden
`firstname.lastname@tu-dresden.de`

Abstract

Compositional matrix-space models of language were recently proposed for the task of meaning representation of complex text structures in natural language processing. These models have been shown to be a theoretically elegant way to model compositionality in natural language. However, in practical cases, appropriate methods are required to learn such models by automatically acquiring the necessary token-to-matrix assignments. In this paper, we introduce graded matrix grammars of natural language, a variant of the matrix grammars proposed by Rudolph and Giesbrecht (2010), and show a close correspondence between this matrix-space model and weighted finite automata. We conclude that the problem of learning compositional matrix-space models can be mapped to the problem of learning weighted finite automata over the real numbers.

1 Introduction

Quantitative models of language have recently received considerable research attention in the field of Natural Language Processing (NLP). In the application of meaning representation of text in NLP, much effort has been spent on semantic Vector Space Models (VSMs). Such models capture word meanings quantitatively, based on their statistical co-occurrences in the documents. The basic idea is to represent words as vectors in a high-dimensional space, where each dimension corresponds to a separate feature. In this way, semantic similarities can be computed based on measuring the distance between vectors in the vector

space (Mitchell and Lapata, 2010). Vectors which are close together in this space have similar meanings and vectors which are far away are distant in meaning (Turney and Pantel, 2010).

VSMs typically represent each word separately, without considering representations of phrases or sentences. So, the compositionality properties of the language is lost in VSMs (Mitchell and Lapata, 2010). Recently, some approaches have been developed in the area of compositionality and distributional semantics in NLP. These approaches introduce different word representations and ways of combining those words. Mitchell and Lapata (2010) propose a framework for vector-based semantic composition. They define additive or multiplicative function for the composition of two vectors and show that compositional approaches generally outperform non-compositional approaches which treat the phrase as the union of single lexical items. However, VSMs still have some limitations in the task of modeling complex conceptual text structures. For example, in the bag-of-words model, the words order and therefore the structure of the language is lost.

To overcome the limitations of VSMs, Rudolph and Giesbrecht (2010) proposed Compositional Matrix-Space Models (CMSM) as a recent alternative model to work with distributional approaches. These models employ matrices instead of vectors and make use of iterated matrix multiplication as the only composition operation. They show that these models are powerful enough to subsume many known models, both quantitative (vector-space models with diverse composition operations) and qualitative ones (such as regular languages). It is also proved theoretically that this framework is an elegant way to model compositional, symbolic and distributional aspects of natural language.

However, in practical cases, methods are needed

---

[*]Supported by DFG Graduiertenkolleg 1763 (QuantLA)

Proceedings of the ACL Workshop on Statistical NLP and Weighted Automata, pages 70–74,
Berlin, Germany, August 12, 2016. ©2016 Association for Computational Linguistics

to automatically acquire the token-to-matrix assignments from available data. Therefore, methods for training such models should be developed e.g. by leveraging appropriate machine learning methods.

In this paper, we are concerned with Graded Matrix Grammars, a variant of the Matrix Grammars of Rudolph and Giesbrecht (2010), where instead of the "yes or no" decision, if a sequence is part of a language, a real-valued score is assigned. This is a popular task in NLP, used, e.g., in sentiment analysis settings (Yessenalina and Cardie, 2011).

Generally, in many tasks of NLP, we need to estimate functions which map arbitrary sequence of words (e.g. sentences) to some semantical space. Using Weighted Finite Automata (WFA), an extensive class of these functions can be defined, which assign values to these sequences (Balle and Mohri, 2012).

Herein, inspired by the definition of weighted finite automata (Sakarovitch, 2009) and their applications in NLP (Knight and May, 2009), we show a tight correspondence between graded matrix grammars and weighted finite automata. Hence, we argue that the problem of learning CMSMs can be mapped to the problem of learning WFA.

The rest of the paper is organized as follows. Section 2 provides the basic notions of weighted automata and the matrix-space model. A detailed description of correspondence between CMSM and WFA is presented in Section 3, followed by related work in Section 4 and conclusion and future work in Section 5.

2 Preliminaries

In this section, we provide the definitions of weighted automata in (Balle and Mohri, 2015; Sakarovitch, 2009) and matrix-space models of language in (Rudolph and Giesbrecht, 2010).

2.1 Weighted Finite Automata

Weighted finite automata generalize classical automata in which transitions and states carry weights. These weights can be considered as the cost of the transitions or amount of resources needed to execute the transitions. Let Σ be a finite alphabet. A weighted automaton $\mathcal{A}$ is a tuple of $(Q_\mathcal{A}, \lambda, \alpha, \beta)$ and defined over a semi-ring $(\mathbb{S}, \oplus, \otimes, \bar{0}, \bar{1})$. $Q_\mathcal{A}$ is a finite set of states, $\lambda : \Sigma \to \mathbb{S}^{Q_\mathcal{A} \times Q_\mathcal{A}}$ is the transition weight function,

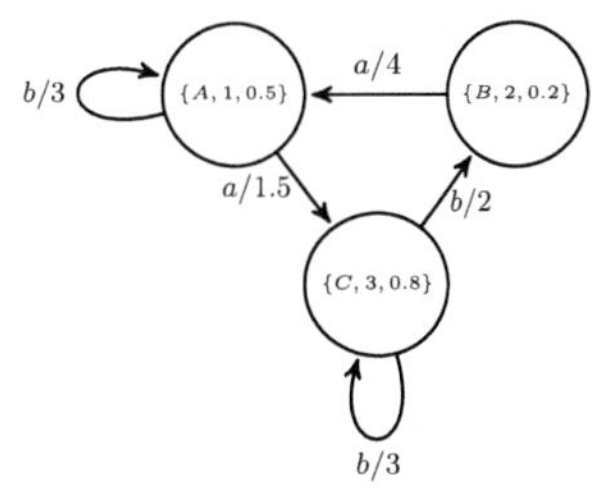

Figure 1: Example of WFA $\mathcal{A}$.

and, $\alpha : \Sigma \to \mathbb{S}$ and $\beta : \Sigma \to \mathbb{S}$ are two functions assigning to every state its initial and final weight. Thereby, for each transition $e = (q, \sigma, q')$, $\lambda(\sigma)_{q,q'}$ denotes the weight of the label σ associated with the transition e between q and q', which are the source and target state of the transition. Moreover, A *path* $\mathcal{P}$ in $\mathcal{A}$ is a sequence of transitions labeled with $\sigma_1 \cdots \sigma_n$, in more detail:

$$\mathcal{P} := p_0 \xrightarrow{\sigma_1} p_1 \xrightarrow{\sigma_2} \cdots \xrightarrow{\sigma_n} p_n$$

with $p_i \in Q_\mathcal{A}$. The *weight* of $\mathcal{P}$ is defined as the $\otimes$-product of the weights of the starting state, its transitions, and final state: $\omega(\mathcal{P}) = \alpha(p_0) \otimes \lambda(\sigma_1)_{p_0,p_1} \otimes \cdots \otimes \lambda(\sigma_n)_{p_{n-1},p_n} \otimes \beta(p_n)$. Now, the weight of a word $x = \sigma_1 \cdots \sigma_n \in \Sigma^\star$ is the cumulative weight of all paths labeled with the sequence $\sigma_1 \cdots \sigma_n$ which is computed as the $\oplus$-sum of the weights of the corresponding paths, also known as a *rational power series*:

$$f_\mathcal{A}(\sigma_1 \cdots \sigma_n) = \bigoplus_{\mathcal{P} \in P_\mathcal{A}(\sigma_1 \cdots \sigma_n)} \omega(\mathcal{P}), \quad (1)$$

where $P_\mathcal{A}(\sigma_1 \cdots \sigma_n)$ denotes the (finite) set of paths in $\mathcal{A}$ labeled with $\sigma_1 \cdots \sigma_n$. So, the function $f_\mathcal{A}$ maps the set of strings in $\Sigma^\star$ to $\mathbb{S}$. In this work, we will assume that $\mathbb{S}$ is the set of the real numbers $\mathbb{R}$ with the usual multiplication and addition. Figure 1 illustrates an example of WFA over $\Sigma = \{a, b\}$. Inside each state there is a tuple of the name, initial and final weight of the state, respectively. As an example, for $x = ab$ we have: $f_\mathcal{A}(x) = 1 \times 1.5 \times 3 \times 0.8 + 1 \times 1.5 \times 2 \times 0.2 + 2 \times 4 \times 3 \times 0.5$.

2.2 Compositionality and Compositional Matrix-Space Model

The general principle of compositionality is that the meaning of a complex expression is a function of the meaning of its constituent tokens and some rules used to combine them (Frege, 1884). More formally, according to Rudolph and Giesbrecht (2010), the underlying idea can be described as follows: "Given a mapping $[\![\cdot]\!] : \Sigma \to \mathbb{S}$ from a set of tokens in Σ into some semantic space $\mathbb{S}$, the composition operation is defined by mapping sequences of meanings to meanings: $\bowtie: \mathbb{S}^\star \to \mathbb{S}$. So, the meaning of the sequence of tokens $\sigma_1 \cdots \sigma_n$ can be obtained by first applying the function $[\![\cdot]\!]$ to each token and then $\bowtie$ to the sequence $[\![\sigma_1]\!] \cdots [\![\sigma_n]\!]$, as shown in Figure 2".

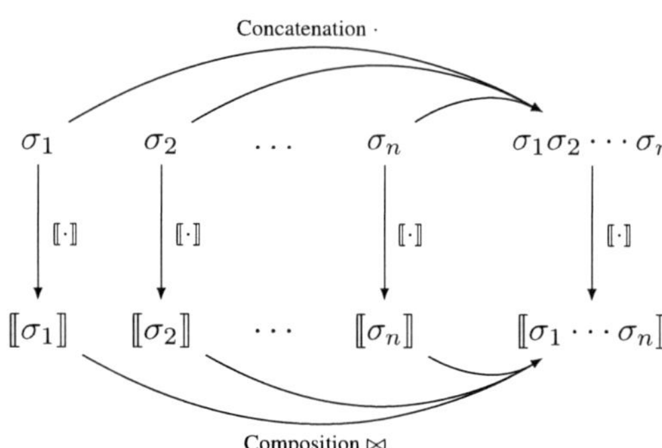

Figure 2: Principle of compositionality, illustration taken from Rudolph and Giesbrecht (2010)

In compositional matrix-space models, this general idea is instantiated as follows: we have $\mathbb{S} = \mathbb{R}^{n \times n}$, i.e., the semantic space consists of quadratic matrices of real numbers. The mapping function $[\![\cdot]\!]$ maps the tokens into matrices so that the semantics of simple tokens is expressed by matrices. Then, using the standard matrix multiplication as the only composition operation $\bowtie$, the semantics of complex phrases are also described by matrices.

Rudolph and Giesbrecht (2010) showed theoretically that by employing matrices instead of vectors, CMSMs subsume a wide range of linguistic models such as statistical models (vector-space models and word space models).

3　Graded Matrix Grammars and Weighted Finite Automata

In some applications of NLP, we need to derive the meaning of a sequence of words in a language, which can be done with CMSMs as described in Section 2.2. In this section, we introduce the notion of a graded matrix grammar which constitutes a slight variation of matrix grammars as introduced by Rudolph and Giesbrecht (2010).

Definition 1 (Graded Matrix Grammars). *Let Σ be*

an alphabet. A graded matrix grammar $\mathcal{M}$ of degree n is defined as the tuple $\langle [\![\cdot]\!], \Sigma, \alpha, \beta \rangle$ where $[\![\cdot]\!]$ is a function mapping tokens in Σ to $n \times n$ matrices of real numbers. Moreover, $\alpha, \beta \in \mathbb{R}^n$. Then we map each sequence of tokens $\sigma_1 \cdots \sigma_n \in \Sigma^\star$ to a real number (called the value of the sequence) using the target function $\varphi : \Sigma^\star \to \mathbb{R}$ defined by:

$$\varphi(\sigma_1 \cdots \sigma_n) = \alpha [\![\sigma_1]\!] \cdots [\![\sigma_n]\!] \beta^\top. \qquad (2)$$

However, as discussed before, to be used in practice, some learning methods are needed to extract graded matrix grammars from textual data. Hence, the target function φ can be generalized to all texts in the language and handle unseen word compositions. To this end, we show the correspondence between the CMSM and WFA, with the consequence that existing learning methods for WFA can be applied to learning CMSMs.

As discussed in Section 2.1, in WFA, for a rational power series f, a value $f(x)$ is the sum of all possible paths labeled with $x = \sigma_1 \cdots \sigma_n \in \Sigma^\star$. However, this computation can be described via matrices by the fact that a walk over a graph corresponds to a matrix multiplication (Sakarovitch, 2009). More precisely, for any $\sigma \in \Sigma$, let $A_\sigma \in \mathbb{R}^{Q_\mathcal{A} \times Q_\mathcal{A}}$ be the transition matrix of σ: $[A_\sigma]_{pq} = \sum_{e \in P_\mathcal{A}(p,\sigma,q)} \lambda(\sigma)_{p,q}$, where $P_\mathcal{A}(p, \sigma, q)$ is the set of all transitions labeled with σ from p to q. Also, the vectors $\alpha_\mathcal{A} \in \mathbb{R}^{Q_\mathcal{A}}$ and $\beta_\mathcal{A} \in \mathbb{R}^{Q_\mathcal{A}}$ are the start and final weights of the states in $Q_\mathcal{A}$, respectively. Then, Equation 1 can be equally expressed as follows in terms of matrices with entries in $\mathbb{R}$ (Balle and Mohri, 2015):

$$f_\mathcal{A}(\sigma_1 \cdots \sigma_n) = \alpha_\mathcal{A}^\top A_{\sigma_1} \cdots A_{\sigma_n} \beta_\mathcal{A} \qquad (3)$$

Hence, we see the correspondence between Equation 2 and 3. In more detail, consider each phrase p and its value r in a natural language. If we extract the words of the language as a finite alphabet Σ in an automaton, then p would be a string in $\Sigma^\star$. The $[\![\cdot]\!]$ function in $\mathcal{M}$ applied over the words constructs $n \times n$ transition matrices of the alphabets in the automaton. Here, n can be the number of states of the automaton. So, estimating the function φ in graded matrix grammar corresponds to estimating the target function of the automaton $f_\mathcal{A}$, which computes exactly the value of a string translated from the phrase p in a language. That is, the representation of a string is done with multiplication of transition matrices of its tokens, which results in a new representation matrix for the string. Then, the suitable predefined vectors α and β translate the resulting matrix to a real number which denotes the value of associated phrase p in the natural language.

The problem of learning WFAs is finding a WFA closely estimating a target function, using for training a finite sample of strings labeled with their target values (Balle and Mohri, 2015). By learning WFAs, one obtains an automaton that is a tuple $\mathcal{A} = \langle \alpha, \beta, \{A_a\}_{a \in \Sigma} \rangle$, and one can compute the target function $f_{\mathcal{A}}(x)$. Since WFA encode CMSMs, and based on this close correspondence between them, learning a graded matrix grammar to estimate the value of phrases can be mapped to the problem of learning a weighted automaton.

4   Related Work

An application of CMSM has been shown in the work of Yessenalina and Cardie (2011). They proposed a learning-based approach for phrase-level sentiment analysis. Inspired by the work of Rudolph and Giesbrecht (2010) they use CMSMs to model composition, and present an algorithm for learning a matrix for each word via ordered logistic regression, which is evaluated with promising results. However, it is not trivial to learn a matrix-space model. Since the final optimization problem is non-convex, the matrix initialization for this method is not done perfectly.

Socher et al. (2012) introduce a matrix-vector recursive neural network (MV-RNN) model that learns compositional vector representations for phrases and sentences. The model assigns a vector and a matrix to every node in a parse tree. The vector represents the meaning of the constituent, while the matrix captures how it affects the meaning of neighboring constituent. The model needs to parse the tree to learn the vectors and matrices.

Recently, new approaches are proposed in learning weighted finite automata in NLP. Balle and Mohri (2012) and Balle et al. (2014) introduce a new family of algorithms for learning general WFA and stochastic WFA based on the combination of matrix completion problem and spectral methods. These algorithms are designed for learning an arbitrary weighted automaton from sample data of strings and assigned labels. They formulate the missing information from the sample data as a Hankel matrix completion problem. Then, the spectral learning is applied to the resulting Hankel matrix to obtain WFA. Balle et al. (2014) also, offer the main results in spectral learning which are an interesting alternative to the classical EM algorithms in the context of grammatical inference and show the computational efficiency of these algorithms.

Moreover, Balle and Mohri (2015) discuss modern learning methods (spectral methods) for an arbitrary WFA in different scenarios. They provide WFA reconstruction algorithms and standardization. it is theoretically guaranteed that for a Hankel matrix with a finite rank, representing a rational power series, there is a corresponding WFA with the number of states equal to this rank and it is minimal.

5   Conclusion and Future Work

In this paper, we introduced a graded matrix grammar for compositionality in language where compositional matrix-space models are employed in different tasks of NLP. However, we need to propose a learning method to train this model for value assignments in NLP. For this purpose, we showed the close correspondence between matrix grammars and weighted automata. So, the problem of learning the CMSM can be encoded as the problem of learning WFA.

Our future goal is to review the existing methods in learning WFA, and adapt them to solve the task of sentiment analysis/meaning representation in NLP. Using learning methods, they allow to automatically learn CMSM and induce the graded matrix grammar.

References

Borja Balle and Mehryar Mohri. 2012. Spectral learning of general weighted automata via constrained matrix completion. In *Advances in neural information processing systems*, pages 2168–2176.

Borja Balle and Mehryar Mohri, 2015. *Learning Weighted Automata*, pages 1–21. Springer International Publishing.

Borja Balle, Xavier Carreras, Franco M Luque, and Ariadna Quattoni. 2014. Spectral learning of weighted automata. *Machine Learning*, 96(1):33–63.

Gottlob Frege. 1884. *Die Grundlagen der Arithmetik eine logisch-mathematische Untersuchung über den Begriff der Zahl.* Verlage Wilhelm Koebner, Breslau.

Kevin Knight and Jonathan May. 2009. Applications of weighted automata in natural language processing. In Manfred Droste, Werner Kuich, and Heiko Vogler, editors, *Handbook of Weighted Automata*, pages 571–596. Springer Berlin Heidelberg, Berlin, Heidelberg.

Jeff Mitchell and Mirella Lapata. 2010. Composition in distributional models of semantics. *Cognitive Science*, 34(8):1388–1429.

Sebastian Rudolph and Eugenie Giesbrecht. 2010. Compositional matrix-space models of language. In *Proceedings of the 48th Annual Meeting of the Association for Computational Linguistics*, ACL '10, pages 907–916, Stroudsburg, PA, USA. Association for Computational Linguistics.

Jacques Sakarovitch. 2009. Rational and recognisable power series. In Manfred Droste, Werner Kuich, and Heiko Vogler, editors, *Handbook of Weighted Automata*, pages 105–174. Springer Berlin Heidelberg, Berlin, Heidelberg.

Richard Socher, Brody Huval, Christopher D. Manning, and Andrew Y. Ng. 2012. Semantic compositionality through recursive matrix-vector spaces. EMNLP-CoNLL '12, pages 1201–1211, Stroudsburg, PA, USA. Association for Computational Linguistics.

Peter D. Turney and Patrick Pantel. 2010. From frequency to meaning: Vector space models of semantics. *Journal of Artificial Intelligence Research*, 37(1):141–188.

Ainur Yessenalina and Claire Cardie. 2011. Compositional matrix-space models for sentiment analysis. In *Proceedings of the Conference on Empirical Methods in Natural Language Processing*, EMNLP '11, pages 172–182, Stroudsburg, PA, USA. Association for Computational Linguistics.

Pynini: A Python library for weighted finite-state grammar compilation

Kyle Gorman

Google, Inc.

111 8th Avenue, New York, NY 10011

Abstract

We present Pynini, an open-source library for the compilation of weighted finite-state transducers (WFSTs) and pushdown transducers (PDTs) from strings, context-dependent rewrite rules, and recursive transition networks. Pynini uses the OpenFst library for encoding, modifying, and applying WFSTs and PDTs. We describe the design of this library and the algorithms and interfaces used for compilation, optimization, and application, and provide two illustrations of the library in use.

1 Introduction

Weighted finite-state transducers (WFSTs) are widely used in speech and language applications. The hypothesis space for tasks like automatic speech recognition (ASR) and optical character recognition can be be represented as a compact, efficiently searchable cascade of WFSTs (Mohri et al., 2002). Manually-generated grammatical resources such as pronunciation lexicons and phonological rules are also naturally represented as finite-state transducers. One advantage of an end-to-end WFST formulation in complex natural language problems like speech recognition is that WFSTs make it easy to combine "big data" statistical components like language models and "small batch" resources like hand-written grammars. For instance, WFST ASR models may be augmented with a series of weighted rewrite rules modeling pronunciation variation (Hazen et al., 2005) to reduce word error rate, or composed with an WFST which restores punctuation and capitalization to improve transcript readability (Shugrina, 2010).

2 Existing WFST libraries

There are a number of publicly available WFST libraries, most of them open-source. Roughly speaking, these libraries can be divided into three groups. First, libraries like Carmel (Knight and Graehl, 1998) and OpenFst (Allauzen et al., 2007) provide efficient implementations of key algorithms for combining, optimizing, and searching WFSTs. However, such libraries provide little support for users who wish to compile a lexicon or a list of grammatical rules into a WFST, so that even basic grammar-building tasks may be a challenge. A second group of libraries, including HFST (Lindén et al., 2013), Lextools (Sproat, 1995), Kleene (Beesley, 2012), and Thrax (Roark et al., 2012), focus on grammar compilation operations and rely upon the aforementioned libraries for core WFST algorithms. Finally, a third group of libraries, including Foma (Hulden, 2009) and XFST (Beesley and Karttunen, 2003), provide algorithms and compilation routines for finite-state transducers, though neither supports weighted transducers required by many real-world applications.

2.1 DSL-and-compiler interfaces

Table 1 summarizes key features of eight libraries which provide some form of grammar compilation support. Among these libraries, the most common interface is a compiler for a library-specific declarative, domain-specific language (DSL). There are some advantages for using a domain-specific language here; for instance, they allow for remarkably terse grammars. However, in our experience, DSL-and-compiler interfaces may also be a substantial impediment to rapid development.

First, these domain-specific languages all make extensive the use of novel operators; e.g., several employ $ as a unary prefix operator denoting the containment of an WFST. Any new language

Proceedings of the ACL Workshop on Statistical NLP and Weighted Automata, pages 75–80,
Berlin, Germany, August 12, 2016. ©2016 Association for Computational Linguistics

	XFST	Lextools	Carmel	Foma	Kleene	Thrax	HFST	Pynini
Gratis	No	Yes	Yes	Yes	Yes	Yes	Yes	Yes
Libre	No	No	Yes	Yes	Yes	Yes	Yes	Yes
Weighted transducers	No	Yes	No	No	Yes	Yes	Yes	Yes
CDRR compilation	No	Yes	No	Yes	Yes	Yes	Yes	Yes
PDT compilation	No	No	No	No	No	Yes	No	Yes
Python bindings	No	No	No	Yes	No	No	Yes	Yes

Table 1: Key features of eight publicly available libraries for compilation of finite-state grammars.

comes with a learning curve, but the use of novel operators (with unfamiliar precedence) may make the curve particularly steep.

More generally, these DSLs lack the libraries, programming constructs, and tooling present in popular domain-general programming languages. A user who wishes to compile a pronunciation lexicon from data stored in an XML file, for example, has little choice but to write a script in some domain-general programming language to rewrite the XML data into a library-specific format supported by the compiler.

2.2 Introducing Pynini

We propose an alternative approach to this problem. We do not introduce yet another competing DSL-and-compiler standard, nor do we attempt to expose a DSL to another programming language, as do Foma and HFST, both of which provide basic Python bindings. Rather we make WFST algorithms and compilation routines "first-class citizens" of an existing domain-general multi-paradigm programming language. The result is a Python extension called *Pynini* (named in honor of Pāṇini, the renown Sanskrit grammarian). Pynini takes advantage of Python's substantial standard library, expressive syntax, and tools for debugging, linting, and interactive development.

Pynini is distributed freely as part of the Open-Grm toolkit under the Apache 2.0 license.

2.3 Outline

In what follows, we describe the design and implementation of the Pynini library, focusing on compilation and optimization routines (§3). We then present two examples illustrating the use of the library (§4–5), and then conclude with future directions for this project.

3 Design of the library

3.1 Software architecture

Pynini is based on OpenFst (Allauzen et al., 2007), an efficient weighted finite-state transducer library written in C++ 11.[1] At the lowest level, OpenFst provides a set of classes (representing WFSTs) and functions (representing WFST algorithms) templated on the semiring of the input FST(s).

A second layer, the OpenFst scripting API, uses virtual dispatch, function registration, and dynamic loading of shared objects to provide a common interface shared by FSTs of different semirings. OpenFst also includes a Python extension module, `pywrapfst`, which exposes the entire scripting API with little additional "syntactic sugar".[2]

Pynini extends this architecture at all three levels. It is implemented with C++ template functions (some of which are shared with Thrax), a semiring-independent scripting interface, and a Python module which extends `pywrapfst`.

3.2 Compilation

Pynini provides a Python class called `Fst`, which represents a mutable WFST with a user-specified semiring (by default, the tropical semiring). The `epsilon_machine` function creates a one-state FST that accepts only the empty string. The `acceptor` function compiles a string into a (deterministic, epsilon-free) FSA. The user may specify how the arcs of the resulting FSA are to be labeled; by default, each arc in the FSA corresponds to a byte in the input string, but the string may also be interpreted as a UTF-8-encoded string—in which case each arc label corresponds to a codepoint in the Unicode Basic Multilingual Plane—or according to a user-provided symbol table. As in

---

[1] At time of writing Pynini depends on OpenFst 1.5.3.

[2] For more information on these APIs, visit `http://openfst.org`.

Thrax, a string enclosed in square brackets are interpreted as a single *generated* symbol rather than as sequences of bytes or codepoints.

Nearly all Pynini functions permit a string to be passed in place of an `Fst`, in which case `acceptor` then is used to compile the string. One such function is `transducer`, which takes two FSA (or string) arguments and compiles a transducer that represents their cross-product. The union of many such string pairs can be compiled using the `string_file` and `string_map` functions. The former reads pairs of strings from a tab-separated values (TSV) file, whereas the latter extracts string pairs from a Python dictionary, list, or tuple. Both functions produce a compact prefix tree representation of a map (or multimap) such as a pronunciation dictionary.

The `cdrewrite` function performs compilation of context-dependent rewrite rules (CDRRs) using an algorithm due to Mohri and Sproat (1996). The `replace` function compiles FSTs from recursive transition networks (RTNs; Woods 1970). An RTN is specified as a single *root* FST followed by a set of one or more *replacement* FSTs, each of which is passed as a keyword argument where the keyword represents the replacement's corresponding *nonterminal*. If an RTN contains any recursive replacements—i.e., if any FST in the RTN contains its nonterminal either directly or indirectly—it lacks a finite expansion and therefore cannot be compiled into an FST, but it can be compiled as a pushdown transducer (PDTs; Allauzen and Riley 2012) using the `pdt_replace` function.

Major functions for constructing FSTs are shown in Figure 1.

3.3 Visualization

Pynini provides several techniques for visualizing FSTs. Invoking Python's `print` statement on an `Fst` prints the FST's arc list, and the `draw` method renders an FST as a GraphViz[3] image. It is also possible to iterate over the states, arcs, and paths of an FST using the `states`, `arcs`, and `paths` methods, respectively.

3.4 Algorithms

All of the major WFST algorithms supported by OpenFst can be invoked via module-level functions which return an `Fst` instance (or raise an exception in the case of run-time failure). A subset of

---

[3] `http://graphviz.org`

OpenFst WFST algorithms, including closure, inversion, and projection, operate destructively (i.e., they mutate their input in-place), and can also be invoked by calling the appropriate instance method on an `Fst` object. All destructive operations return their mutated input so as to allow chaining.

3.5 Optimization

Core FST operations such as composition, concatenation, and union tend to introduce many redundant arcs and states, and therefore it is desirable (and in some cases necessary) to optimize FSTs during grammar compilation. OpenFst provides four algorithms for this task: epsilon-removal, arc-sum mapping (which merges identically-labeled multiarcs), determinization, and minimization. However, there are complex restrictions on the application of these algorithms, making manual optimization something of a challenge.

Pynini provides an instance method `optimize` which applies these four procedures, subject to these algorithmic restrictions and the properties of the input FST. For instance, the minimization algorithm is guaranteed to find a minimal FST only in the case that the input is deterministic, and while any acyclic FST over a *zero-sum-free* semiring is determinizable, this is not necessarily true of FSTs with weighted cycles (Mohri, 2009). Therefore, if an FST is not known to be deterministic and weighted-cycles-free, the optimization routine performs both determinization and minizimation on the FST while it is encoded as if it were an unweighted acceptor (Allauzen et al., 2004).

4 Sample grammar: Finnish harmony

Koskenniemi (1983) provides a number of manually-compiled FSTs modeling Finnish morphophonological patterns. One of these concerns the well-known pattern of Finnish vowel harmony. Many Finnish suffixes have two allomorphs differing only in the backness specification of their vowel. For example, the adessive suffix is usually realized as *-llä* [l:æ:] except when the preceding stem contains one of *u*, *o*, and *a* and there is no intervening *y*, *ö*, or *ä*; in this case, it is *-lla* [l:ɑ:]. For example, *käde* 'hand' has an adessive *kädellä*, whereas *vero* 'tax' forms the adessive *verolla* because the nearest stem vowel is *o* (Ringen and Heinämäki, 1999). Figure 2 provides a Pynini function (`make_adessive`) which generates the appropriate form of a noun stem.

77

```
a = epsilon_machine()
b = acceptor("Red Leicester")
c = transducer("Tilsit", "Never at the end of the week, sir")
d = string_map({"Stilton": "Sorry", "Gruyère": "No"})
e = replace("[COLOR] [CHEESE]",
            COLOR=union("Blue", "Red", "White"),
            CHEESE=union("Leicester", "Stilton", "Vinney", "Windsor"))
```

Figure 1: Examples of various FST construction functions in Pynini.

It first concatenates the stem with an abstract representation of the suffix, and then composes the result with a context-dependent rewrite rule `adessive_harmony`.

5 Sample application: T9 decoding

T9 (short for "Text on 9 keys"; Grover et al. 1998) is a patented predictive text entry system. In T9, each character in the "plaintext" alphabet is assigned to one of the 9 digit keys (0 is usually reserved to represent space) of the traditional 3x4 touch-tone phone grid. For instance, the message *GO HOME* is entered as *4604663*. Since the resulting "ciphertext" may be highly ambiguous—this sequence could also be read as *GO HOOD*, not to mention many nonsensical expressions—a hybrid language model/lexicon is used for decoding.

Figure 3 shows T9 encoding and decoding in Pynini. The first line reads in an language model represented as a weighted finite-state acceptor.[4] The second line reads in the encoder table from a `string_file`, a text file in which each line contains an alphabetic character and its corresponding digit key. By computing the concatenative closure of this map, we obtain an FST (T9_ENCODER) which can encode arbitrarily-long plaintext strings.

The `k_best` function first applies a ciphertext string (a bytestring of digits) to the inverted encoder FST (T9_DECODER) via composition and output-projection. This creates an intermediate lattice of all possible plaintexts consistent with the T9 ciphertext. This is then scored by—that is, composed with—the character LM. Finally, we generate the *k* shortest paths (i.e., the *k* highest-probability plaintexts) in the lattice. In the example given in the figure, the shortest path here is in

fact identical to the plaintext.

6 Conclusions

We have described and illustrated the design and implementation of an expressive and extensible open-source library for weighted finite-state grammar compilation. In future work, we hope to exploit this library to improve the user experience for developers of grammars and of WFST applications more generally.

Acknowledgements

Thanks to all those who provided valuable input during the design of Pynini. Richard Sproat originally suggested to me the idea of developing a Python based finite-state grammar library, discussed many design issues, and contributed the path iteration algorithm. Cyril Allauzen, Steven Bedrick, Myroslava Dzikovska, Mark Epstein, Toby Hawker, Michael Riley, and Ke Wu also provided a lot of useful input. To obtain Pynini, visit `http://pynini.opengrm.org`.

References

Cyril Allauzen and Michael Riley. 2012. A pushdown transducer extension for the OpenFst library. In *CIAA*, pages 66–77.

Cyril Allauzen, Mehryar Mohri, Michael Riley, and Brian Roark. 2004. A generalized construction of integrated speech recognition transducers. In *ICASSP*, pages 761–764.

Cyril Allauzen, Michael Riley, Johan Schalkwyk, Wojciech Skut, and Mehryar Mohri. 2007. OpenFst: A general and efficient weighted finite-state transducer library. In *CIAA*, pages 11–23.

Kenneth R. Beesley and Lari Karttunen. 2003. *Finite state morphology*. CSLI, Stanford, CA.

Kenneth R. Beesley. 2012. Kleene, a free and open-source language for finite-state programming. In *10th International Workshop on Finite State Methods and Natural Language Processing*, pages 50–54.

---

[4]The language model used here is an 8-gram character language model with Witten-Bell smoothing, trained on the Wall St. Journal portion of the Penn Treebank using OpenGrm-NGram (Roark et al., 2012). This is somewhat different than the language models used in mobile phone T9 systems.

```python
back_vowel = u("u", "o", "a")
neutral_vowel = u("i", "e")
front_vowel = u("y", "ö", "ä")
vowel = u(back_vowel, neutral_vowel, front_vowel)
archiphoneme = u("A", "I", "E", "O", "U")
consonant = u("b", "c", "d", "f", "g", "h", "j", "k", "l", "m", "n", "p", "q",
              "r", "s", "t", "v", "w", "x", "z")
sigma_star = u(vowel, consonant, archiphoneme).closure()
adessive = "llA"
intervener = u(consonant, neutral_vowel).closure()
adessive_harmony = (cdrewrite(t("A", "a"), back_vowel + intervener, "",
                              sigma_star) *
                    cdrewrite(t("A", "ä"), "", "", sigma_star)).optimize()

def make_adessive(stem):
  return ((stem + adessive) * ur).stringify()
```

Figure 2: Finnish adessive suffix harmony, implemented with context-dependent rewrite rules.

```python
LM = Fst.read("charlm.fst")
T9_ENCODER = string_file("t9.tsv").closure()
T9_DECODER = invert(T9_ENCODER)

def encode_string(plaintext):
  return (plaintext * T9_ENCODER).stringify()

def k_best(ciphertext, k):
  lattice = (ciphertext * T9_DECODER).project(True) * LM
  return shortestpath(lattice, nshortest=k, unique=True).paths()

pt = "THE SINGLE MOST POPULAR CHEESE IN THE WORLD"
ct = encode_string(pt)
for (_, opath, _) in k_best(ct, 5):
  print opath
```

Figure 3: T9 encoding and decoding with a character LM.

Dale L. Grover, Martin T. King, and Clifford A. Kushler. 1998. Reduced keyboard disambiguating computer. US Patent 5,818,437.

Timothy J. Hazen, I. Lee Hetherington, Han Shu, and Karen Livescu. 2005. Pronunciation modeling using a finite-state transducer representation. *Speech Communication*, 46(2):189–203.

Mans Hulden. 2009. Foma: A finite-state compiler and library. In *EACL*, pages 29–32.

Kevin Knight and Jonathan Graehl. 1998. Machine transliteration. *Computational Linguistics*, 24(4):599–612.

Kimmo Koskenniemi. 1983. *Two-level morphology: A general computational model for word-form recognition and production*. Ph.D. thesis, University of Helsinki.

Krister Lindén, Erik Axelson, Senka Drobac, Sam Hardwick, Juha Kuokkala, Jyrki Niemi, Tommi A. Pirinen, and Miikka Silfverberg. 2013. HFST: A system for creating NLP tools. In *SCFM*, pages 53–71.

Mehryar Mohri and Richard Sproat. 1996. An efficient compiler for weighted rewrite rules. In *ACL*, pages 231–238.

Mehryar Mohri, Fernando Pereira, and Michael Riley. 2002. Weighted finite-state transducers in speech recognition. *Computer Speech and Language*, 16(1):69–88.

Mehryar Mohri. 2009. Weighted automata algorithms. In Manfred Droste, Werner Kuich, and Heiko Vogler, editors, *Handbook of weighted automata*, pages 213–254. Springer, New York.

Catherine O. Ringen and Orvokki Heinämäki. 1999. Variation in Finnish vowel harmony: An OT account. *Natural Language and Linguistic Theory*, 17(2):303–337.

Brian Roark, Richard Sproat, Cyril Allauzen, Michael Riley, Jeffrey Sorensen, and Terry Tai. 2012. The OpenGrm open-source finite-state grammar software libraries. In *ACL*, pages 61–66.

Maria Shugrina. 2010. Formatting time-aligned ASR transcripts for readability. In *NAACL*, pages 198–206.

Richard Sproat. 1995. Lextools: Tools for finite-state linguistic analysis. Technical Report 11522-951108-10TM, Bell Laboratories.

William A. Woods. 1970. Transition network grammars for natural language analysis. *Communications of the ACM*, 13(10):591–606.

Author Index

Association for Computational Linguistics
209 N. Eighth Street
Stroudsburg, Pennsylvania 18360

ISBN 978-1-5108-2771-4